THIS IS YOUR
BRAIN ON JOY

OTHER BOOKS BY DR. EARL HENSLIN

Your Father's Daughter

Man to Man

Forgiven and Free

Off the Cliff: 10 Principles of Business Success

Intervention: Seven Life-Saving Steps

BOOKS COAUTHORED BY DR. HENSLIN

Secrets of Your Family Tree

Inside a Cutter's Mind

THIS IS YOUR BRAIN ON JOY

A Revolutionary Program for Balancing Mood,
Restoring Brain Health, and Nurturing Spiritual Growth

Dr. Earl Henslin

with Becky Johnson

THOMAS NELSON
Since 1798

NASHVILLE   DALLAS   MEXICO CITY   RIO DE JANEIRO

Published in Nashville, Tennessee, by Thomas Nelson. Thomas Nelson is a registered trademark of Thomas Nelson, Inc.

Published in association with the literary agency of WordServe Literary Group, Ltd., 10152 S. Knoll Circle, Highlands Ranch, Colorado 80130, www.wordserveliterary.com.

Thomas Nelson, Inc. titles may be purchased in bulk for educational, business, fund-raising, or sales promotional use. For information, please e-mail SpecialMarkets@ThomasNelson.com.

This Is Your Brain on Joy provides information of a general nature and is not to be used as an alternative method for conditions requiring the services of a personal physician or other health-care professional.

Information contained in this book or in any other publication, article, or Web site should not be considered a substitute for consultation with a board-certified doctor to address individual medical needs. Individual facts and circumstances will determine the treatment that is most appropriate. *This Is Your Brain on Joy* publisher and its author, Earl Henslin, PsyD, disclaim any liability, loss, or damage that may result in the implementation of the contents of this book.

To protect the privacy of individuals, some names and details have been changed, and some stories are composite characters. All of the contextual elements and results, however, are true. Permission has been granted for use of the real names of some clients.

Unless otherwise noted, Scripture quotations used in this book are taken from the Holy Bible: New International Version®. © 1973, 1978, 1984 by International Bible Society. Used by permission of Zondervan Publishing House. All rights reserved.

Scripture quotations marked NASB are from the New American Standard Bible®. © The Lockman Foundation 1960, 1962, 1963, 1968, 1971, 1972, 1973, 1975, 1977, 1995. Used by permission.

Scripture quotations marked NLT are from the Holy Bible, New Living Translation. © 1996, 2004. Used by permission of Tyndale House Publishers, Inc., Wheaton, Illinois 60189. All rights reserved.

Scripture quotations marked MSG are from *The Message* by Eugene H. Peterson. © 1993, 1994, 1995, 1996, 2000, 2001, 2002. Used by permission of NavPress Publishing Group. All rights reserved.

Scripture quotations marked KJV are from the King James Version.

ISBN 978-0-7852-9837-3 (trade paper)

Library of Congress Cataloging-in-Publication Data

Henslin, Earl R.
  This is your brain on joy : how the new science of happiness can help you feel good and be happy / Earl Henslin, with Becky Johnson.
    p. cm.
  Includes bibliographical references and index.
  ISBN 978-0-7852-2873-8 (hardcover)
  1. Joy—Religious aspects—Christianity. 2. Happiness—Religious aspects—Christianity. 3. Joy. 4. Happiness. 5. Brain research. I. Johnson, Becky Freeman, 1959– II. Title.
  BV4647.J68H46 2008
  248—dc22

                    2008038242

Printed in the United States of America

08 09 10 11 QW 6 5 4 3 2 1

To Richard and Marie Henslin.
I want to dedicate this book to you, Mom and Dad.
Thank you for your unfailing love, sacrifice, and the wonderful brain
and heart that you gave me. Thank you for your willingness to share
the stories of our family so that God could use them to help others.
Thank you for your example of growing and changing throughout life.

I love you!
Your favorite oldest son,
Earl

"Pleasure comes and goes, but joy has eternity in it."
—HEATHER KING IN *REDEEMED*

CONTENTS

I am honored to introduce you to my friend, Dr. Earl Henslin. We have been colleagues in helping people through the area of brain study for over a decade.

At the Amen Clinics our mission is to help balance troubled brains. We have seen tens of thousands of patients from all fifty states and sixty-eight countries. We see small children, the elderly, and everyone in between. One of the reasons people come to our clinics is because we use sophisticated brain imaging technology to help us understand and treat our patients—something you'll learn more about in the following pages.

It is through the lens of our brain imaging work that we discovered that when we improve how your brain functions, we help you not only to overcome problems, such as ADD, anxiety, depression, obsession, addiction, and anger, but also to become more thoughtful, creative, energetic, focused, loving, and effective. It is clear to me that a balanced brain is the foundation for a life that is happier, more joyful, wealthier, and wiser.

One question people often ask me is whether the mind is separate from the brain. The answer, after looking at nearly fifty thousand scans over the past twenty years, is *no*. The mind and the brain are completely intertwined. Just think about Alzheimer's disease, which is clearly a brain illness. Do people with Alzheimer's lose their minds? Yes, they do as the disease progresses. When you lose brain tissue, you lose your memory and your ability to be rational.

Or let's consider brain trauma. I recently saw a soldier who'd returned from war. His brain was damaged in an explosion in Iraq, and he'd been discharged from the Army within a year of his injury because he kept getting into fights with other soldiers—something that did not happen before the injury. Does brain damage affect a person's ability to get along with others? Of course it does! Damage the brain and you damage the mind, and usually most everything else in your life.

But what about when we improve the brain? Does that improve the mind? Does it improve the quality of one's life? Yes. Here's an example. When Edward came to see us, he was driving a truck for a living. He had just split from his second wife and frequently had the urge to drive his truck off a bridge. As a child he did poorly in school, and as an adult he struggled to keep both his jobs and his relationships. His scan was consistent with ADD, attention deficit disorder. The very next day, with the right treatment, his brain had already shown improvement. Edward was a gifted artist but was never able to finish the projects he started. As he continued on his treatment, he finished paintings and sold several at a local gallery. Over the next year the demand for his work increased and he was able to stop driving the truck and do the work he loved.

This Is Your Brain on Joy is a thoughtful, practical, life-changing book that will help you take advantage of the latest neuroscience research, combined with biblical insights, to bring more joy and love into your life. This book has wide-ranging implications for individuals, families, the church . . . not to mention our society as a whole.

In my years as a friend and colleague to Dr. Earl Henslin, I have referred many, many people to him, including members of my own family. He is a brilliant, competent, kind, caring man. Early on, he immediately understood the importance of using neuroscience to help individual clients and families and has helped to pioneer this work among psychologists, businesspeople, and church leaders across the United States.

How do you know what's going on in your brain unless you look?

This is a constant phrase Dr. Henslin uses with his patients and colleagues. And for good reason: Did you know that psychiatry is the only medical specialty that never looks at the organ it treats? Most psychiatrists and psychologists today make diagnoses the same way they did in 1840 when Abraham Lincoln was depressed—by looking for symptom clusters and talking with patients. You can try to kill yourself in every major city in the world and virtually no psychiatrist will look at how your brain functions.

Dr. Henslin's insights into what it takes to keep the brain on joy will help lead the way to new avenues of thinking and healing for many people. And through this book he will show you a different way that just may help you change your brain and change your life to find the joy you so richly deserve.

—Daniel G. Amen, MD
Author of *Change Your Brain, Change Your Life*
Newport Beach, California
Fall 2008

ACKNOWLEDGMENTS

Many people have supported and encouraged me in the development of this book. First and foremost, I want to thank my good friend and colleague Daniel Amen, MD. Thank you for your love and affirmation over these years. I am so thankful I took the chance to approach you during your seminar, now twelve years ago. Thank you for the precious time you have given this Curious George of a therapist with an insatiable desire to learn how I can better help my clients through SPECT imaging. You've helped deepen my understanding of the most important and most neglected organ in the body: the brain.

I want to thank Mike Marino, consultant to the Amen Clinics, for the introduction to my agent, Greg Johnson. Without Greg's capable guidance, this manuscript would not have made it into the hands of Joey Paul, vice president at Thomas Nelson. Joey championed this project with all his heart from the moment the proposal landed on his desk. Thank you, Joey. Also, thanks to the village of hard-working editors (Kris and Paula); designers; and marketing, publicity, and sales forces at Thomas Nelson, who take authors' words and package them into books that ultimately change lives.

Greg, I cannot thank you enough for recommending Becky Johnson to collaborate with me on this project. Becky, you are an amazing gift from God. This book would not be in print without your creative contribution and efforts to shape this book into a readable form. You are a great steward of the gifts that God has given you to help his hurting children. It has been an honor to work with you on this project.

By the way, you'll meet Becky in some of the pages of this book, particularly appendix A, where she shares the story of her own visit to the Amen Clinics when she volunteered to be a guinea pig—as "research"—to better explain brain imaging to our readers. Becky can see the humor in just about anything, and so her story should bring a few smiles along with the information. (And she not only lived through the experience but also found it valuable enough that since then, she has recommended several people to our clinic.)

I am privileged to have a gifted and talented group of therapists who have put up with me for many years: David Jarvis, PhD; Daniel McQuoid, PsyD; Martha Schuyler, PsyD; and Dave Osborne, MA, MDiv. I am grateful to Pamela Inman, who is our office manager at Henslin and Associates and who takes care of a hundred details so I can be fully present with our clients; and to Rachel Henslin, founder and president of Henslin Communications: words cannot express my heartfelt gratitude for your hard work in making this book possible. All of you make our weekly staff meetings a joy, as well as a safe place for personal growth, so that we can better minister to God's hurting children who walk through our doors.

Roger and Ann Stull, I want to thank you for your support and encouragement over the years. Your faithful and prayerful support means more to me than you will ever know. Gaylen, as well as the staff and board of Recovery Assistants Foundation, thank you for your support of this project. I know Linda is smiling from heaven, enjoying watching this book finally become a reality.

Steve Yungerberg, president of OAIS Counseling and Performance Enhancement Strategies, thank you for your friendship, prayers, and encouragement over all these years. Dr. Vance Shepperson and Dave Koehn, thank you for your support and friendship—you are mighty men of God.

Kimmie, you and your staff at Kimmie's Café are to me what the Sidetrack Tap was to the fictional citizens of Lake Wobegon. Thank you for your smiles and encouragement in the early hours of the morning when I am writing—and drinking coffee—at the Dr. Henslin booth!

Dr. Bill Ankerberg, pastor of Whittier Area Community Church, your faithful exposition of God's Word has helped me draw closer to the Great Physician, whose guidance I rely on to help bring more joy into the hearts of his children. Thank you for your faithfulness to his calling on your life.

Most of all, I want to thank the many patients and their families that God has brought through the doors of Henslin and Associates. You are the ongoing miracles who provided the stories and desire to write this book. The healing of your brains and hearts and relationships can now bring hope to others who are hurting and need help and encouragement.

Finally, I wish to thank God for my brain. Even though there are days I can't get it geared up enough to find my car keys, it shows up for me every day in the therapist's office as I tune in to my clients, and it blesses me with the creativity to write and speak. It also enables me to enjoy my wonderful family and extended family of siblings, nieces, and nephews.

Now if you'll indulge a proud father (and mother), we are so proud of each of our adult children and grandchildren!

Rachel, thank you for the huge role you have played in developing Henslin and Associates and Henslin Communications. I am so happy for you and Keith, overjoyed that God provided just the right match for you!

Amy, I applaud the risks you have taken during these years in college. You amaze me. Thank you for your honest feedback on this manuscript as it was developing.

Jill, it is so exciting to watch you grow and develop the natural leadership gifts that God has blessed you with. Thank you for your interest and encouragement in this project.

You each bring such great joy to my heart.

And to my son, Ben, and daughter-in-law, Grace, for helping me to celebrate the end of the writing of this book with the birth of a second granddaughter. Your timing was perfect, because holding my newborn granddaughter while her adorable big sister looks on has to be the epitome of pure joy to this grandpa's brain.

Ben, I am so proud of you! You are more of a husband and father than I was at your age. It brings such joy to my heart to see how you and Grace work together so wonderfully in raising these two beautiful granddaughters, Jorja and Lilly.

That is the news from Brea, where this former Minnesota farm boy finds that even here in California (and with a nod to Garrison Keillor) "all the women are strong, the men are good-looking, and the kids are above average."

Healthy Brain, Happy Life

CHAPTER ONE

My First Hug and Other Joyful Brain Matters

Thank you, God, for this good life and
forgive us if we do not love it enough.
—GARRISON KEILLOR

I come from a family of Minnesota dairy farmers, the population that served as fodder for Garrison Keillor's hilariously stoic Lutheran characters in the famed *Prairie Home Companion* skits. Just in case you originate from another, more animated part of the country and wonder if such stiff-upper-lipped (albeit, well-meaning) people actually exist in real life, let me assure you, they do. Though at midlife I embrace the basic tenets of my childhood faith, I have to say—with great relief, some good therapy, and the discovery that God is all *for* being happy—I've gladly dropped the stone-faced expressions that accompanied my religious experience. But my upbringing was straight out of a Lake Wobegon novel, where the citizens feel a sense of unease at potentially emotional moments. Keillor could have been describing my own understated kin when he wrote, "Left to our own devices we Wobegonians go straight for the small potatoes. Majestic doesn't appeal to us; we like the Grand Canyon better with Clarence and Arlene parked in front of it, smiling."[1]

In my family, unbridled feelings of joy and open emotion *were* momentous events: full of danger and potential for sin, and to be avoided at all costs. That's why I'll never forget the moment I received my first open-armed, enthusiastic hug.

3

I was in my early teens, standing in the front yard with my grandfather, grandmother, mom, and dad. About thirty yards from our white clapboard two-story home stood a picturesque red barn on a field of green. We were all gathered together (except for my three younger siblings, whose whereabouts I've forgotten) under the shade of a beautiful maple tree with a trunk about the size of a love seat, its giant umbrella-like branches providing shade on that hot, humid Minnesota day. The whole scene looked like a Norman Rockwell still life. We were lined up in anticipation of meeting my uncle's fiancée. My uncle came driving into the yard in a light blue Thunderbird, and as the dust settled he jumped out and did something I'd never seen before. Truly, it was like watching some bizarre tribal custom play out before our widening eyes. He walked around to his betrothed's side of the car . . . and opened the door. She stepped out, and the world as I knew it was suspended in time.

She was beautiful—a vision of loveliness with brunette hair, sparkling eyes, and doing something I'd not seen often in my family or church: she was smiling! She strode forward with confidence, introduced herself to my grandfather, and did something absolutely unheard of except on *Father Knows Best* or *Leave It to Beaver*.

She *hugged* my grandfather.

My grandfather, whom I felt sure had been born with a King James Bible embedded in his side, had quite the impressive Christian pedigree: Sunday school superintendent, Sunday school teacher, and a rich bass voice for hymn singing. None of his religious training, however, prepared him for this unbidden display of affection, and his whole body went rigid—with shock, I assume. This newcomer had no idea how many centuries-old family rules she had just violated. Topping the list was the blatant sin of a beautiful young woman embracing a man to whom she was not married. Though I know it sounds odd now, I do not recall ever seeing any couples around me hug in public, and hardly ever in private.

Undaunted, this vision of loveliness moved ahead to my grandmother, another hard-working, devout, dependable pillar of the faith. My grandmother suffered from severe asthma and emphysema, and in the horror of being hugged, not only went stiff from head to toe, but also began to wheeze and cough. She frantically searched in her purse, brought out her inhaler, and began drawing breaths from it in an effort to recover her dignity.

Next up, my mother, who is the product of these two. Same song, third verse—only as I watched her brow wrinkle in physical pain as a result of the unprovoked hug, I knew she was getting a migraine that would probably put her out of commission for the next day or two. Bless her heart, the persistent fiancée walked over to embrace my dad next. I had seen my dad try to hug my mom, but she always moved quickly away, dismissing him with, "Oh, Richard!" His knees stiff from years of milking cows, he rarely, if ever, caught her. (Though by the sheer existence of me and my three siblings, there's proof he must have caught her at least four times.)

The young woman hugged my father, and I was expecting the same wooden reaction from him, but to my surprise, he did not let go! In fact, he wrapped his arms around her and held on as if for his life, like a camel that had just walked two thousand miles across the desert, found an oasis, and was determined to quench his thirst until the well ran dry.

Next, the still-smiling lady hugged me. I was, at this point, in the heat of puberty. I had seen girls like her only in my dreams and now felt as though I'd just been transported to heaven on the wings of her soft embrace. After she and my uncle wed, I always looked forward to my aunt's arrival, knowing I would get a warm, tender hug. She did not know or ask about any of my faults, no prodding into sins of omission or commission of which I may have been guilty. She just hugged me.

It was for me, my first real taste of God's unconditional love on earth in human form.

Over the years she'd encourage me to reach out to my warm-on-the-inside, fully-concealed-from-the-outside family. "Earl, hug your family even if they act awkward or withdrawn. You can't hug them when they're dead." It took almost a decade of one-sided hugging, but believe it or not, eventually the folks caught on, and hugs are now a routine part of our family's life.

This is not meant to be a negative comment on my family. They're the salt of the earth—good folks with generous hearts. But they struggled so much with verbalizing affection, demonstrating physical love, and showing open-faced, smiling joy.

So you may be asking, what's a guy from a long line of stoics doing writing a book on happiness? Perhaps it is *because* of my background of sensory deprivation (at least in terms of hugs and smiles), where my family looked upon deeply happy people with a good measure of suspicion, that I developed an almost insatiable curiosity, even fascination, with the subject of joy.

On the one hand, there is the researcher-therapist in me who loves discovering what makes people tick, and tick with a good measure of glee. Deeply joyful people are not terribly commonplace, particularly in my profession where folks usually knock on my door as a last resort for their depressions, obsessions, and traumas. Therefore, when I happen upon people who radiate happiness from the core of their being, it is almost like observing aborigines, a foreign tribe from an altogether other culture. What if I could bottle whatever it is that they have, and share it with the world? It would be perhaps the most meaningful contribution I could make in my earthly existence as a mental health professional and a researcher involved with all things neurological, psychological, and spiritual.

On the other hand, my reasons for writing this book could be, I'll admit it, a bit selfish. For it is said that if we really want something, we should teach or write about it. Embarking on the serious subject of happiness and all its applications and implications has already given me some wonderful personal payoffs. It is impossible to apply your mind to the study of joy without experiencing some surges of insight and all the positive feelings that go along with them. So there, I've said it. Writing this book is just plain fun.

What I've discovered in my research, through reading about the latest scientific breakthroughs, in my experiences with clients in search of happiness, and specifically in studying the brain through SPECT images (more on that later), has been both personally and professionally life-altering. I cannot keep to myself what I've learned about joy: what it is, what it is composed of, and how to find, measure, and keep it. When a man finds a fountain of living water, he doesn't horde it; he shouts about it, shares it.

Jesus spoke of a joy that no man could take away. And it is that joy, that depth of happiness, that we'll be uncovering in the coming pages. What is especially sad to me is how many Christians believe that their lack of joy is due to some spiritual or personal failing or character flaw. "God made some people happy, and some people Eeyores." "There are glass-half-full folks, and glass-half-empty folks."

Is that true? If so, even *partially* so, how much of our natural disposition determines our potential to approach life from the best possible angle? How much can be changed by our thoughts? By spiritual intervention? By medication, foods, supplements, or exercise?

Are you reaching, on a daily basis, your absolute highest potential for happiness? Are you bringing your best, most joyful self to the table of your relationships?

And while we're asking questions, by the way, what *is* happiness or joy? (And is there a difference between the two words?) Is a joyful outlook sustainable during crisis or grief? Do we get it from nature or nurture or supernatural intervention?

Wonderful questions. Questions of the ages posed by centuries of sages. And in time, I'll do my best—by the end of this book—to give you some thoughtful answers gleaned from my study of the Bible and from living life, being a listening ear to friends, and being a professional therapist to clients. And perhaps, most uniquely of all, from what I've learned from my study of and experience with brain science.

What may make this book different, particularly since it is a book written *for* and *from* a faith-based standpoint, is that I believe the most logical and compassionate place to begin our search for joy is not necessarily in the Bible. (Though we *will* get there, I promise.) In fact, we'll eventually spend a full chapter examining the apostle Paul's own personal discoveries about joy, a word used sixteen times in his letter to the Philippians (a book, I believe, that was written at the apex of Paul's spiritual maturity and mental health, not long before his death). But we will not start there.

Neither will we begin by observing deeply happy people and how they got that way though that, too, will be part of this book.

I want to begin by examining the most basic element, the seat of our human potential for joy: that three-pound hunk of gray matter between our ears that we call *the brain.* Dr. Daniel Amen, a dear friend, fellow believer, world-renowned neuroscientist, and author of many groundbreaking books on how neurology affects psychology, has called the brain "the hardware of the soul." (And in fact, he has written a thought-provoking book by the same name.) If our hardware isn't working correctly, Dr. Amen explains, all the software we put into our body's system will be futile, or at best, only work partially well.

I believe that in the Garden of Eden, God created man and woman with beautifully functioning brains. (Yes, brains that were capable of sin and sorrow but healthy, perfect brains equally capable of joy, love, generosity, and goodwill.) After the Fall, everything in creation took a hit, including the hardwiring of our brains. In other words, all brains today are not equal. Dr. Amen goes so far as to assert that though we have free will, depending on the makeup of our brains, human beings do not all have the same amount of free will. "We assumed that we are all equal and have an equal ability to choose right or wrong, good or evil, and heaven or hell. The brain imaging work taught me that we are not all equal, and not everyone has the same power to choose."[2]

Only God knows, sees, and can judge how many of our errors are due to our free wills and how many are due to faulty hardwiring. Let me repeat this: only *God* knows how much of our wrongdoing is the result of pure rebellion or evil intent and how much is caused by brain imbalances. To judge another is to play God's role and is probably the reason the Bible so often urges us not to do it.

When I see brains that are simply not functioning on all cylinders, it stretches my compassion for patients: they may be absolutely doing the very best they can possibly do with the hardware they are driving. For example, Jim was a man with such angry and unpredictable moods that eventually his adult children refused to allow him to see his grandchildren. At his own wit's end with his inability to control his rages, he finally took a risk and had a SPECT brain scan done at the Amen Clinics (again, more about SPECT scans soon). He discovered that his hyperreactivity was due to an injury in the temporal lobes from a concussion while playing football in college. Once he was on a mood stabilizer, this Christian leader gained control of his anger for the first time in his life.

Julie's life had been ruled by panic attacks and migraines. She lived in fear that someday she would be driving with her children in her car and have a panic attack, then an accident, possibly injuring or even killing them all. This all-pervasive fear, along with frequent migraines, would cause her to miss family events, time with friends, and her kids' school functions. Then there was the added guilt of knowing a "good Christian" should not live in fear. She received a new lease on life when she discovered that the medications she'd been on for her headaches were actually contributing to her anxiety! Once the anxiety center in her brain was calmed, she was free to live fully, without debilitating, irrational fear nipping at the corners of her mind.

If only Christians could see what I see—behind the curtain of the skull and into the brain—I believe we'd be much gentler with each other, and our compassion for strugglers in the average church would soar. For many of you, these pages will offer a true lightbulb moment, relief from false guilt, compassion for others (and yourselves), and hope for a brighter tomorrow. Tragically, too often in religious circles we've been trying to pray away or spiritualize a *brain* problem—assuming (however well-intentioned) that we or someone else has a *sin* problem. Or a character flaw. Or a root of bitterness. Or, worse, a demon.

With what I now know about the inner workings of the brain, I believe that trying to pray away sadness or exorcise a demon from a person whose brain is imbalanced is the equivalent of putting a Band-Aid on a gaping wound, walking away, washing our hands of further responsibility, and praying the gash will close itself.

Now don't hear me wrong. Prayer works. Prayer heals. (And you'll read in these pages how science supports this fact.) But there is our part, the part God has allowed us to discover and uncover, that is *just as significant* in our journey toward physical or mental healing. And not just healing our hurts, but also upsizing and expanding the mental health we may already be enjoying.

There's no way to know if someone's joy is being sabotaged by sin or circumstantial sorrow or a brain imbalance until we take a look under the hood, at the hardware. So this is where we will start. (The great thing about being an author is you get to create the agenda.)

One word of clarification: because I am writing this book for the average person in the pew with a layman's interest in joy and the brain, I'll do my best to explain complicated concepts in down-to-earth ways. This means that on occasion, I'll be oversimplifying and "nutshelling" difficult terminology and ideas. So for the scientists, researchers, professional therapists, and medical professionals who read this, forgive me if I take a few liberties in giving general explanations for detailed data.

My specific goal in this book is to bring brain science into the average Christian home where couples are struggling to love each other; where hearts are broken by abnormal behaviors or addictions in family members; where depressed believers are tortured by thoughts that there is something fundamentally wrong with their souls, when the problem lies between their ears, in a very fixable part of their brains' anatomy. So if I sacrifice some scientific specifics on the altar of simplification, please understand my purpose. I'll list resources with the latest and greatest scientific data for those who are curious and want to dive deeper and more thoroughly into the fascinating area of brain study.

I don't think that people of faith can really bring joy to the world before we live a life of authentic, abiding joy as individuals.

Why should anyone want what we believe if it doesn't make us truly, deeply joyful people?

Before we start noodling around in our ol' noggins, however, I'd like to share how I—a family therapist and avid student of Scripture—got stopped in my professional tracks by a grinning doctor and his PowerPoint presentation. Because since that day, when I felt as though God dropped a third piece of the "emotional health" puzzle into my lap, I've been helping people get better in a whole new, and much more successful, way.

CHAPTER TWO

The *Ah-Ha* Moment

But strange that I was not told
That the brain can hold
In a tiny ivory cell
God's heaven or hell.

—OSCAR WILDE

Before we jump right into brain matters, I'd like to start with a more personal matter: exactly how I became interested in brain imaging and how that interest led to discoveries that would bring me to a crisis of faith and career. One meeting would eventually turn upside-down everything I'd learned as a psychotherapist and cause me to ask myself some of the hardest questions I've ever had to answer.

It was over ten years ago that I met Daniel Amen, MD, at a continuing education conference where he talked about the application of SPECT (single photon emission computerized tomography) and its application to attention deficit disorder (ADD). During this past decade I, along with the clinicians that work with me at Henslin and Associates in Brea, California, have worked closely with Dr. Amen. By way of brief introduction, Dr. Amen is a pioneer in brain imaging research and is the author of over thirty professional papers and twenty-two books, including the *New York Times* bestseller *Change Your Brain, Change Your Life*, as well as *Healing ADD*, *Healing Anxiety and Depression*, *Preventing Alzheimer's*, *Making a Good Brain Great*, and the latest book, *Sex on the Brain*. Dr. Amen's high school course, "Making a Good Brain Great," on "practical brain science health education," is now taught in thirty-four states and seven countries. In 2008, PBS stations across the nation aired

Dr. Amen's program, *Change Your Brain, Change Your Life*, which resulted in the book returning to the *New York Times* bestsellers list close to ten years after it first made that list!

Our office has made more than three thousand referrals for SPECT brain imaging and is one of the few outpatient private practices in the United States working daily to integrate brain imaging into the treatment of anxiety, depression, ADD, addictions, eating disorders, phobias, chronic headaches, anger, migraines, chronic pain, and numerous other spiritual, relational, emotional, and physical problems. In fact, Dr. Amen will tell you that the sheer number of patients I sent his direction was a determining factor in his opening up a clinic in our area.

SIN PROBLEM OR BRAIN PROBLEM?

When I first met Dr. Amen (along with two hundred to three hundred other health care professionals) and heard him talk about the brain as we viewed dozens of scans and their common imbalances in a PowerPoint presentation, I could not help but think of the scripture where the disciples asked Jesus: "Rabbi, who sinned, this man or his parents, that he was born blind?" Jesus answered, insightfully and compassionately, "Neither this man nor his parents sinned . . . but this happened so that the work of God might be displayed in his life." (You can read more of this story in John 9:1–7.)

What struck me as I listened to Dr. Amen and pondered this particular verse was that there are conditions that we humans are born with that are not the result of personal sin or our parents' sin. And those conditions don't just include being blind or lame, or the color of our eyes; they include being mentally and emotionally challenged by our particular brain chemistry.

It was one of the most defining moments of my life.

Oh my goodness, I thought, *all the models of psychotherapy that I have learned in my pursuit of two master's degrees and a doctorate have been based on a faulty assumption: that we all have normal brains,* when in fact Dr. Amen pointed out that there really isn't such a thing as a normal brain.

All our brains are uniquely wired. Some of our wiring gifts us with a basic emotional set point that includes mostly thoughts and feelings of happiness and peace and basic sanity. Sadly, however, some of us are wired to experience more anxiety, anger, or depression. Some have mental predispositions for psychological imbalances or illnesses. And many of us are wired with a mixture of everything in between. But here's the reality: much of what we are assuming is volitional sin is not. It is neither the person's fault nor his parents' fault: it is his brain makeup! And most Christian counselors, pastors, and lay ministers do not take any of this research into consideration. Why? Because they don't know about it!

In fact, the Christian books on marriage, marital intimacy, parenting, healing, and recovery, including—and here's a sad confession—the ones I had written, assumed foundationally there was such a thing as a normal brain. (I've updated my books in reprints to include information on brain imaging and issues.) As the day went on, the compelling truth of what Dr. Amen showed in slide after slide hit home. I realized that I needed to make a decision: either I would continue as I had been trained in my practice (which was going fine for me) or take the chance to jump in with both feet and learn a new way of looking at human behavior.

On the one hand, I argued with myself, "Earl, if you don't take this risk and learn all you can about the organic causes of emotional stress, you might miss out on an entirely new way of helping someone, and possibly saving lives." On the other hand, I knew that as in any relatively new science, I might take a professional beating for opening my mind to brain imaging research.

I learned that day that there are over a thousand research studies that have been done utilizing SPECT brain imaging. I was drawn to Dr. Amen because he had done the hard work of practically applying imaging so that he was helping regular people live extraordinary lives. He now has the world's largest database (presently over 45,000 SPECT scans), and that is increasing daily in the four clinics he has around the country. Brain imaging centers, stimulated by Dr. Amen's groundbreaking work, are also developing.

Would I take the chance and wade into new waters of brain scan research, or would I ignore the compelling stories of amazing turnarounds in people who'd been scanned and treated by the Amen Clinics (and often in more dramatic and faster ways than I'd have ever been able to treat them with conventional therapy)? I was growing more and more uncomfortable as God brought to my mind all his hurting children he had brought into our office to help. I realized how much more help I could have given them if only I had known this information. But, once I knew better, God was calling me to be responsible—to *do* better—and to help others with what the latest and greatest research was showing.

The people in my care deserved my best.

WHAT A DIFFERENCE A SCAN MAKES

Let me pause here to give you just one example of how using brain imaging as a part of my practice revolutionized typical outcomes. During the first year of referring people for SPECT brain imaging, I kept track of thirty couples who were headed for divorce at the time of referral. In these situations, one or both spouses had a problem with anger. They were all verbally abusive relationships and were headed down a destructive road straight for the cliff of divorce. At this writing, twenty-nine of the thirty couples are still married. The one couple who did divorce included a spouse who did not follow through on the medication and supplement protocol suggested by Dr. Amen. So the abuse continued, and the marriage dissolved.

Today, all I can say is that I am so thankful I took the jump into the unknown and took a risk in getting to know Daniel Amen. Once this man understood how passionate I was about learning all I could from him, he guided me into the territory of the brain—how it works, how it hurts, how it impacts all that we do, and most of all, how to heal it. Thus began my journey into studying the brain. It also proved to be the beginning of a great friendship.

I took ten years away from writing to learn and study, allowing myself time to be retrained. In this past decade, with the SPECT scan tool as a component of my practice, I've gleaned much from those who I've been helping get better, and after having done the hour-by-hour, day-by-day, month-by-month work required to teach others, I am finally ready to share this life-altering knowledge and the stories of what God has done. My personal and clinical experience only continues to be affirmed through God's Word and the latest research.

TOWARD A MORE COMPASSIONATE CHURCH

Dr. Amen has been quite successful in communicating with health care professionals, as well as reaching the educated layperson with the information in his books. But I have a desire to reach out to people of faith especially with this message. I believe it will widen our hearts and increase our compassion.

By way of example, a forty-five-year-old man was referred to me by his couples' Bible study class. He was the leader of the study, and the class members were concerned for him because of an ongoing battle with depression. The heavy cloud of gloom caused him to have trouble just getting up in the morning to go to work. In the initial session I asked, "Have you suffered any trauma to your brain as a child, teen, or adult?" Dr. Amen and I often have to ask this question in a variety of ways because people tend to forget head injuries from long ago or don't consider them all that serious or significant. And yet, we've learned that even a minor head injury can damage brain tissue and affect behavior.

He shared that when he was in elementary school, he was climbing on a jungle gym and fell. The impact of the fall resulted in his being hospitalized for four days as the doctors monitored the severe concussion. "How did that trauma affect your school performance?" I asked, but before he could fully answer, he began to sob.

He had not made the connection between the concussion and the change in school performance. Prior to the concussion he loved to read, and after the concussion it was a struggle to concentrate on pages full of words. Then he shared how he had felt such spiritual guilt, along with a general sense of shame, when he had to force himself to read Scripture or to keep his mind from wandering when he prayed.

I referred him for a SPECT scan, and the report showed that there was trauma to the prefrontal cortex, the area of the brain involved in attention and concentration. Dr. Amen prescribed 10 mg of Adderall—a medication that improves perfusion, or blood flow, in the prefrontal cortex—for him to take twice a day. I saw this man for a grand total of three sessions because, as his brain began to balance out, most of his other problems began to fade as well.

He was especially excited about the joy he was discovering in his spiritual journey now that he could focus more easily. He was able to read without struggle for the first time in decades. He was able to enter into worship and prayer in a deeper manner.

Perhaps even more personally significant to him was that since puberty he had masturbated every night to calm himself in order to fall asleep—in spite of having a satisfying and fulfilling sexual relationship with his wife. This had been a burdensome secret that he had carried alone for decades. Once he went on the Adderall, there was no need to self-soothe or calm himself in that manner.

What a precious moment it was for me, as his therapist, to watch decades of sexual shame lift away. Talk about joy! To be able to help someone enter into a deeper relationship with the Lord he loved and find freedom from an unwanted sexual impulse and to see him smile, relax, and engage with life was such a privilege. It always is, no matter how many times I watch lives transform when problems are accurately diagnosed and treated, whether it be through therapy, prayer, supplements, or medication.

What helped this good-hearted man get free?

It's significant that his rather fast track to emotional health all began with a few close friends who cared enough to recommend he get some help. Without a brain scan, he might have gone to a general practitioner for his low moods and missed that his depression was stemming from a focus problem, not a mood disorder. The doctor would have begun the normal hit-and-miss prescribing of antidepressants, which in this case wouldn't have helped much with his core brain issues.

Thankfully, someone in his Bible study had heard about our clinic and pointed the way to a door that held solid answers. When the couples saw the change in this man after he'd received our help, it sent a ripple effect through them all. Their compassion increased even more; their understanding grew in spades. Their love for one another expanded. They bonded more deeply as a group and thus became a living portrait of God's love on earth.

Did you know that Jesus' words, "Be *perfect*, therefore, as your heavenly Father is *perfect*" (Matthew 5:48, emphasis mine) might have been more accurately translated, "Be *compassionate*, therefore, as your heavenly Father is *compassionate*"? When I observe the whole of Christ's life and ministry, this second translation makes much more sense to me. In fact, when I ponder what I would like my legacy to be, at least in part it would be for people to say, "Dr. Henslin helped me to be more compassionate to others, and toward myself, through a deeper understanding of the Bible and the brain."

It is my dream to see pockets of God's children, all over the world, experience more compassion and more joy based on a solid understanding of the Bible integrated with what we now know about brain science.

Though nothing in life is 100 percent, we are now extremely confident that when we look at a brain scan, we can recommend the right supplements or medications to help clients perform at their best. (To get exact dosages that work for each individual may take a little tweaking and patient-doctor communication.) In short, we help to restore the health of their minds to a more Eden-like state, one that is closer to the brain God intended we have.

One more story about how this brain information can set off a revival of Christian compassion. During the first year of using scans and brain balancing in my counseling practice, a church approached me about doing a summer series for them based on an earlier book I had written called *Forgiven and Free*. I told the pastor, "I would love to do the series, but I'd like to integrate what I wrote a few years ago with what I'm now learning from neuroscience." He wholeheartedly encouraged me to do that.

During that workshop series, a businessman from the church was so moved with compassion by the information presented that he personally donated $10,000 to the church to help people who needed SPECT scans but could not afford them. The pastor then began personally driving folks, who wanted to be scanned and professionally evaluated, from his church in Brea to Fairfield, California. (At that time, it was the only one of the Amen Clinics in the country.)

Can you imagine what it would be like to have a congregation full of emotionally healthy, brain-balanced people who were ready to receive all that God had for them to experience? (I know. Every pastor's dream, right?) I can only report from firsthand observation that it was incredibly exciting to see so many lives changed for the better in one local church body. So many struggling Christians were deeply relieved to discover that the problems they suffered from weren't just spiritual or psychological—there was a *medical component* in their ongoing battles with depression, panic attacks, addictions, rage, and so on.

I believe that having a better, even simplistic, working knowledge of brain problems will help us better represent Jesus. We can be kinder to ourselves and offer this gift of understanding to others in the body of Christ . . . and beyond. Though I plan to follow up this book with others about how our brain affects relationships, and how our brain affects our faith (balanced brains tend to believe in God), this first book begins where all of us live and touches a desire of the human heart worldwide.

The infamous pursuit of happiness.

How does our brain affect our experience of daily joy and happiness? So glad you asked. Let's begin by taking a little tour of your brain, or, as I like to call it, the ultimate head trip.

CHAPTER THREE

A Head Trip to a Happier Life

My own brain is to me the most unaccountable of machinery
—always buzzing, humming, soaring, roaring, diving, and
then buried in mud. And why? What's this passion for?
—VIRGINIA WOOLF

C an you actually see happiness? Are there real pictures of people's brains
. . . on joy? Amazingly, yes. Through the miracle of modern science, we
can actually see joy on the brain.

One of the most fascinating outcomes of clinical studies on happiness, joy,
and well-being is that scientists are now able to observe brains in a state of
relaxed joy. A couple of the most interesting studies involved Tibetan monks
and Franciscan nuns, both during their time of meditation and prayer, and also
when they went about their normal, daily routines. Since the nuns used mental
words to form a prayer (a technique called *centering* or *contemplative prayer*), a
part of their brain (the part that forms verbal thought) lit up that didn't light
up in the monks, who try to empty their minds of all conscious thought.[1]

However, both groups showed familiar brain imaging patterns: the area
of the brain that was most lit up was an area at the front, mostly on the left
side—the region associated with clarity and happiness. Areas that were sub-
dued were in the lower back part of the brain—an area that is involved in
fear memory, often called the *reptilian brain*, which activates an automatic
fight-or-flight response. It is also an area that helps us orient ourselves in
space, showing that while in prayer or deep meditation, we are able to let go
of our need to control and simply relax and go with the flow.

What was most interesting was that both groups of daily supplicants

19

experienced a deep sense of well-being, peace, and joy during meditation *and*—most interestingly—this feeling of serenity followed them throughout the routines of their days, even through their lives. You've heard the expression that "an apple a day keeps the doctor away." Well, it may also turn out to be true that a few minutes of positive, prayerful meditation a day will help keep the blues at bay.

This time of quieting the mind of its typical worries, basically "letting go and letting God," allowed the study participants to handle negative circumstances with grace, to slow down automatic reactions of anger or frustration by using their thinking brain (or the prefrontal cortex) to talk their fearful brain centers (namely, the basal ganglia and amygdala) down from the ledges. Other studies on the healing effects of prayer, both to the people praying and the people being prayed for (even if they are unaware of the fact), are fascinating and encouraging. In short, doctors, scientists, and researchers have been so impressed by how prayer changes brain and body chemistry for the better that many hospitals are incorporating and encouraging prayer for their patients as an adjunct to traditional healing therapies.

Hey, Doc. Whoa there! some of you are probably saying to yourselves right now. *I get the prayer thing, but let's back up to the middle of that paragraph you just slipped by me. Left prefrontal cortex? Basal ganglia? Amygdala? Are you kidding me? All of this is very interesting, but if I have to learn all these new and difficult-to-pronounce words to understand how the brain affects my experience of happiness, I'm already not feeling like a very happy camper.*

Understood.

The terminology that us nerdy neurologist types throw around on a daily basis can cause the average person's eyes to glaze over in less time than it takes to say "anterior cingulate gyrus." And yet, I am passionate about sharing this information with everyone. So what's a brainiac to do?

Think like an architect, that's what.

After all, most of us are familiar with houses and their basic construction, so, though I'll admit that some of my scientist friends may accuse me of oversimplification, this model works for most. Virginia Woolf once wrote, "I like going from one lighted room to another, such is my brain to me; lighted rooms." Indeed, our brains are a lot like lighted rooms, as you will read.[2]

This cartoon graphic may help you to visualize your brain as a house with emotion-packed rooms.

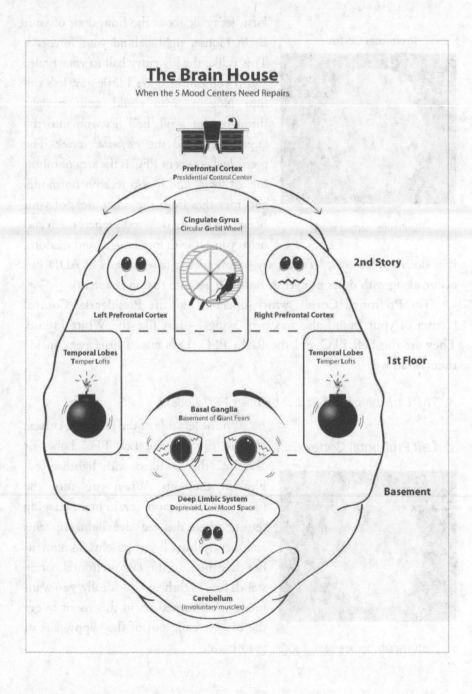

THE PRESIDENTIAL CONTROL CENTER
(THE PREFRONTAL CORTEX)

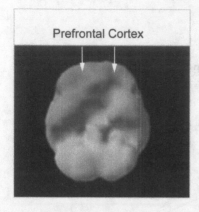

Prefrontal Cortex

(Underside, surface view)

First, let's talk about the front door of your Brain House, right behind your forehead. This is like the big entry hall to your brain; and if you can imagine a little guy, let's call him Noggin, who could walk straight through your skull, he'd first run into the large area called the *prefontal cortex*. The prefrontal cortex or PFC is the area of thinking, of logic, and it also receives hormones and messages from the other areas of your brain. If working well, it deciphers them and helps you act with forethought and wisdom.

If it doesn't work well, let's just say it isn't pretty: several types of ADD can occur, along with other problems. But we'll get into that in chapter 6.

The Prefrontal Cortex, which operates like the Presidential Control Center of your brain, also has two "wings"—just like the White House. They are the Left PFC and the Right PFC. Let's take a brief peek inside them, shall we?

A. The Lighthearted Left Lobby (Left PFC Lobe)

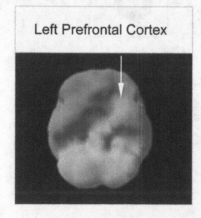

Left Prefrontal Cortex

(Underside, surface view)

On the left side of the prefontal cortex, Noggin can see the Left PFC Lobe, or "Lobby," that is filled with lighthearted, pleasant thoughts. When you turn the lights on in this room (or, in brain imaging terms, when the red dye lights up this area), everything is just peachy. So remember that the L in the *Left* prefrontal cortex stands for "Lighthearted." Ideally, you want more lights turned on in this room to get the biggest bang out of the happy part of your brain.

B. The Ruminating Right Lobby (Right PFC Lobe)

To the right of the neocortex, however, there is the (duh . . .) Right PFC Lobe, which rounds out the Lobby. This room in the brain should be lit up some but not too much, or it is not much fun at all. When the lights are too bright here, it goes from being a nice logical balancer (that helps you see potential problems) to a runaway ruminator that can go on rants and, simply put, ruin your day. So we just turn a couple of lamps on in this room and avoid that overhead bright light switch because too much

Right Prefrontal Cortex

(Underside, surface view)

light in this room in the brain usually means we have a troubled, worried, and unhappy person on our hands. So remember, the R in the *Right* prefrontal cortex stands for "Ruminating."

By way of orientation, if you were to reach up with your right hand and touch the right side of your head, this is the location of the Right PFC. From Noggin's viewpoint, facing the brain, it would be on the left, which reminds me of something I should probably explain right now. When looking at most of the brain scans in this book, sometimes the right side of the brain shows up on the left side of the page depending on the camera angle (whether it's a picture from the top down, or the bottom up). I've found it helpful to imagine the brain as a turtle shell: some views of the shell are from the top down, but in many scans, the camera takes pictures of the underside of the brain as if someone kicked the turtle shell over on its back and then took pictures. In addition, some of the scans are side views, allowing a look from the side of your head where your ears and temples are located. To keep this from driving you nuts, we'll help you by labeling the scans and letting you know from which camera angle the pictures are taken. Also, you'll notice there are two types of pictures that we take: one is a surface scan, the other is an active scan. More details on that in the next chapter.

CIRCULAR GERBIL WHEEL (CINGULATE GYRUS)

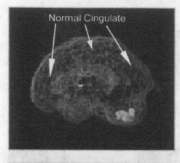

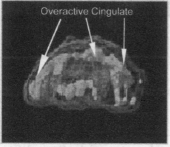

(Side, active view; forehead on left)

Actually, starting in the middle of the prefrontal cortex (which houses both the lovely and luminous left side and that runaway, ruminating right side), there's a hallway straight down the middle of your head. This is the area called the *cingulate gyrus*. Borrowing the C from cingulate and the G from gyrus, we're going to think of this as the Circular Gerbil Wheel hallway. If the lights are ultra-bright in this room, it almost looks like the cingulate has grown from a small dot to a big log running down the middle of your head. When it is fully lit up, our little friend Noggin can get caught in a gerbil wheel of nonstop negativity and worrisome thought that is tough to get out of. Round and round and round your mind goes in the same old rut. Ranting is common in those with cingulate issues.

This is the area of concern with inflexible thoughts (*cognitive inflexibility* is the therapeutic term) and those with obsessive-compulsive symptoms. We'll discuss this more in future chapters, but for now, just remember that problems in this area cause "stuck thinking"—when people just can't let go of a thought or a grudge. They are like a dog with a bone, and no matter how much logic you use to convince them that if they let go of the bone, there's a juicy steak waiting for them in the kitchen, they aren't about to let go of what they know and feel is right.

THE DEPRESSED LOW-MOOD SPACE (DEEP LIMBIC SYSTEM)

Now, we've got to sink deeper into the middle of the brain. So imagine that Noggin is taking an elevator down, down, to the center of the earth—well, actually, to the center of your head. The Limbic System houses both good and bad feelings. On a scan, when we see too much lighting up this area of the brain, we know this person is probably struggling with depressive thoughts. In fact, we've got a saying around the clinic: "When the limbic system is hot, you're not." We're going to learn a lot about this storehouse of emotionally charged memories, both wonderful and painful. But for our brief tour here, just remember that an imbalanced deep limbic system is often responsible for depression and lethargy and can be a real party pooper if the lights in the room are too bright!

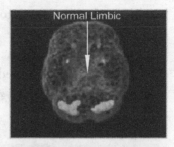

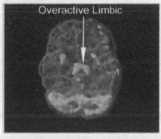

(Underside, active view)

Note: Many scientists include other parts of the brain, such as the basal ganglia and amygdala, as part of the limbic system. For our purposes, we found it helpful to divide out those parts and discuss them seperately. This is why I call this area the Deep Limbic System.

THE **B**ASEMENT OF **G**IANT FEARS (**BASAL GANGLIA**)

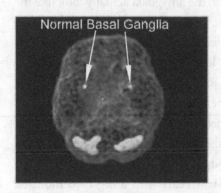

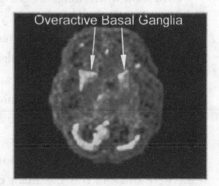

(Underside, active view)

Just when you think you've seen the worst of the rooms in the Brain House (yes, some minds really can be a scary place to go into alone!), hold on to my hand as we watch Noggin go down the elevator a little lower, to nearly the base of the skull. Here we enter the Basal Ganglia—or as I call it, the Basement of Giant Fears. Actually, the basal ganglia looks less like a room and more like a curve-horned creature with two almond-shaped eyes, called the *amygdala*. (Actually, *amygdala* is derived from the word for "almond.")

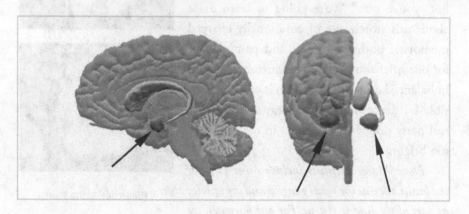

The round marble-looking "eyeballs" attached to the horn-like basal ganglia are called the *amygdala*. (A single one is called the *amygdale*.) In the side view on the left, you see half of the structure. In the view on the right— from the front of the brain—you can see the twin-horned structures with amygdala "eyes."

On a scan, when things are going well, the amygdala actually look like the friendly little dotted eyes on a smiley face. When this area is overlit, however, the "almond eyes" grow bigger and more fearful. Panicked and anxious. It's like having Chicken Little with eyes bulging, living in your head when this critter is overactivated. Again, when there aren't too many big red, lit up "eyes" going on in here, things are pretty calm, and the basal ganglia and amygdala (some-times called the *reptilian brain*) actually help you avoid many real dangers.

The problems begin if this area of the brain starts sensing nearly every-thing as a threat or danger and your body stays on hyperalert, as if Noggin really were stuck in this Basement of Giant Fears with a big-eyed monster. You can imagine how hard it would be to suppress these fears if your brain believed they were real. Fear is a drag on your ability to be happy, as your lighthearted lobby has little chance to take charge when the basement lights are blaring and the scary creatures are stomping around.

THE TEMPER LOFTS (TEMPORAL LOBES)

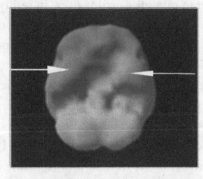

Right Temporal
Lobe

Left Temporal
Lobe

(Underside, surface view)
Imagine a turtle shell flipped on its back, so in this picture
the left side of the brain is on the right side of the page.

Finally, Noggin is ready to float back up and out of the brain, and he is taking the path up the side of the head. Well, actually, Noggin would have to split into two people—so imagine that in a cartoon-like image—and take the path up *both* sides of your head, near your ears to the temporal lobes (that's right, by your temples!), and what have we here? Many helpful processes. But if they are lit up like a Christmas tree, guess what? We may have a very angry person under our scan, perhaps, someone who rages inappropriately and is easily set off. Someone who makes others feel as though they always have to walk on eggshells in order to avoid triggering their explosive temper. So let's call the Temporal Lobe rooms, on either side of the Brain House, the Temper Lofts. As you can imagine, anger is one of life's most common joy robbers.

TRIAL RUN THROUGH THE BRAIN HOUSE

In fact, now that you've had the basic head trip around the ol' Brain House, let's do a little trial run around some of the rooms. Let's say that you are a child, Jay, who has to live with a father who has the lights turned to high beam in his Temper Lofts. What part of little Jay's brain will light up in coping with an angry father? You bet: the basal ganglia, the Basement of Giant Fears, with its frightened almond-eyed monster (amygdala). And at this point in the boy's life, the fears are real and valid. The child needs to be hyperaware of his surroundings in order to minimize getting hurt. In reality, his brain is protecting him. Since most children choose flight over fight, they usually do some form of hiding: disappearing to a bedroom, trying not to disturb anyone, remaining still and silent.

Now let's say, years later, Jay grows up and marries a loving, safe, and emotionally healthy woman named . . . Joy. Of course, even the most emotionally balanced woman has times when she feels angry or irritated. For Joy, it's usually about once a month. (Pre-monster . . . er, I mean pre-*menstrual* symptoms can turn the sweetest woman into someone even she doesn't recognize sometimes.)

Imagine that Joy speaks harshly to Jay when she discovers he's left a mess in the kitchen. A man raised in a home without fear will think before reacting, and probably apologize for the mess, but also ask his wife to speak to him in a kinder tone of voice. (Emotionally healthy, brain-balanced people tend to think compassionately toward others and toward themselves.)

But how would a man react whose lights are nearly always blazing in the Basement of Giant Fears? (After all, Jay was basically trained to keep the lights on, always, in order to best protect himself.) Most likely, he'd go into automatic hyperanxiety: fight-or-flight mode. He'd totally shut down in silence and sneak into his man cave, or he'd overreact, mimic what he saw in his dad, and explode in a rage.

And that, my friends, is just one small example among millions of how we human beings can get so confused in the head. We under- or overreact, we lose our joy, we miss opportunities for connection and happiness; we think God, society, our wife, or our kids are out to get us. We see giants in the basement even when there's no reason for fear anymore.

THIS IS YOUR BRAIN ON JOY

So what does a happy brain look like? Funny you should ask—ironically, it looks a little like a smiling face!

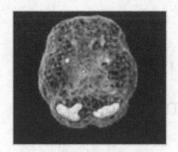
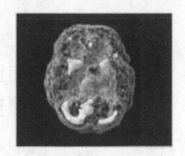

A joyful, peaceful brain   A brain in emotional pain
(Underside, active view)

The picture on the left is a normal, happy, balanced brain. You can see that the limbic system looks like a little dot of a nose in the middle of the brain. The light is on, but just enough, like a nice, soft white lamp light. The same is true for the basal ganglia (which looks like a couple of cute little button eyes). No giants in the basement here and, therefore, no major fears. The part where there is a lot of white is the cerebellum, and it is like the lowest basement of the brain, near your brain stem. This should always be lit up quite a bit because it controls automotive motor skills. Because the focus of this book is on joy and moods rather than other brain processes, we won't spend much time talking about the cerebellum.

Now take a look at the contrasting picture of the brain on the right. It is lit up like the Fourth of July in the areas of the brain that produce fear and sadness. When I see scans like this, I feel two distinct and contrasting emotions. On the one hand, I feel great empathy and compassion for the people who are courageously facing each day with such a burden of sorrowful and fearful emotions at play in their brains. On the other hand, I feel so thankful that I can help them. I have the tools to calm the savage beasts that have ravaged their minds and, often, their lives and relationships. Not only that, but I have the tools to help them get beyond a baseline of normal feelings. I can help them upsize their experiences of life, help them trade their worries for wonders, their sorrows for joy.

And now, because of the tremendous privilege I've been given of writing this book, I'm delighted and grateful to share the same information with you.

After all, joy is a terrible thing to waste.

CHAPTER FOUR

Testing, Testing . . . All Brains Need a Little Help Sometimes

Shaped a little like a loaf of French country bread,
our brain is a crowded chemistry lab,
bustling with nonstop neural conversations.[1]

—DIANE ACKERMAN

Now that you've been on the official tour of the Brain House, it's time to take a test. Don't worry. I won't be testing your memory on the names of the various areas of the brain. Actually, I left out my favorite brain name: the medulla oblongata, or the brain stem. For the sheer pleasure of impressive pronunciation, nothing beats learning to say *medulla oblongata* over and over again. Even five-year-olds get a kick out of repeating it. But, alas, the medulla oblongata doesn't have anything to do with mood or emotion or feelings of joy. In fact, it is part of the unconscious, autonomic nervous system and helps control things like breathing, blood pressure, heart rate, swallowing, vomiting, and defecation. Not nearly as fascinating to me as mood, passion, emotion, and joy! So as Forrest Gump might say, "That's all I have to say 'bout that." Hope you enjoyed the medulla oblongata's brief, one-time mention here, and perhaps find that adding it to your vocabulary might come in handy to impress your peers or amuse small children so that this paragraph won't be entirely wasted. (Did I mention that my particular brain type tends to meander off track now and then? I embrace the battle cry of the attention-challenged: "Life's too short to stay on topic!")

With that rabbit trail out of my system, let's get refocused and talk about the big, fun brain test.

Dr. Amen has graciously allowed me to put his diagnostic screening tool into this book. He created the checklist that begins on page 33, and though it may look simple, trust me, years of research and fine-tuning went into this amazingly helpful test. Though not nearly as accurate as a brain scan coupled with therapeutic observation, the test can point many people in the right direction for help. How? By helping a doctor identify areas of the brain that are most probably over- or underactive.

It should be said here that not all minor imbalances need scanning or medication. Most don't! In fact, some of our personality traits come from the unique ways that our brains light up at rest or under stress. Remember that there is really no such thing as a totally perfect brain (although I would have loved to have scanned the brain of Jesus!). I would venture to say that 100 percent of us could use at least a little help to improve our mood and brain function. Most successful business partnerships, and many successful marriages, come from two people whose brains are synergistic when put together. When Jerry Maguire, the lively sports agent movie character who was "great at friendship, bad at intimacy," was finally smitten by the real thing, he told his girlfriend, "You complete me." There's some truth to that. You may have highly functioning parts of your brain that help complement or make up for your partner's weaker areas. And vice versa. Human beings were created to help complete each other. Paul even referred to the church as being like the body of Christ, each part playing a part to help complete and complement the other.

So in balance, completing each other can be a beautiful duet to observe. We all know cases of the scatterbrained wife with a big heart who is married to a steady, rock-solid, organized guy who sometimes seems to be lacking what Jennifer Aniston's character in *Friends* so aptly termed "a sensitivity gene." But together, somehow, they make a whole, functioning couple. "As iron sharpens iron, so one man sharpens another," Solomon once said (Proverbs 27:17). In balance, again, this is absolutely true.

On the other hand, out of balance, things can go downhill quickly. Perhaps you've seen the movie *Mrs. Doubtfire*, where Robin Williams played the fun and funny, creative but irresponsible father paired with his high-need-for-order wife, played by Sally Field. She was seething in ever-escalating anger for always having to play the bad cop in childrearing while her husband also let her take all the major day-to-day responsibilities. It proved to be a formula for a movie divorce. I often see this happening in marital therapy and sometimes will turn to the exhausted spouse and say, "You look like you are tired of being his prefrontal cortex." By that I mean, "Your marriage is sinking under the strain of your mate letting you do all the thinking, planning, and organizing while he (or she) goes out to play (or leaves dishes in the bedroom, cabinet doors open, and often credit cards maxed out)."

How will you know, after taking the test, whether or not you may need more than a lifestyle change or wake-up call to feel more personally balanced—or to help own your responsibility for your part in your closest relationships? One way to know is to think back on the times when you've tried to change and, perhaps, were able to do so but only temporarily. It was as though a window of positive change opened in your life—through a good therapy session, a sermon, a poignant book, or the sincere plea of a loved one—but within a relatively short time, the window automatically slammed shut, and you were unable to continue the change. If, despite desire, good input, and proactivity, you are still suffering from anxiety, anger, depression, or obsessive thoughts, you may need some extra brain help: most likely some targeted supplements or specific medication to help balance you out and also to help you absorb the good sermons, books, and advice.

One young man put it like this: "No matter how many times I tried to control my anger, I failed. Prayer, sermons, pleading from others would touch me for a time but never stick. Part of my brain was like Teflon. Even books and tapes on anger management, though helpful, could not tame my tendency to flare up the moment I felt slighted. It's like everything I'd learned flew out the window when I was faced with a circumstance that triggered my rage. Finally, after an arrest, I consented to try the medication recommended to me. Within a week, my brain was able to absorb and hold on to anger management techniques, and it stuck when tested in the heat of provocation. My brain now allowed me the split-second moment I needed for my thinking brain to overtake my fight response in the emotive, reactive part of my brain."

If you are having trouble applying all the nonmedical recommendations we'll make in these chapters, or the exercises don't seem to have "sticking power," then you may want to consider getting a good, professional workup and learn about the possibility of either supplementation or medication.

AMEN BRAIN SYSTEM CHECKLIST

Please rate yourself on each of the symptoms listed below using the following scale. If possible, to give the most complete picture, have another person who knows you well (such as a spouse, partner, or parent) rate you as well.

Never: 0   Rarely: 1   Occasionally: 2
Frequently: 3   Very Frequently: 4   Not Applicable/Not Known: NA

Other   Self

___ ___   1. Fails to give close attention to details or makes careless mistakes

___ ___   2. Trouble sustaining attention in routine situations (such as homework, chores, and paperwork)

___ ___   3. Trouble listening

___ ___   4. Fails to finish things

___ ___   5. Poor organization for time or space (such as backpack, room, desk, and paperwork)

___ ___   6. Avoids, dislikes, or is reluctant to engage in tasks that require sustained mental effort

___ ___   7. Loses things

___ ___   8. Easily distracted

___ ___   9. Forgetful

___ ___   10. Poor planning skills

___ ___   11. Lacks clear goals or forward-thinking

___ ___   12. Difficulty expressing feelings

___ ___   13. Difficulty expressing empathy for others

___ ___   14. Excessive daydreaming

___ ___   15. Feels bored

___ ___   16. Feels apathetic or unmotivated

___ ___   17. Feels tired, sluggish, or slow-moving

___ ___   18. Feels spacey or "in a fog"

___ ___ 19. Fidgety, restless, or trouble with sitting still

___ ___ 20. Difficulty remaining seated in situations where remaining
         seated is expected

___ ___ 21. Runs about or climbs excessively in situations in which it is
         inappropriate

___ ___ 22. Difficulty playing quietly

___ ___ 23. "On the go" or acts as if "driven by a motor"

___ ___ 24. Talks excessively

___ ___ 25. Blurts out answers before questions have been completed

___ ___ 26. Difficulty waiting turn

___ ___ 27. Interrupts or intrudes on others (for example, butts into
         conversations or games)

___ ___ 28. Impulsive (saying or doing things without thinking first)

___ ___ 29. Excessive or senseless worrying

___ ___ 30. Upset when things do not go own way

___ ___ 31. Upset when things are out of place

___ ___ 32. Tendency to be oppositional or argumentative

___ ___ 33. Tendency to have repetitive negative thoughts

___ ___ 34. Tendency toward compulsive behaviors

___ ___ 35. Intense dislike for change

___ ___ 36. Tendency to hold grudges

___ ___ 37. Trouble shifting attention from subject to subject

___ ___ 38. Trouble shifting behavior from task to task

___ ___ 39. Difficulties seeing options in situations

___ ___ 40. Tendency to hold on to own opinion and not listen to others

___ ___ 41. Tendency to get locked into a course of action, whether or
         not it is good

___ ___ 42. Becomes very upset if things are not done a certain way

___ ___ 43. Others complain that you worry too much

___ ___ 44. Tend to say no without first thinking about question

___ ___ 45. Tendency to predict fear

___ ___ 46. Frequent feelings of sadness

___ ___ 47. Moodiness

___ ___ 48. Negativity

___ ___ 49. Low energy

___ ___   50. Irritability

___ ___   51. Decreased interest in others

___ ___   52. Decreased interest in things that are usually fun or pleasurable

___ ___   53. Feelings of hopelessness about the future

___ ___   54. Feelings of helplessness or powerlessness

___ ___   55. Feels dissatisfied or bored

___ ___   56. Excessive guilt

___ ___   57. Suicidal feelings

___ ___   58. Crying spells

___ ___   59. Lowered interest in things usually considered fun

___ ___   60. Sleep changes (too much or too little)

___ ___   61. Appetite changes (too much or too little)

___ ___   62. Chronic low self-esteem

___ ___   63. Negative sensitivity to smells/odors

___ ___   64. Frequent feelings of nervousness or anxiety

___ ___   65. Panic attacks

___ ___   66. Symptoms of heightened muscle tension (headaches, sore
               muscles, hand tremor)

___ ___   67. Periods of heart pounding, rapid heart rate, or chest pain

___ ___   68. Periods of trouble breathing or feeling smothered

___ ___   69. Periods of feeling dizzy, faint, or unsteady on feet

___ ___   70. Periods of nausea or abdominal upset

___ ___   71. Periods of sweating or hot or cold flashes

___ ___   72. Tendency to predict the worst

___ ___   73. Fear of dying or doing something crazy

___ ___   74. Avoids places for fear of having an anxiety attack

___ ___   75. Conflict avoidance

___ ___   76. Excessive fear of being judged or scrutinized by others

___ ___   77. Persistent phobias

___ ___   78. Low motivation

___ ___   79. Excessive motivation

___ ___   80. Tics (motor or vocal)

___ ___   81. Poor handwriting

___ ___   82. Quick startle

___ ___   83. Tendency to freeze in anxiety-provoking situations

___ ___ 84. Lacks confidence in own abilities

___ ___ 85. Seems shy or timid

___ ___ 86. Easily embarrassed

___ ___ 87. Sensitive to criticism

___ ___ 88. Bites fingernails or picks skin

___ ___ 89. Short fuse or periods of extreme irritability

___ ___ 90. Periods of rage with little provocation

___ ___ 91. Often misinterprets comments as negative when they are not

___ ___ 92. Irritability tends to build, then explodes, then recedes;
               often tired after a rage

___ ___ 93. Periods of "spaciness" or confusion

___ ___ 94. Periods of panic and/or fear for no specific reason

___ ___ 95. Visual or auditory changes, such as seeing shadows or hear-
               ing muffled sounds

___ ___ 96. Frequent periods of *I* (feelings of being somewhere you
               have never been)

___ ___ 97. Sensitivity or mild paranoia

___ ___ 98. Headaches or abdominal pain of uncertain origin

___ ___ 99. History of a head injury or family history of violence
               or explosiveness

___ ___ 100. Dark thoughts, may involve suicidal or homicidal thoughts

___ ___ 101. Periods of forgetfulness or memory problems

Answer Key

Prefrontal Cortex (Presidential Control Center) Symptoms, Questions 1–28
   If nine or more symptoms are rated 3 or 4, this indicates a problem with
   the prefrontal cortex. (1–18 indicate a more "inattentive type" ADD;
   19–28 may indicate ADHD, which includes symptoms of hyperactivity
   along with attention problems; see chapter 6.)

Cingulate Gyrus (Circular Gerbil Wheel) Symptoms, Questions 29–45
   If five or more symptoms are rated 3 or 4, there's a high probability that
   the SPECT scan will show an overactive cingulate (see chapter 7).

Deep Limbic System (Depressed Low-Mood Space) Symptoms, Questions 46–63
   If five or more of symptoms are rated 3 or 4, you may need to consider

an antidepressant or a supplement with antidepressant qualities (see chapter 9).

Basal Ganglia (Basement of Giant Fears) Symptoms, Questions 64–88

If five or more symptoms are rated 3 or 4, then there is a high likelihood that a SPECT scan would show overactivity in the basal ganglia, the area of the brain associated with fear and anxiety (see chapter 8).

Temporal Lobe (Temper Lofts) Symptoms, Questions 89–101

If five or more symptoms are rated 3 or 4—in my personal experience over the past ten years, 100 percent of people scanned have had temporal lobe overactivity or underactivity in either or both the left and right temporal lobes—you may struggle with mood swings: times of high energy or mania that may shift suddenly to dark depressions or volatility (see chapter 10).

There now, that wasn't so bad, was it? Remember, you can't get a good or bad grade on this test. You just get information to help you get happier sooner.

Now that you know where you may be having some brain issues, you may want to skip to the chapter that applies to you right this very minute (especially you ADD types; I know you all too well). That's fine. However, before we leave this chapter and get on with the *what's wrongs* and *how do I fix its*, I have one final piece of information I want to share with you.

GOOD NEWS! YOUR BRAIN IS PLASTIC!

Just when you think you've mastered all the big words you can handle, I want to quickly introduce you to one more brain buzzword: neuroplasticity. If you take the word apart, it basically describes a phenomenon that has only been discovered in recent years: your *neurons* (that make up the communication system in your brain) are *plastic*. Of course, this doesn't mean your neurons are made by Rubbermaid or purchased in Hong Kong (though, on a tough day, some of you may feel like your brain was "made in China"). In brain terms, when something is plastic or shows plasticity, it simply means it is malleable, changeable, pliable, and able to grow, stretch, and change.

It can now be proven that human beings literally change their own brain makeup and that this process continues (as long as you continue to learn and grow) until the day you die. For a long time, scientists thought that at a certain point, adults no longer could grow any new neurons or make new neuron connections. They thought, *Yeah, sure. You can teach an old dog new tricks, but it won't be easy because the old boy has to use the same, tired, midlife brain cells he's stuck with until he's ready for dog heaven.* Alas, take heart, middle-aged dogs—and people—of the world. This is simply not true. Old dogs not only can learn new tricks, but when they do so, their neurons start reproducing and branching wildly, just like those of young pups. And the more they learn, the friskier they feel. This helps explain why, in part, curious and involved older people often walk around with silly grins on their faces. There's always one eternally smiling, eager, mature returning student in every college class, sitting at the front of the room, impressing the professor, asking questions with enthusiasm, ruining the grade curve for everyone else, and generally having the time of his or her life. Learning something new is one of life's greatest pleasures, no matter your age.

There is a myth about brain function that once the brain is injured or cells are lost, it's "So Long, Farewell, *Auf Wiedersehen*, Good-bye." Research has shown that this, too, is simply not true. For people who stay mentally active throughout their lives, there are areas of the brain that will continue to grow, particularly if you learn something completely new or different. Think of Winston Churchill learning to paint after mastering the art of war. Or the famed Dallas Cowboy running back Emmitt Smith cha-cha-ing his way to the *Dancing with the Stars* championship.

Okay, maybe some of you he-men don't really want to think of this. Still, there are dozens of new, exciting creative skills for you *Wild at Heart* guys to learn beyond watercolor painting, doing the tango, or baking a mean blueberry muffin (or what I call the *mild*-at-heart man skills). There's always rock climbing and sky diving and alligator rasslin' and snake huntin'. The world is full of interesting new stuff to learn, and all of it makes your brain cells become fruitful and multiply. And this tends to put a smile on your face (even if it might put a dent or two in your budget).

How do new neurons multiply and connect and branch wildly in our brains? Research shows they are stimulated to grow in three ways:

1. *By a change in outside circumstances*—the things you view or read and that surround you
2. *By a change within*—your thoughts or determination to try new things
3. *By what we physically feed them*—medication, supplementation, nutrition, and exercise

All this means you can begin *today* to change your brain into a happier, more peaceful, fun hunk o' burnin' gray matter.

As you might imagine (now that you are getting pumped up about your future brain on joy), research and findings in the study of neuroplasticity are causing quite a stir of hope and excitement in the brain-health community. Perhaps you may have also seen articles on this subject in several popular magazines from *Time* to *Newsweek* to *Reader's Digest*. Even *O, The Oprah Magazine* and *Woman's Day* are talking up the brain and its plastic parts these days. Baby boomers like me are thrilled to hear about anything that keeps them young at heart and away from depressing images of themselves shuffling along in a nursing home muttering nonsensical threats to dust balls. Brain science is no longer just a hot topic among nerds without girlfriends; it's now *cool* to be into the brain. (I knew my moment in the cool spotlight would eventually come!)

When you really grasp the fact that our brain is literally shaped and changed by our experiences (inner or outer), it upsizes the sense of control you have over your own happiness. What you choose to do, think about, surround yourself with, and put in your gullet make a difference. It *all* matters to your experience of joy on this planet.

In fact, God has wired in our DNA that we change throughout life. We were never designed to be static, unchanging sticks in life's mud.

Thinking outside the brain for a moment, did you know that even the skeleton that you have now is not the skeleton that you had three months ago? Every molecule and atom that makes up your skeleton will change within three months. The cells in your stomach change every five minutes. (I sure wish the cells in my system that love a good cheeseburger and fries would die off and be replaced by ones that crave carrots and celery.)

"We are not stuck with the brain we were born with," writes Sharon Begley, author of *Train Your Mind, Change Your Brain*. "Connections among neurons can be physically modified through mental training," she explains, in much the same way that we build up our biceps by working out at the gym.[2]

For example, people who proactively and diligently use their mind to train their brain (or their prefrontal cortex to balance their mood systems) through daily prayer and meditation can literally go from an anxious, fearful mood state to another more peaceful, joyful one that can be seen on a brain scan. (Prayers of gratitude, compassion, and love are particularly effective.) Not only that, but the more years that you practice the daily art of calming your brain in quiet, focused prayer or meditation, the more those changes stick and become part of a whole new, kinder, gentler you. Even when you are not actively centering yourself in prayer, if you incorporate compassionate, simple, prayerful meditation and weave it into your daily routine for years, you'll be happy and you'll know it because your SPECT scan will surely show it.

Now that you've taken your test, and you know that you've got a wonderful, plastic, bendy brain in your hands (actually, on your neck), we're ready to do the work on your Brain House. We'll go room by room, a chapter at a time, and take a look at what's happening and how to make each area the best it can be. We'll use all the methods available to us to help you give yourself a do-it-yourself brain makeover: outer circumstances and information; inner tweakings of your thoughts and habits; and physical changes like nutrition and exercise, along with recommendations for supplements or medications, if needed.

After reading this book, some of you with more complicated issues may want to consider taking a couple of days out of your life to come to Southern California where I live and work and get a "tan and scan." My collaborator on this book, Becky Johnson, recently came out to California to visit with Dr. Amen and me, to gather more information as well as to get her own brain scanned as part of the research in assembling this book. If you'd like to read about her experience from walking into the Amen Clinics to walking out with pictures of her beautiful brain and a few recommendations on how to make her brain even more gorgeous, see appendix A: The Day I Had My Head Examined.

You also may want to take a peek at appendix B: Common Questions About SPECT Scans. This information helps you better understand the scans in the coming chapters. Finally, appendix C gives a more detailed explanation of post-traumatic stress disorder (PTSD) and the *diamond pattern* (affecting three mood centers) that usually shows up in a scan of someone with PTSD symptoms.

PILLSBURY DOUGH HEAD AND OTHER BRAIN IMAGES

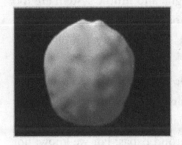

Normal Brain

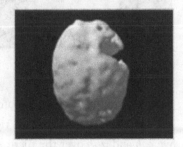

Forty-eight-year-old who fell off roof.
Problems with memory, listening, concentration, and temper.

(Top-down, surface view)

In brief, when you see a brain scan that looks a bit like an oblong ball of tie-dyed bread dough, this is called a SPECT *surface* scan. It is used to help us detect underactivity in the brain. We often see, in this form of scan, pictures that look like someone has poked their finger in some poor soul's psychedelic brain dough. And sadly, in some pictures, where there are a lot of *poked holes* (showing lack of desired activity), the person is usually suffering from problems from a variety of sources (stroke, brain injury, substance abuse, or dementia).

When you see a SPECT *active* scan, in color, it will look somewhat like red and white fish caught in a net in a blue, brainy sea. This scan is taken while someone is doing a concentration task on a computer, and it measures problems with overactivity in the brain. The back of the brain, near the cerebellum, *should* show up bright red, revealing a lot of activity because it controls so many motor functions. But the rest of the brain, except for three little red dots (that look like eyes and a nose on the next scan) should be a sea of blue. (Note: The black-and-white scans included in this book are an economical necessity, I'm afraid. If we had used color scans, we'd have to charge you $100 for the book. If you have access to the Internet, you can

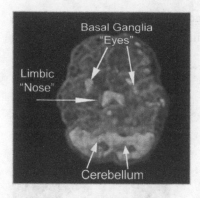

(Top-down, surface view)

view color scans on Dr. Amen's site at www.amenclinic.com.) In the black-and-white scans, the *hot spots* in the brain are the darker areas.

In this scan, the cerebellum is normal—it is always supposed to be "lit up"—but the basal ganglia and limbic system are too "hot" and should be smaller. This person probably has some anxiety coupled with depression.

When Dr. Amen and I see a holey—over/underactive—brain become a smooth, healthy brain with activity in just the right amounts in just the right places, especially after successful treatment, we *ooh* and *ahh* over the pictures like a pair of proud papas. For we know: not only do the pictures look nicer, but the person is feeling much happier.

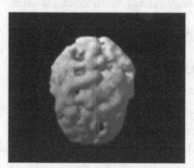

Alcohol, Meth, and Cocaine

One Year Sober

(Top-down, surface view)

All right then! You've taken your test and now, hopefully, you are ready to explore more. You may want to skip to the chapter that most applies to you, but be sure to come back and read chapter 5 at some point because 1) it's a quick and fun read with vital applications and healthy prescriptions for all brain types, and 2) it will give you some brief research as to the *whys* behind the prescriptions for upsizing your brain's joy.

CHAPTER FIVE

Joy Boosters: The Science Behind Pleasure Prescriptions

When your brain works right, you work right.

—DR. DANIEL AMEN

To help summarize activities that increase your joy to your brain, I've divided the following joy boosters into three neat categories:

- *Enriching your outer world* (creating a joyful, brain-stimulating environment)
- *Enriching your inner world* (feeding your mind and soul with nourishing thoughts)
- *Enriching your body-mind chemistry* (through what you put in your mouth and how you move your muscles)

Obviously, some of these areas overlap. For example, a good argument could be made that music is both an *outer* world and *inner* world activity, with listening to the score from *Phantom of the Opera* an outer activity, but singing "Oh! Susannah" while strumming the banjo originating from inner impulses. But people, *people.* Let's not quibble! Life's too short to argue about categories—let's just get down to the business of absorbing and applying all the resources at hand that will upsize our daily experience of happiness, shall we? And if you obsessive-compulsive types cannot rest easy until the categories work for you, by all means, get out your red pen and mark up this section until it feels right. (Or neatly type out a whole new list since the stray red marks could make your eye start to twitch.)

To bring the points home, I want to offer you some tidbits of interesting backup research so you'll understand the *why* behind the reason I am going to be sprinkling the following joy boosters into the next five chapters—chapters where we explore the five major mood areas of the brain and how to turn down the angst and turn up the joy in each unique room.

ENRICHING YOUR OUTER WORLD

Rat Park: A Case for "Enriching Environment" in Joy and Brain Health

One study that had been mostly forgotten or overlooked but is making its way back into several books on happiness is an experiment dubbed *Rat Park*. You've probably heard of studies done on rats that prove they'll do anything for a pleasure fix. Typically the scientists put the rat in a cage with a lever that allows them to give themselves drugs that activate their pleasure center (alongside a lever for food and water, which often remains untouched). The rats will hit the pleasure lever until they pass out in exhaustion and then wake up only to hit it again until they eventually die from exertion or starvation.

So the assumption has been that humans will certainly do the same thing, given free access to certain drugs. Bruce Alexander, a rebel researcher from Canada, was skeptical about these results. He noticed that the rats in the experiments were stuffed alone in a boring cage with little else to do. *If I was strapped down alone in a cage,* he thought, *I'd probably want to get high too.*

So he built a *rat park*—a large, intricate, brightly painted, and heavily padded structure to make the rats happy. They also had plenty of rats to socialize with and make rodent love to. Toys, rat wheels, and mazes along with good food, fresh water, rat friends, and—glory!—lots of room to roam.

Then he put half of the rats in the normal cages and half in the park and gave both equal access to morphine-laced water. The rats in the cage got addicted while the rats in the park stayed away. Even when he sweetened the morphine source with sugar water (rats have a sweet tooth), the rats in the park (sometimes after trying it once or twice) avoided it.

Then, even more strikingly, he took some rats from the small cages (who'd had fifty-seven days to get addicted to morphine) and put them in the park. Even though they'd been addicted in the cage, those rats suddenly stayed away from the drugs too. They even voluntarily detoxed—trembling and shaking but still staying off the drugs.[1]

What does this remarkable study say to us? Life itself was meant to be our original natural high. You can imagine that life in the Garden of Eden—filled with everything pleasant for the eye to see, mouth to taste, and with both earthly and godly companionship—was especially conducive to a blissful state of mind. Does this mean that kids who grow up surrounded by beauty and love and healthy pleasures in our society will not abuse or get addicted to drugs? It probably *would* mean that if their brains were also processing their outer environment realistically. Sadly, humans are more complicated than rats and thus sometimes sabotage wonderful life circumstances with poor or skewed thinking. So that is why we want to take a three-pronged approach to joy—covering outer circumstances as well as inner thoughts and chemical balancing.

That said, however, here are a few examples of how to proactively create an environment conducive to *natural* highs. There are many more that could be put in this list, but this will give you a random sampling of environmental enrichment.

Village of Support

It really does take a village to help most of us feel happy. The success of twelve-step recovery programs shows the power of close-knit, authentic community in overcoming life's stresses—particularly when leaving an addiction behind in order to experience life's natural highs. It's no wonder that many consider AA the world's largest church. More *real* church is probably happening in many of these meetings of honest people in rented office spaces than in some of our greatest and most beautiful cathedrals.

Areas of the world where generations of families live close to each other tend to have the highest happiness rates. As an aside, they also have less cancer and heart disease, and this is without making any of our typical "healthy" lifestyle changes. It does not seem to matter how much these close-knit clans eat, drink, or exercise—the joy that comes from being part of a connected community is truly life-giving, often trumping the standard medical prescriptions for longevity.[2]

It is important, however, that you have relatives who are supportive and loving overall, not just in close proximity. Surrounding yourself with positive people who believe in and champion your dreams is vital to bouncing back from sorrow or stress into joy. (And for some people, they have to escape a dysfunctional family and re-create a sense of family among good friends.) Being in a loving marriage, bonding with a baby, and even stroking a beloved pet can reduce anxiety and raise happiness hormones.

Surprisingly, few human connection studies show a greater rise in pure happiness than when you are involved, in some way, in voluntarily helping someone else. Bishop T. D. Jakes has said, ". . . your ministry will be where your misery has been," and encourages you to get out of your "hospital bed" as soon as you can to make room for others who need emergency aid and comfort—often just the sort of aid and comfort that you can best give them (because you remember, all too well, what it was like to feel sick).[3]

One study in England found that people living in areas where the citizens routinely volunteered their time for charitable causes "enjoyed better health, suffered less crime, and claimed to be 'very satisfied' with their lives." Students also achieved higher grades. So volunteering is good for your soul, and puts a grin on your face.[4]

A more recent study showed that the happiest people tend to give more money to charity. It didn't matter how much they earned—across the board low- and high-income families who gave a part of their money to help someone else were much happier.[5] It really *is* more blessed, in a dozen ways, to give than to receive as Jesus said it would be. (I always grin when science finally catches up to scriptural truths.)

The Scent of Happiness

One of the most interesting bits of news to come out of the science lab is how a variety of scents affect mood states. Researchers have found that even a low-level scent—one that is hardly noticeable—can help people relax or feel more focused. Consider the following:

- P. J. Person and Mary Shipley, authors of *Aromatherapy for Everyone*, write that of all the senses, "smell hits the brain first. Faster than a speeding bullet, it's the 'Superman of Senses' with a direct path to the brain."[6] In fact, the olfactory nerve fibers run a path directly to the limbic system—the mood center of the brain—bypassing the runaround that the other senses go through. So this is why you may feel suddenly and inexplicably happy when you walk by the scent of a fresh orange tree or romantic when you get a whiff of a gardenia or comforted by the smell of vanilla. Scent activates your memories before your thinking brain kicks in. It's a major reason why aromatherapy has become such a popular joy booster. It works, and brain studies prove it.

• Retailers have embraced the scent/mood connection and are offering many tailor-made lines of scents to help get you in a desired mood. Whole Foods has entire sections of the store devoted to aromatherapy products, and Bath and Body Works has introduced a new line of products, from soaps and lotions to roll-on scents, to help soothe or perk up your mind. (C. G. Bigelow has one of the most pleasant, all-natural lemon-scented product lines available on the market today and is available through Bath and Body Works.)

• A word about candles and air fresheners: although they may smell great, they can also be toxic to your system. Look for natural, organic soy candles and air fresheners, or use essential oils that are chemical free. (Some essential oils cannot be used on the skin, so check the bottles.) It is worth any extra cost to get the purest form of scents you can buy.

In the following chapters, we'll explore which scents tend to calm or stimulate each area of the brain under discussion.

Music

Music therapists (and yes, there is such a thing) have known for years that certain types of music can calm and lift people out of depression. "Music can be—and often is—used for the treatment of mental health issues," says Al Bumanis, a board-certified music therapist and spokesperson for the American Music Therapy Association.[7]

In addition:

• Music has an effect on brain chemistry, and the right kind of music can decrease stress hormones, resulting in relaxation.

• Lyrics coupled with the sounds of music tend to bypass the thinking part of the brain and go straight to the mood center. Music can bring down defenses, help patients who need to cry get all those tear toxins out of their system, cheer and console, and—used wisely and proactively—can put us in the best frame of mind for any particular moment.

• One simple way to do music therapy on yourself is to go back to the songs that lightened your mood or were uplifting to your soul in the past. Keep a journal of the tunes that make you smile. Arrange them on one or two personally made CDs or put them in your iPod. You may want to make one CD for soothing songs, another for getting your happy energy up, and another for putting you in the mood for love.

• Rachel St. John Gilbert, author of *Wake Up Laughing,* says, "My younger girls, ages five and seven, love silly songs. Buck Howdy, for example, is a fun and funny musical artist who caters to kids. I had a friend from Georgia, recently and tragically widowed, who loved belting out songs with her two school-aged sons in the car, and observing the fun they had inspired me to do the same. My teenage son, Trevor, is a budding actor and vocalist, and we've always enjoyed listening to soundtracks of Broadway shows. *Phantom of the Opera, Wicked,* and *Les Miserables* are some of our favorites. Last summer on a trip to New York, we got to see some of our favorite Broadway musicals together. What a memory, made sweeter because we knew every word to every song!" She added, "Incorporating music into my parenting has been one of life's greatest pleasures. In addition, I usually keep soft classical music on in our home to help keep a more peaceful and calm state of mind even in the middle of noisy kids and family messes."[8]

Exercise

Dr. Amen is fond of pointing out a study where researchers put a control group of moderately depressed people on a daily exercise plan and another control group on Zoloft—both for twelve weeks. At the end of the twelve weeks, both groups of people showed improved mood, and in fact, their moods had improved to equally sunny levels. However, many of those on Zoloft suffered the unwanted side effect of lower libido and sexual impotence while those who exercised not only felt better but had better bodies and a higher libido. As a joy booster, it is hard to find a more healthful and effective "cure" for the blues than exercise. (Now for those who suffer from deeper, clinical depressions, the medications can be lifesavers and help the deeply depressed to feel like getting out of bed and moving around again. But more on that later.)

Humor

A merry heart really does work like medicine for the brain, body, and soul. Take the opportunity to laugh at yourself at least once a day. A sense of humor can be trained; it just takes noticing life's irritations as if they could be funny—as if written up by a humor columnist or made into a skit. Learn to break for funny movies, cartoons, books, and comics—or whatever tickles your funny bone.

According to Marci Shimoff, author of *Happy for No Reason*, "People who maintain a sense of humor, an indication of inner happiness, outlive those who don't." She points out that the survival advantage "is particularly large for people with cancer," with one study showing that a sense of humor cut a cancer patient's chance of dying prematurely by around 70 percent.[9]

Cinematherapy

How many of you could name a movie that made you cry, opened your heart, cheered you up, or calmed your soul? When you think of that movie, a smile may cross your face as you recall the lines, the scenery, the actors, and the music. Think for a moment of the opening scene in *The Sound of Music*—with Maria bursting onto the screen amid the Alps, singing her heart out with joy. Just the full-bodied memory of this and other gorgeous, happy scenes from this classic musical can suddenly put you in a mood to climb every mountain and ford every stream.

Movies are so powerful because they envelop you in a full sensory experience. But can movies really be considered therapeutic? Many therapists believe so and are writing books to support movies as a legitimate supportive therapeutic treatment. (Watch one Jimmy Stewart film, and call me in the morning when you wake up to your *wonderful life*.)

"One aspect of most movies," says Birgit Wolz, PhD, MFT, the inspiration for the Web site www.cinematherapy.com, "is that they serve as allegories, in much the same way as do stories, myths, . . . or dreams, which can all be utilized in therapy." She points out that we have seven intelligences or types of IQ—such as musical, visual-spatial, linguistic, and logical learning—and that movies access all of those intelligences, thereby helping clients learn and absorb information faster.[10]

For a happiness boost on a down day, choose movies that provoke laughter or inspire you to rise above your circumstances. The oft-quoted research from Norman Cousins about how he recovered from cancer by watching funny shows such as *Candid Camera* and *I Love Lucy* is just one example of the healing and pain-relieving power of laughter.

When it comes to what kinds of films inspire a smile, we are all unique. One sensitive woman said, "A couple of movies that I feel are a feast for the eyes and soul are *Babette's Feast* and *Enchanted April.* Both move at a slower pace, have beautiful scenery, and a deeply moving and uplifting message of redemption." When men speak of movies that have healing effects on their lives, they often mention *A River Runs Through It* or *Field of Dreams* because these touch the father-son issues so embedded in men. *Braveheart* or *Gladiator, Saving Private Ryan* or the *Band of Brothers* series are often among the movies that men say elevate their masculine soul: the desire to fight for a cause greater than themselves perhaps—along with the bonding of brothers in such a fight—stirs them. Then there's *Dumb and Dumber* and *Anchorman*—not exactly your soul-stirring movies, but they've provoked a lot of laughter in the male species, and hey, though it's not Hemingway, silly comedy is therapeutic too.

Try asking your friends for good film recommendations, or query a group of people for a great conversation starter: "So tell me about the movies that encourage or lift your spirits in some way." Not surprisingly, many people mention movies they saw at happy points in their childhood as being especially joy-producing today. No need to wait until you have a child to rent *Snow White* or *Cinderella*. If a *Tom and Jerry* cartoon makes you smile, by all means, go there. Nostalgic television reruns like *Father Knows Best* or *Leave It to Beaver* often bring up warm, fuzzy feelings. And many of us would not consider it Christmas without watching the timeless *White Christmas, It's a Wonderful Life*, or newer classics such as *Home Alone* or *How the Grinch Stole Christmas.*

Never underestimate the power of a two-hour movie, chosen for its joy-inducing qualities, to brighten your day.

Beholding Beauty

Think of all the beauty still left around you and be happy. —Anne Frank

If little Anne Frank, hiding from the Nazis, could find pockets of beauty in her limited world, then surely we can upsize our ability to look for and absorb the beauty around us that brings an inner smile. Even photos of natural beauty have proven to be calming to the brain. Having lunch in a city park can make the difference between smiling on your way back to the office or feeling closed in and morose. Architects and interior decorators have long recognized the connection between mood, color, arrangement, and style. Try noticing rooms or pictures of rooms in magazines that make you say *ahh* on the inside. Then try to incorporate some of those colors and styles into your own nest. Rearranging or decorating is a pleasurable mental and physical exercise that packs a punch in increasing your daily joy quotient.

ENRICHING YOUR INNER WORLD

Books: A Well-Stored Mind

Gloria Gaither, beloved songstress and author, admits to being a bibliophile—a lover of books. If books are one of your brain's love languages, then you'll understand Gloria's favorite obsession, for she is one who never leaves home without a book.

Gloria confesses that one of her phobias is the fear of getting stuck in a variety of situations—from sitting on a plane, to the hospital waiting room, to Starbucks—without a book in hand. "And when I have come closest to losing my faith in God and mankind," she says, "it has been a book that has come to my rescue."[11]

My love of reading comes directly from my father. He is now seventy-nine years old and has a box of books in the trunk of his car. He reads three to four books per week on a variety of topics. Reading and learning any kind of new information helps prevent Alzheimer's and dementia. So if you love books, indulge yourself, knowing that with every new idea you read about, you are causing neural growth in your brain.

Well-written books of all genres—from self-help to spiritual growth to mysteries and allegories, memoirs and romance—entering our lives at the right moment, have all been used to lift our souls. In what is believed to be one of Paul's last books, 2 Timothy, he requested that Timothy "bring . . . the books, especially the parchments" (4:13 NASB) to help him redeem his final hours in prison. The Greek word for *books* is used to describe books written on cheaper papyrus that could have been authored by any number of people. The parchments, however, were printed on costly vellum and believed to have been the Old Testament Scriptures. Paul found comfort mostly in the Scriptures, but apparently he also had a fondness for a good read too.

The Great Thought Exchange

Dr. Amen often speaks of ANTs infestations: Automatic Negative Thoughts that disrupt and sometimes kidnap our experience of joy. Learning to question our own thoughts and ponder alternative and more positive ways of "reading" situations is a skill that can be integrated with practice. Our thoughts often lie to us. By distancing ourselves from their messages, we can evaluate any automatic painful paths (or ANTs infestations) and point our minds toward new and more upbeat directions. This internal thinking skill may be the most valuable tool you take away from this book because it can, with proactive practice, become more automatic for you to think positive than negative.

In the coming chapters, we share quotes from Scripture and famous folks to give you specific thoughts that you can use to replace your old ANTs.

Relaxation Responses

Made popular by the research of Herbert Benson, MD, the relaxation response is a physical state of deep rest that changes the physical and emotional responses to stress when eliciting the relaxation response:

• Metabolism decreases
• The heart beats more slowly, and muscles relax
• Breathing becomes slower
• Blood pressure decreases

If practiced regularly, relaxation can have lasting effects. Repeating words of comfort (such as "The LORD is my shepherd" [Ps. 23:1]), prayerful meditation, progressive muscle relaxation, and mindful breathing are some of the ways our brains can help our bodies release the relaxation response.

The basics of progressive muscle relaxation are easy. One mom says, "I used this with my children when they had headaches or couldn't get to sleep. It's a wonderful technique to help your kids learn to self-soothe at night, and enjoy peaceful dreams. Or help them relax enough to sleep when they don't feel well." Lie down in a comfortable position and simply tighten and then relax your body in sections from head to toe. Imagining that each part of your body is initially heavy and full of lead also helps to totally relax each area as you imagine it becoming lighter. Another helpful relaxation trick is to imagine yourself walking down a set of stairs, slowly descending into a peaceful scene (green pastures and cool waters work for me).

Prayer

The apostle Paul wrote about praying for others "with joy" (Phil. 1: 4)—describing the emotional state he was in during his prayer time. And for good scientific reason. Prayer for others, particularly prayer for their happiness and well-being, lights up the left prefrontal cortex—the happiness spot—of the human brain. In fact, few activities foster more feelings of joy than praying a blessing over someone else. Not only that, but there is also research pointing to the effect of those prayers on others: they feel better, and often *get* well when others are praying for them, even if they are unaware of those prayers. ₁

Visual prayer is a way of connecting several joy-boosting practices at once: contemplating a scene of beauty while relaxing and praying for your own well-being or that of someone else's is a marvelous way to be a more joyful person. Perhaps this is why the Twenty-third Psalm is so popular. It is one of the most visual, relaxing, and joyful prayers in the Bible, and its picture of God's shepherding nearness—even through the dark valleys—is immensely comforting to anxious spirits.

Getting Your Zzzz

Thomas Edison used to take several naps a day because he discovered he was most creative in the moments when he had just woken up. So he'd fall asleep in a chair with a ball bearing in each hand and pie tins nearby. Once he would drop off to sleep, the ball bearings would fall from his hands, hit the pans, and wake him up. Then he'd grab pen and paper and do what a well-rested Thomas Edison enjoyed most: invent.

In the book *Take a Nap! Change Your Life*, author Sara C. Mednick, PhD, asserts that taking a nap isn't being lazy; it's taking control of your life.

Mednick says naps can:

- Increase alertness
- Boost creativity (the Thomas Edison factor)
- Enhance libido
- Reduce stress
- Aid in weight loss
- Keep you looking younger
- Reduce the risk of heart attack
- Elevate mood
- Strengthen memory
- Clarify decision making
- Improve productivity
- Feel *great*[12]

In fact, if you ask the philosophical question, "What does mankind truly yearn for?" my guess is that it would be to enjoy a guilt-free nap and a good night's sleep. We'll help you enjoy both in the coming pages.

Learning Something New

When you are totally immersed in learning something new, something that you enjoy thinking about or participating in, your brain buzzes with joy. And when you have to concentrate hard, your neurons begin to branch and grow, like one of those time-elapsed science films of a tree growing branches. The state of mind that scientists call *flow* occurs when you are so caught up in the task or joy of learning and creating that time no longer exists.

An author friend of mine tells me that she'd get struck with an idea for a chapter, then head to her office to start to write at 8:00 in the morning and suddenly look up—in complete shock—to see her kids home from school. *Could it already be 3:30?* she'd wonder incredulously. When she was in true, deep creative flow, she literally didn't feel the passage of time.

One fun joy booster is to write down all the things you'd love to learn how to do before you die. Play the saxaphone? Play golf? Drive a racecar? Go deep-sea fishing? Play tennis? Whittle a redbird? Photograph the Sistine Chapel at sunset? Let your mind go free, and write everything down; then promise yourself to sign up for one class or research how to begin, and get started on learning one new activity this month. Aim for a new learning experience every year. For example, this could be the year you *learn to knit*. Next year, *learn to create gourmet meals*. The next year, *learn how to do brain surgery*. Well, that last one might be a stretch for most, but you get the gist.

Or perhaps you already love golf but need to adjust your swing or get some putting lessons. Maybe you know how to make crepes but would love to learn how to start a fast-food "crepery" restaurant where you stuff crepes with everything from chicken to chocolate. New learning can be found in a familiar and beloved hobby—just upsize it or change how you do it.

Being a lifelong learner—a Curious George—is fabulous for your brain and your happiness. And when you become interested in life, you become an interesting person. People are attracted like magnets to others who never lose their love of learning.

ENRICHING YOUR BODY-MIND CHEMISTRY

Nutrition

Dr. Kirsten Rokke, staff nutritionist at the Amen Clinics, believes that in most cases, "if you give me a person who is wholly devoted to changing their nutrition and adding in regular exercise, they will experience enormous, positive changes in their mood within a month's time." In the chapters to come, we incorporate some of the recommended foods to fuel and nourish your brain and increase your smiles per mile. For now, take note of the list of Joy Food below. It's a good, healthy start for all brain types.

Supplements

One of the wonderful things about working with Dr. Amen is that though he is enormously thankful for—and prescribes—medications when needed to balance the brain, he is also knowledgeable and grateful for the many supplements that can have a tremendous effect on brain health, without side effects. Probably the number-one supplement we recommend for brain health and for happiness is high-grade fish oil. Studies consistently show that the happiest people on our planet eat a lot of fish, particularly wild-caught salmon. Fish oil is one of the easiest ways to help our land-bound citizens experience the joy that our cheerful coastal cousins partake of on a regular basis. I am convinced absolutely *everyone* should take a good, high-quality fish oil capsule or two every day. (Studies are showing that pregnant mothers, especially, should be taking them for their baby's ultimate brain health.) There's nothing better you can do for your brain, your mood, your heart, and your longevity. Enteric-coated capsules are a bit more expensive, but if you are avoiding fish oil because of the aftertaste, the enteric brands are worth it. Also, try to get a capsule that is as mercury and contaminant free as possible (although most toxins are in the flesh of the fish, not in the oil, so most fish oils are very safe).

Today there are also many flavored versions of liquid fish oil that taste pretty good if you don't want to take pills. We've seen some amazing results using fish oil with children who have childhood arthritis or who are hyperactive. Check out http://kidsneedusnow.org to view a couple of omega-3, fish-oil-based products that we've found children (and adults) really enjoy taking.

Amino acids like 5-HTP or L-tyrosine have also proven to be as effective as prescription drugs for many mild to moderate brain imbalances. I highly recommend both of Dr. Amen's books and *The Mood Cure* by Julia Ross, a particularly helpful book on supplements (especially amino acids) and diets that can help lift several types of false moods resulting from a shortage of feel-good neurotransmitters.

Medication

Finally, medication can be a true godsend when needed to balance a brain. Some of our clients are in such emotional pain that, from our experiences, we know that they need to feel better fast—and usually that means medicinal intervention. Others are more mildly affected and committed to trying a more natural protocol for a while. If it works, wonderful! A win-win for all. But we've got medication as our backup plan should diet, exercise, and supplements prove not to be enough to bring the relief needed.

JOY FOOD

The good news is that what is good for your mood is good for your brain, good for your heart, and good for your weight!

Fat Heads

One of the surprising and perhaps most delightful bits of brand-new research is that two kinds of saturated fats—from whole milk products and butter, as well as coconut oil—do not affect your body negatively when taken in normal doses as do some of the other saturated fats (corn oil, vegetable oil, and so on). And, in fact, they add the yummy touch of comfort and taste in small portions to calm, soothe, and lubricate your brain. (See *The Mood Cure* and Nina Planck's *Real Food*—both excellent books that speak to the subject of healthy fats with news that may surprise and delight you. Another fascinating book on the physiology of eating quality food with mindful, relaxed pleasure is *The Slow-Down Diet* by Marc David.)

When our nation went fat-free for a decade (remember the T-Factor Diet fad of the '80s and '90s?), we not only got fatter but also more depressed . . . in droves. We were feeding our bodies more sugar and less healthy fat, creating one giant brain crisis. Your brain is largely made up of fat and, therefore, needs regular amounts of it in small doses to keep the membranes nourished and healthy and for you to remain calm and clear.

Farm-Raised Folks

The old-fashioned, natural way of eating—a lean protein, a glass of milk, some veggies and whole grains, and fruit as snacks and dessert—was pretty much the best diet our country ever had for nourishing the brain. Basically, anything that brings us *back to the farm*—the way a family would eat if they had to grow their own food, milk their own cows, churn their own butter, and kill their own chickens—seems to be the best diet for the brain after all. And of course, adding in the exercise of plowing and harvesting and milking and churning to your daily routine couldn't hurt.

Looking back on my childhood, I was raised on a Minnesota Farm Diet, where we grew and ate our own veggies and always had a large freezer full of what would now be called *organic* beef. Our neighbors, who had time to go fishing in the Land of 10,000 Lakes, would bring us fresh fish. Milk came straight from the cow each day. (We did pasteurize it first.) Actually, there was very little purchased at the store.

How we can improve today on that classic diet is to emphasize even more fish than beef and get really creative with fruits and veggies until we are eating a quart of them a day. Also, by adopting the Mediterranean's heart-healthy use of olive oil in our cooking, we are protecting our brains and hearts.

For those who can tolerate milk and milk products, raise your frosty mug and enjoy that milk mustache again. In studies where people ate the same amount of calories but half the group had a good amount of dairy in their diet, the dairy eaters lost more weight and were healthier and felt more satisfied overall. If you can't tolerate milk, you can try lactose tablets or yogurt, substitute soy products, or try organic, hormone-free milk products. You may be surprised to discover that it wasn't the milk but the hormones in it that caused negative reactions.

A Word on Organic

I know it is expensive. However, the fewer toxins your body has to process, the happier your liver will be and the more vitamins you'll be getting. By shopping for what's on sale and stocking up if you can, it isn't hard these days to eat organic, at least partially organic, on a budget. Trader Joe's and Sunflower Market often offer great deals on organic produce, dairy, and meat. And most major grocery chains have jumped into the organic pond, cutting costs for all of us. It is safer to eat the nonorganic produce if it is thick skinned—such as bananas or navel oranges or pineapples. In fact, most tropical fruits are generally less exposed to toxic chemicals. So use your budget to buy organic berries, peaches, apples, and other thin-skinned produce.

Also, if you are consuming a lot of one product—for example, milk or hamburger—try to use the organic or antibiotic-free brands. Sam's Club carries milk products that are hormone free (though not organic) . . . and at a very reasonable cost.

Buy bags of frozen organic berries in bulk when they go on sale because they will last a long time and can be used to make ice cream–like frozen desserts in seconds with the addition of a little yogurt and honey in a blender.

Sprinkle with toasted nuts or wheat germ and you'll never know you aren't eating Italian gelato. A high-quality blender, the best you can afford, will be an investment in your family's health too. The Vita-Mix brand is expensive; however, you can toss a whole apple or carrot in there—complete with all its fiber—and it goes down in a silky, pureed juice form, smoothly and deliciously. You can toss in a carton of cottage cheese and blend it on high until absolutely smooth, and it tastes like sour cream or cream cheese, only with so much more protein and less fat. Add a little maple syrup and vanilla, and use like whipped cream on warmed fruit (pears heated with fruit juice and cinnamon are nice), then sprinkle with granola or nuts, and you've got an amazing dessert that is full of protein and fiber.

When you do decide to sweeten a sauce, smoothie, hot tea, or other recipe, try real maple syrup, honey, agave nectar (90 percent fructose but low glycemic), stevia, or a spoonful of frozen apple juice or white grape juice concentrate instead of refined white sugar or artificial sweeteners. A little goes a long way and does less harm to your blood/brain balance. The absolute worst (and commonly used) sugar you can put in your body is corn syrup—it gets to your blood even faster than table sugar. Try to avoid buying products that use this as an ingredient whenever you can.

Now to the brain food!

LEAN PROTEIN

Fish

Salmon, especially Alaskan salmon caught in the wild (the farmed variety is not as rich in omega-3 fatty acids), tuna, mackerel, and herring (which are *oilier* fishes), and all fish—mahi-mahi, cod, orange roughy, and tilapia—is nutritious, full of protein, and easy to digest. Once you find a few recipes you like, you'll get hooked on the way you feel after you eat fish.

Fish tacos are a great place to start if fish has never been your favorite food. Or just pat any of the spices you love along with a sprinkle of salt and pepper into fish filets and sauté on medium-high in olive oil (finish in the microwave or oven if the outside gets crispy before the insides are done). Make fish nuggets by rolling small fish chunks in a thick teriyaki sauce, and then again in nuts or sesame seeds, and bake at 350 degrees for about 15 minutes. Or roll filets in egg whites, then in seasoned bread crumbs (Japanese panko crumbs are incredibly light and crunchy), and sauté . . . delicious!

Note: To purchase the safest, most toxin- and mercury-free fish, of particular concern for pregnant and nursing women and children, you can download a handy wallet-sized safest-fish list at http://www.coopamerica.org/programs/livinggreen/safeseafood.cfm.

Poultry

Chicken and turkey, a little skin (crisped!) is okay for you, especially if you are suffering from a low mood; it will help the uptake of nutrients that calm your brain (see *The Mood Cure* and *Real Food*). One of the worst things about no-fat and low-fat diets is that they are terrible for moods and disastrous for the brain. Every brain cell in your body needs fat to function. The best fats? Olive oil (keep it on your counter near where you cook; it is a very stable oil that doesn't go rancid easily), a little real butter now and again, and full-fat coconut milk (the fat rises to the top and is delicious to cook with). You can get cans of coconut milk in the Asian section of any grocery store. It makes an amazing addition to smoothies: mix with ice and pineapple for a healthy piña colada.

Avoid trans fat, which, thankfully, has become easier to do. With increased awareness of trans fat dangers, groceries, restaurants, and even fast-food eateries are making changes toward using healthier oils.

Alternatives

- Meat: Lean beef and pork
- Eggs: Enriched DHA eggs are best
- Tofu and soy products: Whenever possible, choose organically raised. Don't overdo soy because of how it affects hormones, but one-half cup to one cup a day is good for you.
- Dairy products: Low-fat, not no-fat, dairy, particularly when you are trying to balance low moods. It's easier to be satisfied on a half-cup of dairy with some fat in it than on one cup without any fat. If you are feeling happy, it's okay to use no-fat dairy again, as long as you are getting olive oil and fish oil in your diet.

- Beans: Especially garbanzo beans (hummus is a good way to get these) and lentils (also a good carbohydrate source)
- Nuts and seeds: Especially walnuts (also listed under fats). Toasting them just a minute or two and sprinkling with a pinch of sea salt really brings out their flavors. Great in salads.

COMPLEX CARBOHYDRATES—FRUITS, VEGGIES, AND GRAINS, OH MY!

Try getting four cups of fruits and veggies (one quart) a day, and if you manage to do that—plus get your protein, a little fat, and some grains—you can't gain weight and will probably lose weight if needed. All that fiber fills you up, and there's just not room for donuts. (If you can slowly work your way up to consuming 35 grams of fiber per day from a variety of sources, you'll not only feel great but also find it easier to lose or maintain your weight.) And soon, the desire for donuts will fade anyway. Two tricks: make a smoothie out of your fruit requirement; eat salad or veggie-based soup to help with your daily veggie consumption.

Eat from the Rainbow

Mixing colors is a good way to think about healthy fruits and vegetables. Strive to eat red things (strawberries, raspberries, cherries, red peppers, and tomatoes), yellow things (squash, yellow peppers, small portions of bananas, and peaches), blue things (blueberries), purple things (plums), orange things (oranges, tangerines, and yams), green things (peas, spinach, and broccoli), and so on.

Here are some of the best brain-healthy fruits and veggies and whole grains:

- Berries. Especially blueberries (Dr. Amen calls them *brain berries*), raspberries, strawberries, blackberries. Use one cup of frozen mixed berries in a smoothie as a base for a fabulous-tasting, nutrition-dense shake. Use one to three tablespoons of protein powder—non-flavored whey is great; you can't taste it—and you've got breakfast or lunch in a cup. Or just leave berries whole and defrost just slightly, add a little drizzle of pure maple syrup and a tablespoon of half-and-half. Delicious.

- Oranges, lemons, limes, grapefruit. Get an orange juicer—a cheap plastic hand juicer will do—and squeeze your fresh juice in the morning. You'll get hooked. Citrus peel is loaded with antioxidants, so investing in a good citrus zester will not only add punch to your cooking but nutrition to your meals.
- Cherries. Good for arthritis too—100 percent cherry juice is a common aid to those who suffer with joint pain.
- Peaches, plums.
- Broccoli, cauliflower, brussels sprouts, cabbage.
- Oats, whole wheat, wheat germ. Oatmeal needs to be the slower-cooking kind because instant has a higher glycemic index since the manufacturer has broken down the fiber to speed cooking time and basically made it a refined carbohydrate. I don't leave the long-cooking oatmeal on for very long because I like it less mushy. Same goes for bread. Look for at least three grams of fiber. Try the new double-fiber breads!
- Red or yellow peppers. Much higher in vitamin C than green peppers— green peppers are simply unripe red peppers. Try roasting red peppers yourself; just put them over the open flame of your gas burner until they are black all over. Put in a plastic baggie to let the skin loosen in the steam. Then rub off the skin and there you go—roasted red peppers ready to add flavor to any meal or soup.
- Pumpkin, squash, carrots.
- Spinach. Works wonderfully as a salad or a cooked vegetable and adds fiber and nutrients.
- Tomatoes. Both fresh and canned are great. Actually, tomato paste and sauce are richer in some cancer-fighting nutrients than fresh tomatoes.
- Yams/sweet potatoes.
- Kale or any deep-green leafy veggie. Kale is one of the most nutrient-dense veggies in the produce section, but how many of us have even tried it? (Hint: Try removing the stems first.) If you cook kale in water, toss out the water, and you'll eliminate any bitterness. But it is delicious sautéed, without the stems, in a little olive oil with mushrooms, salt and pepper, and a dash of nutmeg. Deglaze the pan when it's done with a little dash of wine, cook a few more minutes, and serve.

- Brown rice and other whole grains. Leftover brown rice with dried fruit, nuts, and a little cinnamon or honey and a little milk makes a tasty hot cereal. Bulgur or brown rice can make a wonderful pilaf—toss in toasted nuts, some dried cranberries, and any herbs you like, and you've got a tasty, nutritious side dish. Don't forget to use grains in cold, summer salads. Tabouli (bulgur with cucumbers, parsley, tomatoes, garlic, lemon juice, and olive oil) is always refreshing, but you can create any number of grain-based salads by mixing equal parts grain and chopped fresh veggies or beans, a handful of herbs, and your favorite olive oil–based salad dressing.

Note: Almost any veggie tastes amazing steamed and then tossed with a little bit of butter, a squeeze of fresh citrus (orange, lemon, or lime), and a dash of salt and pepper. Also, try tossing a bowl of cut-up veggies in Italian dressing and olive oil; then spread on a cookie sheet and slow-roast for 30 minutes at 300 to 350 degrees or until tender and almost caramelized. Try roasting sweet potato wedges or rounds like this. Yummm!

FATS

- Avocados (guacamole!)
- Extra-virgin cold-pressed olive oil
- Olives
- Salmon (also listed under protein)
- Nuts and nut butter: Especially walnuts, macadamia nuts, Brazil nuts, pecans, and almonds (also listed under protein)
- Real butter in reasonable amounts: Just a tad will go a long way to make food taste better. Clarifed butter or ghee can also be used in cooking and won't burn easily.

LIQUIDS

- Water
- Green or black tea

- Milk: Calcium is good for your bones, and studies show that dairy is also an aid in weight loss. The no- or low-fat versions will help keep calories down, but you need to make sure you are getting enough fat in your system through olive oil and nuts and other good sources to optimize mood and brain function. If not, go ahead and enjoy the full-fat versions of milk products. And if you need to gain a little weight, by all means enjoy whole milk products, especially if you don't have any dairy allergies.
- Juices: Used in small amounts, unsweetened fruit juice can make a good base for smoothies. But there's so much sugar in most juices that I would not recommend them without the fiber included to slow down the absorption of sugar. So go ahead and squeeze juice from an orange, but scrape in the pulp as well. Or enjoy whole fruit smoothies instead.

PROBIOTICS = HEALTHIER GUT, HEALTHIER BRAIN

In his book *The Brain Diet*, author Alan C. Logan advocates using probiotics to help keep the gut healthy, improve immunity, and ultimately boost brain health. There are many good products to help "reseed" the gut with friendly bacteria, but one of the best researched and most easily accessible is the DanActive yogurt drinks. They are small, tasty, and may help keep inflammation in your body down, resulting in fewer illnesses, fewer digestive problems, and yes, ultimately even a healthier brain.[13] (For the peer-reviewed research on this helpful new product, see www.dan-active.com/danactive_scientific.html.)

Raising Your Joy Quota in the 5 Mood Centers

CHAPTER SIX

The Prefrontal Cortex:
The Presidential Control Center

I'm sorry; I wasn't paying attention to what I was thinking.
—SHELLEY CURTIS

In early October of 1945, President Harry Truman unwrapped a package sent from a friend, Fred M. Canfield, a United States Marshall from Missouri. Truman must have chuckled aloud as he read the words painted on the gift—a little wood-and-glass sign, a tad over a foot long and less than three inches tall. It said—as you are probably guessing by now—"The Buck Stops Here." ("I'm from Missouri" was painted on the other side, in case you are curious.)

The saying "The buck stops here" came from the expression "Pass the buck," originally a poker term. In the frontier days, poker players would use a marker—frequently a knife with a buckhorn handle—to indicate whose turn it was to deal. If the player didn't want to deal, he could pass along the responsibility by passing the *buck*, what the marker came to be called, to the next player.

That famous sign would appear at different times on Truman's desk until late in his administration. On more than one occasion the president referred to it in public statements. In his farewell address to the American people, Truman referred to this concept very specifically in asserting that "The President—whoever he is—has to decide. He can't pass the buck to anybody. No one else can do the deciding for him. That's his job."[1]

MAY COOL HEADS PREVAIL

Now, let's imagine our friend Noggin walking into our prefrontal cortex, which is like the White House, the control room, the CEO of your brain. Nicknamed for the purposes of this book as the Presidential Control Center, it sets the thermostat for your Brain House. In healthy, functioning brains, the buck really does stop here, and our thinking center helps mediate and control our moodier, potentially hot-and-bothered rooms from taking over. This is why, when choosing a president for our country, most of us vote for the man or woman we believe will have the coolest head in the toughest times. From Pearl Harbor to the Cuban missile crisis to 9/11, when the going gets horrendous—no matter our political persuasions—the country looks to the president in its hour of fear to calm the national angst. (Personally, I would be in favor of having all of our potential presidents undergo a SPECT scan along with their routine physicals.)

Now imagine for a moment what it would be like to not have a president. To have no place for the buck to stop. No cool head to prevail.

What would happen if decisions were made in our country according to the opinion of the newspapers or talk radio? Freedom of expression is a beautiful concept in our nation, yet at some point there needs to be someone who makes the final decision; someone who is willing to take the tough road for the long-term benefit of the country, even when all the voices may be calling for an easier, softer way. Someone who also knows when to lighten up and laugh and assure the Chicken Littles of the world that the sky is not falling, that everything will work out just fine. Chaos would reign in our society if there were no chief executive.

Similarly, unless you have a healthy, functioning prefrontal cortex, there is chaos at large in your body. The rest of your emotional brain rooms would run amok, acting out every impulse, and eventually your life and relationships would mirror the bedlam in your brain. When not working correctly, this is one of the brain types that will most often turn to self-medication. In fact, 60 to 80 percent of all addicts have ADD. Cocaine and meth addicts tend to have lower blood flow in the prefrontal cortex and reach for a stimulant drug. Those with ADD coupled with anxiety tend toward using or abusing alcohol and marijuana, which have a depressive effect.

The prefrontal cortex (Presidential Control Center), as the executive part of the brain, also plays a significant role in building, maintaining, and growing intimacy. It contains two lobes, *Lobbies* as I like to call them. You may recall the left one is Lighthearted Lobby, and the right one is Ruminating Lobby. Research has shown that in people who are generally happy and at peace, there is more activity in their left PFC than in their right PFC. Best-selling German science writer Stefan Klein, PhD, found that people who have more activity in the right half of their brains have less control over negativity and tend to walk on the pessimistic side of life's street. Therefore, they are often introverts who are more paranoid, get depressed more easily, and find that happiness often eludes them. On the other hand (the other side of the prefrontal lobe), those with more activity in the left prefrontal cortex ". . . usually prove to be true Sunday's children. They are self-confident, optimistic, and often in high spirits." They tend to be social butterflies and are contentedly joyful, keeping to the sunny side of life most of the time. In fact, often when someone has a severe injury to their left PFC, the capacity to feel and express joy is numbed to a tragic degree. Interestingly, when the right PFC has been injured, people can still feel a lot of joy and happiness but often lack the reasoning to be realistic about their blissful state of mind. They are gullible and impressionable, and if you tell them they have no arms, for example, they may believe you; but the upside is, they'll think being suddenly armless is delightful. All in all, if you have to have a bad blow to the right or left PFC, you'll be happier if you lose right PFC functioning. But you'll probably be annoyingly, illogically giddy for those who have to care for you.[2]

For the purpose of this chapter, I want to focus mostly on the overall functioning of the PFC when both Lobbies or lobes are healthy and balanced. The chart on the following page will give you a good snapshot of what's happening just behind your forehead in the Executive Wing of your brain.

Areas Controlled by Prefrontal Cortex	Healthy Prefrontal Cortex in Life & Relationship
Focus	Ability to pay attention while interacting and to follow a topic and not jump from subject to subject.
Forethought	Consideration of impact of words and behavior before they are expressed.
Impulse Control	Thinking before saying or doing something. Can hear a little voice that says, "No . . . that may cause pain or distance in the relationship." Stays with a spending plan, eats moderately, not ruled or governed by the thought or feeling of the moment.
Planning	Able to take a complex goal and break it down into reachable steps.
Judgment	Exercises common sense; able to make choices and decisions for the benefit of the relationship. People with poor prefrontal cortex problems will often sacrifice relationships for immediate pleasure.
Empathy	Ability to feel what the other person is going through and articulate that in a manner such that the other person feels cared for or understood. Self-centeredness is a problem when the PFC isn't working well, seeking own needs and desires first without sufficient consideration of the consequences to others.
Emotional Control	Able to stay in touch with feelings and control responses and reactions. Poor PFC functioning results in an impulsive expression of thoughts and feelings that tends to cause distance or undermine intimacy in marriages, to strain friendships, and to make parenting a child with PFC problems the ultimate challenge.

Areas Controlled by Prefrontal Cortex	Healthy Prefrontal Cortex in Life & Relationship
Insight/Intuition	Aware of function as a person with a sense of how another person is feeling. Picks up on social cues with relative ease. People with injury or poor functioning in the PFC area will have difficulty reading faces and emotions and, thus, in making changes in relationships. They often have trouble with intuiting subtleties and picking up on nuances that normally signal "something isn't right." (In other words, if your mate has ADD, don't expect him to pick up on your mood or catch shifts in body language. You've got to hit him over the head with exactly what you want and need.)
Learning from Mistakes	When entering familiar situations, a person with healthy PFC will recall past experiences and add new information and will avoid repeating a mistake. Not so with poor PFC. When entering similar situations, these persons often do not learn from mistakes but will repeat the same undesirable behavior over and over. Similarly, they may not remember the little things that help a relationship grow, don't have an internal reminder that prompts them to give a flower or write an encouraging note or follow up on requested desires.
Organization	People with poor PFC have trouble maintaining order in the environment. Car, office, or house may be in disarray. They are often unrealistic about what can be accomplished in a given amount of time and have problems organizing and planning days.

HONEY, CAN I BORROW YOUR BRAIN?

As you can imagine, life without a functioning prefrontal cortex would be a challenge, not only for yourself but also for anyone who loved you. In counseling, I often sense that one person in a relationship feels as though he has to take over the responsibility of his mate's executive functioning. This can be an endless source of frustration and resentment! A functioning prefrontal cortex is essential for an adult-to-adult relationship. In a mature marriage, for example, each person takes clear-cut personal responsibility for bringing his best self to the relationship. If the prefrontal cortex is not functioning well, there is not the neurocircuitry needed for a partnership of equals. Too often, one partner ends up feeling as though he is parenting the other. Of course, when these differences are there—but minimal—you can see positive synergy in well-matched couples. I'm thinking of George Burns and his wife, Gracie—the classic comedy team who also enjoyed a lifelong love affair. Burns, who played the quintessential straight man to the giddy, scatterbrain Allen, kept their marriage from careening into organizational chaos; Gracie kept George laughing. It worked.

Then there's Marie and Nick. Though their names are fictional, I assure you they are very real clients in my practice. And they are classic cases of what happens when the neurobiological aspects of a relationship are ignored and dysfunctional: resentful gridlock sets in and makes two people miserable for decades.

When flighty-as-air Marie and responsible, hard-working Nick were with other couples, Marie would often say, "I am in charge of outgo, and Nick is in charge of income." There were times when Marie would add a cute postscript, "Why put money in the bank? It only collects dust," and Nick would smile and laugh along with everyone else. However, as the years went on, the fights about money became increasingly frequent and intense. Expressions of affection seemed to be farther apart. Rather than walking hand in hand as they did when they were young and first in love, Nick often found himself walking a little ahead of Marie, or other times Marie was walking just a little ahead of Nick. As a therapist, I'm a *noticer*, and I have learned that the body language between couples can tell me as much as anything they are saying. So when a couple doesn't walk side by side or turn toward each other, it can be symbolic of the lack of partnership. Typically, one of the mates is playing the parent and the other the role of a child. Again, in healthy, fun marriages, these roles can be charming in small doses—but in healthy marriages, couples take turns with these roles. One day you may pamper your hurting wife. The next, she may baby you when you have a headache.

Personality differences turn into trouble only when one partner feels he or she is *always* "containing a child" rather than "partnering with a teammate." Then, living with a person with prefrontal cortex issues is no longer cute, fun, or charming. It's maddening.

In Nick and Marie's case, lovemaking was reduced to maybe one to two times per month with a continuing downward trend in passion and feeling. The bed was fast becoming just a place to sleep, rather than a place of love, comfort, and passion.

THE BLOOD JUST DRAINED FROM MY BRAIN!

It was not a surprise, then, that when Marie took the Amen Brain System Checklist, her scores reflected high likelihood of attention deficit disorder. The SPECT scans confirmed that under stress (which we measured by having her perform a fairly complex computer task), Marie's prefrontal cortex had a drop in perfusion (good blood flow) to that area of the brain: a classic clue that someone may have ADD. This may come as a surprise to many who think of ADD as only being a disorder that affects little boys. I would venture to say that problems with attention and focus in the PFC are one of the most common and yet undiagnosed problems in millions of adults.

Her surface SPECT looked as though it had dents or holes in

it—representing too little activity there. People with good PFC functioning will typically see an increase in blood flow to the Presidential Control Center when performing a concentration task. People with ADD do just the opposite. Just when they really could use some good perfusion to make a solid, wise choice, all the blood flows, instead, to the impulse center of the brain.

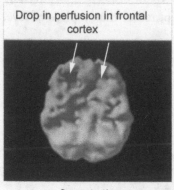

Drop in perfusion in frontal cortex

Concentration

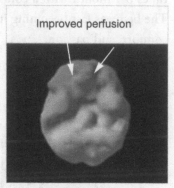

Improved perfusion

Adderall aids perfusion in the prefrontal cortex

(Underside, surface view)

This is why people with poor PFCs make impulsive choices. Marie's lack of executive control in her brain was reflected in the monthly bills from Visa, MasterCard, and American Express. Oh, and in Nick's ever-rising blood pressure as he opened the billing statements.

Parents and teachers of children who have poor PFC functioning are often at a loss, exhausted from efforts to help the child focus, be attentive to the feelings of others, or remember where he put his school backpack or shoes or lunchbox (every single day). Imagine how the child must feel. He or she is often simply labeled that *bad boy* or that *ditzy girl* and knows enough to suffer a loss of self-esteem but doesn't have the brain tools to make the changes that others are screaming for him or her to make. As one mom put it, "One of us had to have some relief. Either my child needed medication, or I would need it soon—in the form of a tranquilizer!"

If you add hyperactivity to the mix of a child or adult's attention problems (ADHD), the poor parents or spouses are usually at their wit's end by the time they stumble into my office for help. I've thought of creating a designated cry room just for parents, teachers, and spouses of those with ADHD, especially before their child or mate is treated. The good news is that when ADD is properly treated—neither under- nor overmedicated—not only does the client feel happier and more in control, but the rest of the family, the mate, the office, or the classroom also gets an upsurge of pure relief and joy.

ADD is not the only evidence of poor PFC functioning, but I would say it has to top the list. What I've learned from Dr. Amen, who is an expert on ADD, is that there are several kinds of ADD, depending on how the PFC is interacting with the other rooms in the brain. So if you suspect ADD and a need for medication, this is one of those situations where I generally implore my clients to bite the bullet and pay for a scan. (Even if your insurance won't cover it, the cost of the scan will save you so much more money in the long run because you won't have to spend as much in trial-and-error experiments to balance the brain.)

Here are the different types of ADD that we see in our practice.

ADD

Type	Personality	Problem
Temporal Lobe	Passionate, intense, and driven. Is committed to goals and values of the family, business, team, or church and will walk through walls for them.	Under times of stress, will be prone to explode over minor issues. Generates fearfulness in others. People will walk on eggshells and avoid bringing problems to light for resolution. Families suffer because, though they may have the appearance of unity, many of them are really suffering in silence under an explosive spouse or parent who has difficulty admitting wrong. This ADD type is usually reluctant to take responsibility for basic human errors (errors that could have allowed him to model that it was okay to make a mistake, learn from it, and move on).

Type	Personality	Problem
Limbic	More sensitive to their feelings and those of others. Can be highly responsible in making sure relationship is okay. Bothered if relationships at work are not doing well.	Can be prone to depression, feelings of hopelessness. Struggles to be optimistic and hopeful during difficult times. Will bring the mood of the marriage or family down. Family members of this ADD type may describe themselves as feeling as though they are "living with Eeyore."
Avoidant	Will tend to be positive and encouraging to team or family members. Feels better when others are feeling better. Will not generate conflict for the sake of generating conflict.	Lives with high degree of anxiety and physical tension. Chronic problems with headaches, backaches, colitis, IBS, and so forth. Avoidance of problems to the point that problems can create crises or financial problems because of unwillingness to face the problem when it was small.
Overfocused	Great organizational skills. Excellent goal-setting skills. Will follow project through to its completion with details taken care of. Great at adhering to budgets and contracts.	Under times of stress, will be stuck in black-and-white thinking. Obsessed with details. Will notice everything wrong without encouraging and building up people. Coworkers, friends, spouse, or family members can end up focusing so hard on "not messing up" that positive, creative, progressive growth can be stunted. It is hard to deeply exhale and relax around a person like this.

Type	Personality	Problem
Inattentive	Spontaneous, creative, and great at generating new ideas. Will motivate people, likes excitement, and is interested in new ideas, new strategies, and new technologies. Seems to shift easily from one project to another.	Will tend to focus under times of stress on activities that are highly stimulating. Will have poor follow-through on projects and avoid follow-through because anxiety increases. Will not use good judgment regarding time. Has problems accurately estimating the amount of time it takes to complete a project. Will often require a crisis for the motivation to complete difficult projects or make a significant change.
Classic	Most likely has the highest creativity of all the types. Will see dimensions of problems that no one else sees. Can be inventive and loves finding new paradigms or models of doing things.	May help create new models or programs but is the worst of all the subtypes in the follow-through. Consistently following a project through to completion (if it gets mundane) often is not enough stimulation for this type to stay interested and motivated. Can have many projects going at one time. Multitasks yet struggles to bring projects to fruition.
Ring of Fire	Passionate, intense; can easily persuade and motivate people. At times may be amazingly sensitive and intuitive.	Under times of stress there is nothing anyone can do to calm or please this type. Will disrupt relationships within the organization or family. Pits one person against the other, and when confronted, acts as if he did nothing. Can be highly manipulative and deceptive (more on this fiery brain issue in chapter 11).

After reading this chart, perhaps you can see why I like to see a scan, or at least gather the answers from the Amen Checklist (from chapter 4), before recommending a medical protocol. Most general practitioners will simply prescribe Adderall or Ritalin to those who say they have focus problems, not realizing that by doing so, they may leave other areas of the brain untreated, or worse, exacerbate moodiness or anger or depressive symptoms that coexist with ADD PFC issues.

FAMOUS ADD CHARACTERS WE KNOW
AND LOVE (AND PICK UP AFTER)

One thing about people with ADD: you don't tend to forget them. In fact, they often make for fascinating and fun people, as long as their ADD is balanced enough to keep them happy and functional. (In fact, many are very fun-*ny*. Lots of comedians, perhaps the majority, have some form of ADD.)

Here are a few examples of some of my favorite ADHD (with an accent on the *hyper*) personalities:

- Tigger, from Winnie the Pooh, eternally ready to party: "Has anyone seen any fun waiting to happen?"
- The hyperactive, lovable-but-pushy, talks-before-he-thinks Donkey from *Shrek*. One attribute of ADHD folks is that they often do not have a filter and may say inappropriate or insensitive things, quite innocently: "Wow, that was really scary, and if you don't mind me saying, if that don't work, your breath will certainly get the job done, 'cause you definitely need some Tic Tacs or something 'cause your breath *stinks*!"
- Robin Williams, playing almost any part resembling his real-life, off-screen, overactive, brilliant personality, beginning with the hyper, lovable space alien named Mork in the '70s sitcom hit *Mork and Mindy*; followed by his roles as the hilarious, fast-talking DJ in *Good Morning, Vietnam*; the laugh-a-minute doctor in *Patch Adams*; and my personal favorite, the genie from Disney's *Aladdin*—who bursts on the screen like an Arabian comic high on caffeine.

Another common subtype of ADD is what we call inattentive ADD. Not usually hyperactive, people with inattentive ADD are generally more spacey and forgetful but inwardly thoughtful—they are so busy looking at the beautiful blue sky and tuning in to the birds singing, that they walk right into the mailbox. Often. (It goes without saying, they can also be accident prone.) Because inattentive ADD folks are generally pleasant in temperament (though infuriating in their lack of organization), parents aren't usually rushing their little daydreamers into my office, begging for relief, as they will their more exhausting ADHD offspring. However, many inattentive ADD types can be helped with routines, systems, supplements, or smaller doses of Adderall when needed. A classic case of inattentive-type ADD would be Dory, the scatter-brained but lovable blue fish from Disney's charming movie *Finding Nemo*, whose short-term memory loss provides unforgettable moments of comic relief (and for me, personally, moments of identification).

In the character of Dory, we see so many typical inattentive ADD traits, such as an inability to pick up and retain many details and, generally, a lack of concern about either deficit. Upon encountering a whale, Dory tosses out the following options with complete nonchalance: "Okay, he either said, 'Move to the back of the throat,' or 'he wants a root beer float.'"

Most happy, well-adjusted, productive inattentive ADD types will tell you they have an assistant or a super-organized friend or a helpmate with a memory like Rain Man. Pick up just about any big business success story, read the history of the company and how it runs today, and you'll find there is always someone following behind the charming ADD entrepreneur/visionary, carrying his daybook or reminding her of what to do next. Or pointing out to the CEO, who is driving while on his phone wheeling and dealing, that he just . . . *uh hum* . . . parked in a flower bed.

Near the end of this wonderful film, Dory illuminates the vulnerable heart beneath most ADD minds. Afraid of losing her newfound and helpful companion she pleads, "Please don't go away. Please? No one's ever stuck with me for so long before . . . I just, I remember things better with you. I do . . . when I look at you . . . I'm home."

Any inattentive ADD type who's found someone who loves him and helps him to be the best he is capable of being can understand Dory's attachment to her compassionate, more organized little fishy friend.

HOW TO UPSIZE PFC HEALTH AND HAPPINESS

In his book *Healing ADD*, Dr. Amen explains the six types of ADD, each with different brain function issues and treatment protocols. Following is a list of the usual supplemental support and a typical prescription protocol should medication be needed or desired.

Note: Information on medication and/or supplements is for informational purposes only. Always consult your prescribing MD when considering a change in medications or supplement use. Supplements can disrupt the effectiveness of various medications, and there are medications that will be affected by the use of supplements.

Six Different ADHD Types with Common Medical and Supplemental Recommendations

Type 1: Classic

Symptoms: Primary ADD symptoms plus hyperactivity, restlessness, and impulsivity

SPECT: Usually low prefrontal cortex with concentration

Supplements: Multiple vitamins, high-quality fish oil, L-tyrosine, or DL-phenylalanine

Medications: Stimulant medications (such as Adderall, Concerta, Ritalin, or Dexedrine)

Type 2: Inattentive

Symptoms: Primary ADD symptoms plus low energy and motivation, spacey, and internally preoccupied. Type 2 is diagnosed later in life, if at all. It is more common in girls. These are quiet kids and adults, often labeled lazy, unmotivated, and not that smart.

SPECT: Usually low prefrontal cortex with concentration and low cerebellar activity

Supplements: Multiple vitamin, high-quality fish oil, L-tyrosine, or DL-phenylalanine

Medications: Stimulant medications (such as Adderall, Concerta, Ritalin, or Dexedrine)

Type 3: Overfocused

Symptoms: Primary ADD symptoms plus cognitive inflexibility, trouble shifting attention, sticks on negative thoughts or behaviors, worrier, holds grudges, argumentative, oppositional, need for sameness. Often seen in families with addiction problems or obsessive-compulsive tendencies.

SPECT: Usually high anterior cingulate activity plus low prefrontal cortex with concentration

Supplements: Multiple vitamin, high-quality fish oil, 5-HTP, L-tryptophan, or St. John's wort plus L-tyrosine

Medications: Antidepressant Effexor, or a combination of an SSRI like Prozac and a stimulant

Type 4: Temporal Lobe

Symptoms: Primary ADD symptoms plus a short fuse, misinterprets comments, periods of anxiety, headaches or abdominal pain, history of head injury, family history of rages, dark thoughts, memory problems, struggles with reading. Often seen in families with learning or temper problems.

SPECT: Usually low temporal lobe activity plus low prefrontal cortex with concentration

Supplements: Multiple vitamin, high-quality fish oil, GABA or taurine for irritability, or Brain Vitale or NeuroMemory (available from the Amen Clinics) for memory issues

Medications: By themselves, stimulants such as Adderall or Ritalin usually make people with this type more irritable. Can be effectively treated with a combination of antiseizure medications (such as Neurontin) and stimulants.

Type 5: Limbic

Symptoms: Primary ADD symptoms plus chronic mild sadness, negativity, low energy, low self-esteem, irritability, social isolation, and poor appetite and sleep patterns

SPECT: Usually high deep limbic activity plus low prefrontal cortex at rest and with concentration

Supplements: Multiple vitamin, high-quality fish oil, SAMe, or DL-phenylalanine

Medications: Stimulating antidepressants such as Wellbutrin. However, by themselves, stimulants usually cause depressive symptoms or problems with "rebound"—depression that returns after a short period of relief.

Type 6: Ring of Fire

Symptoms: Primary ADD symptoms plus extreme moodiness, anger outbursts, oppositional, inflexibility, fast thoughts, excessive talking, and very sensitive to sound and light. I named it Ring of Fire after the intense ring of overactivity that I saw in the brains of affected people.

SPECT: Marked overall increased activity across the cortex; may or may not have low prefrontal cortex activity

Supplements: Multiple vitamin, high-quality fish oil, NeuroLink (contains a balanced combination of 5-HTP, GABA, and L-tyrosine, along with other supportive amino acids and B vitamins)

Medications: Anticonvulsants (such as Neurontin) and SSRI medication, or the use of the novel antipsychotic medications such as Risperdal or Zyprexa, though this type is usually made much worse by stimulants

COMMON TREATMENT RECOMMENDATIONS FOR ALL TYPES OF ADD

These are Dr. Amen's general recommendations for all ADD types and subtypes. I consider him to be the foremost authority on ADD. He also has great empathy because he has parented ADD kids.

Note: Although you may find some wonderful, high-quality supplements at your local health food store, my experience has been that the products from the Amen Clinics are among the highest quality and have been formulated specifically to help with better brain function. They are also reasonable in cost and can be shipped to your home. (And there are often sales and specials offered on the Web site: www.amenclinics.com/store.) So I will often recommend these name brands because of my own familiarity with the products and their results in the patients I see.

1. Take a 100 percent multiple vitamin every day. Studies have reported that they help people with learning and help prevent chronic illness. (The Amen Clinics have an excellent multivitamin called NeuroVite in a formula for both adults and kids. NeuroVite is a comprehensive, highly concentrated, pharmaceutical-grade vitamin and mineral trace element daily supplement containing more than fifty nutritional ingredients, all in a special herbal green food base.)

2. Adults, take 2000 to 4000 mg of high-quality fish oil a day (1000 to

2000 mg for children). For types 1 and 2, NeuroEPA from the Amen Clinics is a high-quality brand. For types 3 to 6, NeurOmega is best. For children or adults who have problems digesting fish oil, check out the Coromega product: a fish oil that tastes like orange pudding with no fishy aftertaste. In fact, as more is known about the powerful and positive effects of fish oil, more manufacturers are finding ways to make it more palatable to the public—including putting it in chocolate. Some people find that the lemon-flavored fish oil capsules (such as Natrol, available at Walgreens) or enteric-coated capsules (which often smell like vanilla) do not produce "fish burps."

3. Eliminate caffeine from your diet. It interferes with sleep and the other treatments.

4. Get intense aerobic exercise for thirty to forty-five minutes daily. If you cannot find a safe exercise for your kids (no brain injuries, please), take them on long, fast walks.

5. Turn off the television and video games, or limit them to no more than thirty minutes a day. This may be hard for kids and teens, but it can make a huge difference.

6. Food is a drug. Most people with ADD do best with a higher-protein, lower simple-carbohydrate diet. Barry Sears's book *The Zone* is a good place to start.

7. In dealing with kids, employees, even spouses—*no yelling*! Many people with ADD seek conflict or excitement as a means of stimulation. They can be masters at making other people mad or angry (and often enjoy playing the mental/relational game called *Let's Have a Problem*). Do not lose your temper with them. If they get you to explode, their unconscious, low-energy prefrontal cortex lights up and likes it. Never let your anger become their medication. They can get addicted to it.

8. Test ADD kids and adults for learning disabilities. They occur in up to 60 percent of people with ADD. Local schools are often set up to do this for school-age children. See the Amen Clinics Learning Disability Screening Questionnaire in *Healing ADD*.

9. Apply for appropriate school or work accommodations. (See *Healing ADD* on how to do this properly.)

10. Never give up seeking help.[3]

ON NUTRITION AND NEUROTRANSMITTERS

There are two primary neurotransmitters that influence the prefrontal cortex or Executive Branch of the brain—norepinephrine and dopamine. Amino acids that help to produce these are tyrosine for dopamine and phenylalanine for norepinephrine. Foods high in protein help produce these amino acids.[4]

Since I have ADD and have learned about how diet affects my brain function, I have noticed that it's important for me to eat higher-quality proteins for breakfast and lunch to keep my dopamine levels high throughout the day. If I eat pasta, breads, or potatoes at lunch, I will feel sleepy in the afternoons, which—trust me—my therapy patients do *not* appreciate.

How much protein do you need at each meal? Look at the palm of your hand (no fair adding your fingers . . . just the palm). Each protein serving should be about the size of your palm. This is true whether you are talking about chicken, beef, tofu, or seafood. For women, this amounts to 3 to 4 ounces, and for men that is 5 to 6 ounces.

Vegetables and salad work well with protein, but stay away from the complex carbs if you want to enhance dopamine and norepinephrine. Protein powders are wonderful for breakfast or lunch, and sometimes are easier for people than making breakfast or lunch. A protein powder can be mixed with a glass of juice or milk, plus some fresh or frozen berries (blueberries are a great brain food). Lactose-intolerant people will do better with rice milk or soy milk, but check the label to make sure you are getting more protein than carbs.

For those in a real hurry, you can just mix a tablespoon or more of soy, whey, or rice protein powder with one of the premixed smoothies so popular now, such as the Naked Juice brands. They are tasty little on-the-go, highly nutritious snacks for business and vacation travel. (Check the fiber content since some brands are more fiber rich than others.) Starbucks is even carrying a variety of Naked Juice smoothies now, so you can find them wherever a Starbucks can be found. (And it seems a Starbucks can be found . . . nearly everywhere now.) Starbucks has also introduced a couple of new protein- and fiber-rich smoothies (Vivanno) that will keep your energy going and your tummy happy much longer than the typical sugar- and caffeine-loaded coffee drink.

Jamba Juice stores (and their ilk) are gaining in popularity as a fast, convenient source for nutritional boosts in a cup while on the run. Just make sure to add protein to your smoothie so you don't "carb out" and get sleepy instead of energized and focused. Eggs (or just the egg whites if you are watching cholesterol) are an easy source of protein to add to a variety of foods.

In addition to protein at each of your three daily meals, make sure to mix some with a couple of snacks as well. A handful of nuts, low-fat cottage or ricotta cheese with your favorite fruit or flavoring mixed in, a slice of cheese, or even a spoonful of nut butter and half a glass of skim milk will tide you over and give you the long-lasting, stable energy you are wanting (rather than the bursts of quickly fading energy you get from sugar or caffeine).

SUPPLEMENTS TO AID PFC FUNCTIONING

Here is a more detailed description of common supplements used to help minor to moderate ADD imbalances.

Supplement	Recommendations
L-tyrosine	NeuroStim is a product designed by Dr. Amen to help with prefrontal cortex function. It contains 500 mg of L-tryosine.
Ginkgo Biloba	Ginkgo is an antioxidant that helps improve circulation, energy, concentration, focus, and memory. The usual recommended dosage is 60 to 120 mg twice per day.[b] Since it helps with circulation, you will often see it combined with tyrosine and other supplements. (As a side benefit, many happy midlife males have found that ginkgo helps their sexual performance as well.)
D-phenylalanine and L-phenylalanine or DL-phenylalanine (DLPA)	The precursor for norepinephrine comes in these forms. Most stores carry the L form, but the D form is more easily converted in the brain (though harder to find in stores). The L form is a bit more stimulating for daytime energy; any form with D in it is going to be more relaxing. See *The Mood Cure* for more details on recommended dosages for specific situations. Because the L form can be stimulating, you need to watch for signs of overstimulation, and people with high blood pressure will want to monitor their numbers to make sure this supplement doesn't raise the numbers.

Supplement	Recommendations
Protein Powder	Rice, soy, vegetable, whey, and egg protein powders will help enhance dopamine and noreprenephrine.

THOUGHTS THAT HELP FOCUS AND SOOTHE THE PFC MIND

Tell yourself these tried and true sayings when you get overwhelmed or frustrated and are having focus problems:

- One day at a time.
- Inch by inch, anything is a cinch.
- How do you eat an elephant? One bite at a time.
- "I can do everything through him who gives me strength." (Phil. 4:13)

QUOTES TO CHEER THE PFC-CHALLENGED

- "If a man does not keep pace with his companions, perhaps it is because he hears a different drummer. Let him step to the music which he hears, however measured or far away." —Henry David Thoreau
- "The best non-pharmacological treatment for ADD is exercise, sex, and humor." —Dr. Edward Hallowell, coauthor, *Driven to Distraction*
- "I prefer to distinguish ADD as attention abundance disorder. Everything is just so interesting . . . remarkably at the same time." —Frank Coppola, MA, ODC, ACG[6]

ACTIVITIES THAT HELP WITH PFC ORGANIZATION

- Make a to-do list each morning. Then put it in the same place every day—preferably tacked up where it cannot be moved, dropped, torn, burned, lost, folded, spindled, or mutilated.
- If you consistently lose an item on a near-daily basis, pause and consider

a system to help you. For example, a key rack, a library book box, or a shoe crate by the front door. If you thoughtfully make a place for everything, at least most of the time, things will end up in their place.

- If you need and lose several pairs of reading glasses, buy them by the dozen at the dollar store and put one in every room in your house.
- Hire or marry someone who is nonjudgmental and loves to organize. Or if your budget can take it, hire a professional organizer to help you clean out and set up systems that will work for you. A fabulous investment in your life and career.
- Put a clock in every room, especially the bathroom. Use a kitchen timer in the bathroom to help you keep on task when you are getting ready to go somewhere and don't want to be late.
- Only buy appliances with automatic shut-off systems for your safety and that of your family.
- Hire an ADD life coach. And yes, there is such a thing. (See ADDcoaching. com for just one of these services.) Life coaches are wonderful for entrepreneurs with PFC challenges or anyone who needs help staying focused on tasks and works best with positive, regular accountability.
- When you are overwhelmed by a mess, start in one corner of the room with a wastebasket and a put-away box, and work your way around the room as you clean and organize. Even if you come across a box of old love letters you are dying to read, force yourself to finish the task at hand and then reward yourself with the love letters afterward.
- When cleaning the kitchen, work in a circle, putting things that go in the fridge or pantry in a stack next to it and putting dishes in the sink and trash in a "trash bowl," à la Rachael Ray. Once the counters are clear, wipe them down and then put the food away, place the dishes in the dishwasher, and dump the trash out of the trash bowl. Create systems like this to help you stay focused on all the tasks you have to do each day.
- Use a computer tool such as Microsoft Outlook to plan your day/week; the automatic reminder feature is wonderful for forgetful types. And the big plus to using your computer as your Day Planner is that it is really hard to lose a whole computer. Generally, my home computer stays where I put it. (How many ADD types have bought several planners, list pads, and calendars, only to have lost them within forty-eight hours? Even my laptop is

iffy. I just left it at a restaurant this week! Thankfully, the waitress knows me and held it for me. Oh, the joys and trials of us ADD folks. Among all the brain types, we are the most likely to depend on the kindness of strangers to help us through life. But our gift is that we can make other people feel really, really needed.)

- Have one main focus per day. Rather than trying to do several different things every day, plan your week with a different emphasis or focus for each day. For example, let Monday be your Catch-Up Day—the day you catch up on e-mail, laundry, errands, and bills. Tuesday could be your Focus Day when you do the thing that takes the most energy and brings in the most income, such as your sales calls or your writing. Plan a Free Day at least once every two weeks, if at all possible, where you take off and do nothing but what you love to do. (ADD types thrive on unplanned, daydreaming time.) Plan a Romance Day with your spouse once a month. Ditto with your kids. You get the gist. Just try to have a unique overall focus for each day of the week.

- Keep your to-do list streamlined: columns for Things to Do, one for Errands/Purchases and one for Contacts to Be Made (e-mails or phone calls).

- Plan your menus on Saturday or Sunday and tape the list on the refrigerator door. You'll be able to see what you need to thaw at a glance, and this method frees up so much mind space.

- Use baskets or boxes instead of shelves whenever possible for ease of organizing, especially in kids' rooms. It is so much easier to toss something in a box than to line it up on a shelf.

- Use rituals to your advantage. Bedroom a mess? For one week, make your bed as soon as you get out of it until it becomes an automatic habit. Hate waking up to a messy kitchen? Before you go to bed, give it a quick cleaning (or better yet, make the family help you). Again, you'll have to concentrate on doing this for a week or two or three. But if you keep at it, soon you'll clean the kitchen before bedtime every night, on autopilot, the same way you brush your teeth. Keep disposable cleaning wipes on the bathroom counters for easy, quick cleanups—train the kids to wipe the sinks and counters before leaving the room after they've made any mess.

- Watch organizational shows like *Clean Sweep* or *Mission: Organization*. They are full of tips and encouragement, and they usually make you feel a whole lot better about yourself. "Well, at least I can *find* my living room floor!"

- Take advantage of school testing for ADD. If tested positive, your child may get permission to take tests in a room away from distractions so that she can concentrate better and her test scores will improve. One father said, "Our son's test scores rose dramatically when he was allowed to test away from classroom distractions. In fact, it made the difference between his scoring high enough to enter a university and barely scoring enough to limp into a junior college."

SCRIPTURES TO RELAX AN OVERACTIVE PFC

- "Come to me, all you who are weary and burdened, and I will give you rest. Take my yoke upon you and learn from me, for I am gentle and humble in heart, and you will find rest for your souls. For my yoke is easy and my burden is light." (Matt. 11:28–30)
- Be still, and know that I am God. (Ps. 46:10)
- To help you focus: "Let your eyes look straight ahead, fix your gaze directly before you." (Prov. 4:25)

VISUALIZATION

To Calm Hyperactivity

When overwhelmed, think of a favorite, relaxing place, perhaps even one where you went as a child: imagine yourself sitting in a tree house or lying on the grass looking up at the clouds as they roll by. Visualize the scene again with all the sights, smells, and sounds. If you relax best at the beach, for example, imagine the sounds of the ocean and seagulls, the smell of salt in the air, the contrast of the cool turquoise sea with the soft tan sand. Imagine sipping your favorite beverage. Relax your body from head to toe. Picture God beaming a warm ray of love, like rays of sun, all over you. (And remember, when you visualize a lovely memory again, your brain sends the message to your body, which can respond as though you are actually there again. Also, the more vivid you make good memories and the more you bring them to mind, the more they will stick in your limbic system and help you feel better all around.)

When Needing to Focus

Imagine you have blinders on—like a race horse—and can only see the task directly in front of you. Focus on doing that one thing until all other distractions fade from view. Imagine yourself feeling strong and energetic and winning the race in front of you, and all the fans cheering you from the sidelines. Then get up, stop procrastinating, and get that task done.

Prayers to Help Focus and Calm Your PFC

This is from St. Patrick, a very small portion of a beloved Celtic prayer that is also called "The Lorica" or "The Breastplate Prayer." It is a wonderful, repetitive, simple visual that can help scattered minds to focus on who we are in Christ—surrounded by him on every side, cocooned by his strength and love.

> Christ with me, Christ before me, Christ behind me,
> Christ in me, Christ beneath me, Christ above me,
> Christ on my right, Christ on my left,
> Christ when I lie down, Christ when I sit down, Christ when I arise.

Contemplative prayer and meditation are paths of Christian prayer that can be of tremendous help in calming and focusing a scattered mind. Calvin Miller, one of our nation's most gifted Christian writers and professors who has also been a pastor for decades, has written a wonderful book, *The Path of Celtic Prayer* (IVP), along with an accompanying DVD, available on his Web site: www.calvinmillerauthor.com. People of faith who have ADD often struggle with traditional or Western forms of prayer—which are generally long and require sitting still—and can be encouraged by the great variety of prayer-types that these ancient believers used and integrated with their everyday lives.

Music

In one controlled study, the music of Mozart was found to be especially helpful for ADD children. A group of children who listened to Mozart reduced their theta brain wave activity (slow brain waves are often excessive in ADD) to the exact rhythm of the underlying beat of the music and displayed better focus and mood control, diminished impulsivity, and improved social skills. Among the subjects who improved, 70 percent maintained that improvement six months after the end of the study without further training. For more information and resources, visit www.mozarteffect.com.

Exercise

Exercise is one of the best gifts you can give to your brain if you have any form of ADD or ADHD. We all know that physical activity is great for our bodies, right? But did you know that exercise also increases blood flow to the brain, stimulating the release of compounds that the brain just loves, including growth factors and a substance (BDNF) that promotes branching of neurons. These substances—by-products of exercise—keep the brain running like a well-oiled engine.

- Aerobic activity is especially helpful to burn off hyperactive energy. Parents and teachers have known the value of letting the kids run off steam for decades and for good reason. Make sure your ADD or ADHD child is not withheld from physical activity as a form of discipline—it will only make things worse. Give him or her a physical chore to do instead.
- Running, jogging, dancing, spin classes, kickboxing . . . all are great for ADHD. Organized sports that are not threats for brain injury are also great for kids.
- Other forms of ADD (inattentive types) may need slower-paced exercises requiring concentration, focus, and balance, such as ballroom dancing, stretches, Pilates, or yoga-type movements.
- Good ol' walking is great for any type of ADD, as you'll tend to naturally walk at a pace that is soothing for your brain type.

An excellent resource for those interested in learning more about the latest and greatest breakthroughs in the exercise/brain/mood connection is the book *Spark: The Revolutionary New Science of Exercise and the Brain* by John J. Ratey (Little, Brown & Company, 2008).

Aromatherapy

Try putting a few drops of lavender or chamomile in a hot bath to calm overactive feelings. On the other hand, if you need to focus and energize, try a natural citrus smell to perk up your brain. Even breathing in the happy scent of fresh lemon or orange peel can do the trick.

Essential Blends (www.essentialblends.com) has a formula especially for ADD/ADHD to help calm some brain areas and stimulate others. The blend is a mixture of tangerine, cardamom, lavender, sweet almond, and jojoba.

Cinematherapy

Here are a few movie genres that ADD types tend to enjoy:

- *The Blues Brothers* never ceases to make me laugh with its hilarious pair of wild and crazy (ADD) guys gone wild. Just pure fun, and if you are ADHD, you can relate.
- Almost any of Robin Williams's funny films or Monty Python's *The Holy Grail* or *The Princess Bride*—movies with fast-paced wit that require a sharp mind and attentiveness. Humor is highly stimulating and fun for most ADD types.
- Fast-paced thrillers with plots that require concentrated thought, such as *The Pelican Brief* or *Mission: Impossible*, are also very pleasurable to the PFC.

Support Village

Interestingly, most ADD types I know prefer to hang out with calmer, laid-back, easygoing friends and usually prefer not to be with too many people at once. They tend to choose people who are good listeners, patient, easygoing, and cheerful to counterbalance their more frenzied selves.

Those with inattentive ADD are especially calmed and encouraged by loyal, steady, cheerful, naturally organized and nurturing personalities. People with ADD need a village of patient, kind, and laid-back support—friends and family who admire their talents and gifts and aren't easily overwhelmed by their bursts of energy. In short, all Tiggers need a laid-back Pooh or two, along with a wise and accepting Christopher Robin in their life.

Bibliotherapy

Self-Help

- *Healing ADD: The Breakthrough Program That Allows You to See and Heal 6 Types of ADD* by Daniel G. Amen
- *Driven to Distraction: Recognizing and Coping with Attention Deficit Disorder from Childhood through Adulthood* by Edward M. Hallowell and John J. Ratey

For Fun

- Fast-paced thrillers and books that are about totally absorbing subjects are perfect for ADHD types. Your son may not read *War and Peace*, but if he is into sports, he may read a book about his favorite sports hero or a copy of *Sports Illustrated* from front to back. Look for books that are of high interest to your ADD child and that move at a quick pace.
- Whether or not you agree with the content, books such as *Harry Potter*—with intense, page-turning plots—tend to pull even reluctant readers in. *The Chronicles of Narnia* by C. S. Lewis or J. R. R. Tolkien's *The Hobbit* can absorb a child's imagination and elevate his mind. However, you may want to get them hooked on the series by reading aloud or playing the book on tape. Soon your child will be anxious to see what happens next and will want to read the book for himself or herself.
- Women with ADD tend to prefer nonfiction and fiction that is filled (or at least heavily dotted) with humor and moves quickly and gets to the point. How-to books with bullet-point lists, shorter paragraphs, and interesting sidebars hold interest. Deep, meandering, lyrical prose tends to put ADD types to sleep. (Actually, it may be good to put this type of book next to your bedside to induce drowsiness at night.)

Beauty Therapy

Walking outside into a nature scene is almost instantly calming to ADD types. I encourage ADD employees to try to take their lunch out-of-doors whenever they can.

Even high-strung babies tend to calm out-of-doors. One mom suggests placing the baby swing or high chair facing a big window that opens to the backyard as one way to calm and focus a fussy little one.

Using a minimalist style of decorating, such as clean lines, calming paint colors, and easy-care storage, can ease the ADD mind at home—unless you are the ADD artsy type who thrives on lots of stimulating colors and vibrant accents. Experiment with your mood by checking how you feel as you walk in and out of a variety of room décors. You may want to keep your bedroom simple and calm, to relax you. But perhaps you want your kitchen to be bright and colorful to stimulate creativity and appetite. Your gut responses will help you decide your decorating style. Just pay a little more attention to the mood-décor connection, and the results may surprise and enlighten you.

"There are many positives with ADD," says Sari Solden, author of *Women with Attention Deficit Disorder*, "including a surplus of ideas, creativity, excitement, and interest which accompany this kind of mind."[7] I would have to agree, as people with ADD tend to be some of the most interesting, dynamic men and women in the world, and often use their energy to accomplish great tasks. One of the most common fears of those with ADD or ADHD is that they'll lose their creative edge if they get treated. I always assure them, "I will work with you to balance your brain, not to turn you into a zombie! When your medication or supplements or activities are right, you'll actually be more creative, more focused and effective. You'll gain that bit of control you need to harness your energy effectively without some of the more destructive elements of ADD getting in your way."

And now, let's wave good-bye to the PFC and meander down the hall for a little visit with the cingulate gyrus or (as I like to call it) the Circular Gerbil Wheel.

CHAPTER SEVEN

The Cingulate Gyrus:
The Circular Gerbil Wheel

Make it your habit not to be critical about small things.

—EDWARD EVERETT HALE

One of my most memorable clients, Dawna, struggled in relationships with her family and friends. A devout Christian, she prided herself on her perfectionist standards even though her "rightness" proved to be like an invisible bubble around her, keeping her from true intimacy with others. She puzzled over why she felt so alone when she was trying so hard to be very, very good. And discerning and, well, almost always *right*.

But her friends seemed to avoid returning her phone calls, showing little enthusiasm about getting together for lunch. When her adult kids called home, they usually gave her a brief, polite hello but asked to speak to their dad more often than not for any real sharing of their lives. (*Such a waste,* thought Dawna. She had so much pent-up advice to give them.) Conversations with her adult children stayed strictly at the level of news, weather, and sports. To find out what was really going on with her children, she had to rely on her husband to share any problems they were struggling with or even their latest funny stories, which she'd hear him laughing at on the phone.

She grew more and more resentful of her husband as the years passed. After all, she had been the one there for them while they were growing up, all the while holding down a part-time teaching job. Her husband? Why, he was rarely home during those years when working so hard to make his career a success.

In the last few years, when she did talk to her children or friends, she felt an inner compulsion, which she felt sure was from the Lord, to correct and reprove their mistakes and wrong thinking. (Isn't that what good Christians do, after all?) Dawna arrived in the counseling office due to the encouragement of her family physician, who had determined that her chronic headaches and acid reflux were due to stress of an undetermined nature. She was taking the antidepressant Effexor, a medication that was supposed to help calm her anxiety. She did feel less depressed, but her anxiety was escalating—causing the headaches to occur with increasing frequency. She was also finding it harder to fall asleep at night. As soon as her head hit the pillow, one thought after another would pop into her consciousness, keeping her from the experience of restorative sleep.

No matter what she tried—counting sheep, clouds, bunnies—she could not calm or self-soothe her frazzled mind. She tried praying, but even that didn't help slow down her internal loops of negativity.

So you've probably guessed what I did next. I pulled out a copy of our handy dandy Amen Brain System Checklist, gave her a pen, and let her answer the questions. The results showed eight symptoms that were indicative of a highly overactive cingulate gyrus, the Circular Gerbil Wheel, an area of the brain where thoughts get stuck like bubble gum to a shoe.

With this information, I encouraged Dawna's family MD to introduce Neurontin, which is a drug that helps calm the anxiety centers in the brain. Her headache pain soon began to subside, and as her cingulate calmed, she began to notice, with increasing frequency, the positive responses of her husband and adult children. She found herself being able to focus on the good and overlook small irritations. She stopped going on and on about the imperfections in others and, in fact, became aware of a few of her own flaws and faults. For the first time ever, she stopped picking at the perceived splinter in everyone else's eyes and got down to the business of removing the telephone pole from her own.

It wasn't long before Dawna's adult children noticed their mother was listening more, talking less. Encouraging more, criticizing less. Once they realized this was not a short-term trick but a permanent change, they began dropping by the house more often and sharing their lives with her on the phone. She realized that expressing God's love and acceptance made for much happier and closer relationships than her role as the Moral Police of the family. She was able to see clearly now that the mental, negative Circular

Gerbil Wheel had stopped turning and churning in her mind. She saw that it often hurt feelings when she offered unsolicited advice. Her cingulate-minded ways had alienated her from the people she loved and cared about most. But with her brain calmed, she was in a better place to live and let live, go with the flow, and not always have to be right, have the last word, or insist things go her way.

The following chart illustrates the role of a healthy cingulate and what happens when one is unbalanced (usually overactive).

Healthy Cingulate	Overactive Cingulate
Flexible, able to move from one thought to another.	Black-and-white thinking.
When wronged, able to forgive and let go.	Will store hurts, angers, and resentments. Has difficulty forgiving and moving on. In conflict, will bring up hurts, anger, and resentments from years ago.
Able to see the positive and hold onto it.	Will notice everything that is wrong in a relationship. Has difficulty seeing the positive.
Able to create order in environment, but disorder does not cause anger or fear.	Can be compulsive about order and cleaning. Upset if anything is left out or system of order is disrupted.
When a negative or self-critical thought enters the mind, able to refocus on the positive.	Unable to let go of negative or self-critical thoughts; will replay them over and over in mind, which can increase anger, hurt, or fears. Will actually rehearse negative thoughts about spouse and will play a role in the relationship deteriorating.
Allows mind to see options.	Tunnel vision. Will see limited options, which will make for difficulty in conflict resolution. "My way or the highway" is the rule. "Agree to disagree" is not an option. Overactive cingulate results in a person feeling pressure to resolve his own anxiety, then being surprised at the destructive effect it has on building intimacy.

Healthy Cingulate	Overactive Cingulate
Comfortable with others having choices in the relationship.	Unless people in relationship make choices that meet person's expectations, person becomes upset. Experienced at "controlling" in relationships.
Lives more in present. Does not look at future with fear.	Tendency to predict fear when thinking about future events.

People with cingulate hyperactivity tend to get stuck on that Circular Gerbil Wheel of thoughts and have trouble shifting their attention from thought to thought. (Dr. Amen refers to the cingulate as the brain's gear shifter. When working well, it helps slide us easily from one thought to another. When stuck, you just can't get out of first gear.)

This brain pattern shows increased blood flow in the top-middle portion of the prefrontal lobes (cingulate area of the brain).

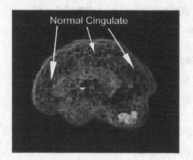 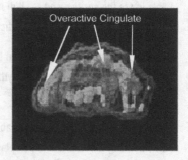

(Side view, active scan;
front of head, left side)

This brain pattern may present itself differently among family members. For example, a mother or father with cingulate hyperactivity may experience trouble focusing, along with obsessive thoughts (repetitive negative thoughts) or compulsive behaviors (hand washing, double- and triple-checking, counting and recounting, and so on). The son or daughter may be *oppositional*—getting stuck on saying "No!" or "No way!" or "You can't make me!"(If severe, this is known as ODD or *oppositional defiant disorder*.) Another family member may find change very hard. And yet another believes he is right and the entire world is wrong.

People who have been labeled as having narcissistic personality disorder—what therapists have traditionally called an *incurable* disorder because these personalities cannot see anything wrong with their thinking and, thus, are therapy-resistant—often have cingulate issues. When given supplementation or medication, this incurable disorder can get a whole lot better; though as with Dawna, it will most often be a family member who brings the person to get help because people with severe cingulate issues often cannot see anything wrong with themselves. If they are willing to get a scan, and we can show them a picture of their brain with its *hot* cingulate, many of their arguments fade away. It's difficult to argue with a picture of what's really going on in their heads.

Other cingulate-related disorders with repetitive, *stuck* thoughts include eating disorders ("Food is disgusting! Food is disgusting!" or "I am fat! I am fat!"), gambling addictions ("I've got to win! I've got to win!"), shopping ("I need that! I need that!"), rage ("I'll make you pay! I'll make you pay!"), and even chronic pain ("My back aches! My back aches!"). By the way, two excellent books to read for chronic, inexplicable back pain are *Mind Over Back Pain* and *Healing Back Pain*, both by Dr. John E. Sarno. More of our back and neck pain comes from unconscious anxiety and stress than most people realize. Also, the supplement DPA has been found to help many people with lower back pain while also acting as a calming neurotransmitter. See all the free tidbits of advice you get for the price of this book?

A very common finding is that there is a combination of brain issues happening in these cases: a lessening of blood flow in the prefrontal cortex with the cingulate firing on all cylinders. So basically, the Presidential Control Center abdicates its throne to the Circular Gerbil Wheel. And everybody knows that it is just not a good idea to put a gerbil in charge of your mind. Perhaps the most common disorder involving the cingulate is obsessive-compulsive disorder (OCD) in its various forms ("Unclean! Unclean!" or "Count every crack, or you'll break your mother's back!").

Here are some common obsessions that are sometimes called OCD *spectrum* disorders, meaning they are disorders that are related to OCD and cingulate issues in particular:

- Obsessions about dirt and contamination
- Obsessive need for order or symmetry
- Obsessions about hoarding or saving
- Obsessions with sexual content
- Repetitive rituals
- Nonsensical doubts
- Religious obsessions (scrupulosity)
- Obsessions with aggressive content (fear of harming another)
- Obsessions with food and weight
- Superstitious fears
- Compulsions about having things just right
- Checking compulsions (checking and rechecking to see if the door is locked, the oven is on, and so forth)

Other compulsions include the following:

- Pathological slowness in carrying out even the most routine activities
- Blinking or staring rituals
- Asking over and over for reassurance (if you're not sure, ask a loved one if you have this symptom)
- Behaviors based on superstitious beliefs (such as fixed bedtime rituals to ward off evil or the need to avoid stepping on cracks in the sidewalk)
- A feeling of dread if some arbitrary act is not performed
- The overpowering need to tell someone something or to ask someone something or to confess something
- The need to touch, tap, or rub certain objects repeatedly
- Counting compulsions: counting panes in windows or billboards along a highway, for example
- Mental rituals, such as reciting silent prayers in an effort to make a bad thought go away
- Excessive list making[1]

Tourette's syndrome and trichotillomania (compulsive hair-pulling) may also be related to an overactive cingulate. Anger issues can also be found here—though it may be a low-grade, constantly grumpy and critical bad mood rather than the explosive anger involved in the temporal lobes (discussed more at length in chapter 10). There's also a common correlation between an angry, ruminating, irritated cingulate (acting as kindling) and the more volatile temporal lobes (that burst into sudden, raging emotional flames). A good anger management program can do wonders in reprogramming the software of the brain as long as the hardware—any chemical imbalance—is also addressed.

IT'S ALL A MATTER OF DEGREE

When we speak about brain areas and imbalances, keep in mind that all problems are on a continuum from mild, to medium, to major issues. With milder problems, we often find that milder solutions such as therapy or retraining thoughts or using nutritional or supplemental changes will help tremendously. But when the cingulate is turned up to high volume, people often need medication to bring the fastest relief. (Once the worst of the symptoms are under control, if a person desires, we can help wean them off the medication, transferring them to more natural life changes down the road.) When it comes to cingulate issues, those with obsessive-compulsive symptoms often need medication to bring relief. (An antidepressant, such as Prozac, also has antiobsessive qualities that not only help elevate low-mood but help release the person from obsessive thoughts.) The good news is that we can help, and usually quickly. In fact, studies show that the vast majority of people who use a combination of medication and behavioral therapy get well.

OCD TYPES TO LOVE, LAUGH, AND OBSESS WITH

Interestingly, some of the funniest TV shows and movies have been based around polar opposites—usually someone with PFC issues (scattered, messy, laid-back) forced to live or work with someone with overactive cingulate issues. Classic case in point? *The Odd Couple*, with cingulate, uptight Felix, of whom his messy roommate, Oscar, once declared, "You're the only man in the world with clenched hair."

One of today's most popular shows is *Monk*, about a detective with a boatload of OCD symptoms. Not surprisingly, someone with an overactive cingulate has a particular nose for details and a unique stick-to-itiveness that come in handy should you be, say, an accountant or a lawyer or have a career sleuthing as Adrian Monk does. However, living with and loving someone like this can be a real pain.

Here are a few examples from this show to demonstrate some of the more common cingulate problems:

- An OCD person rarely forgets . . . anything (which comes in handy when solving a crime but not so much when you'd like him to forgive something you did back in 1982).
  Sharona Fleming: So you remember how many empty boxes you saw?
  Adrian Monk: It's a blessing, and a curse.

  Director's Assistant: [astounded] You memorized the play in one viewing?
  Adrian Monk: I'm really sorry.

- They make great lawyers and debaters because *logic rules*. Of course, it is always *their* logic that rules.
  Capt. Stottlemeyer: Does everything have to make sense, Monk?
  Adrian Monk: It kinda does. Unless I'm wrong, which, you know, I'm not.

- Then there is the common list of phobias or rituals that folks with a touch of OCD can recite at a moment's notice.
  [Due to a loose snake, Monk is standing on the kitchen table of a house he and Capt. Stottlemeyer are investigating.]
  Capt. Stottlemeyer: I thought you were afraid of heights.
  Adrian Monk: Snakes trump heights. It goes: germs, needles, milk, death, snakes, mushrooms, heights, crowds, elevators.

- Most cingulate types really think that there's a verse in the Bible that says, "Cleanliness is next to godliness." (There's not although many an OCD parishioner has tried to write it in.)
  Adrian Monk: [after accidentally wiping his hands with a cloth covered in oil] Sharona, I really need a wipe. Hurry! Oh, the humanity!

> Adrian Monk: [after accidentally touching the ground] Nature! I've got
> Nature on my hand! Get it off!

- When it comes to intimacy, a person with a stuck cingulate can find 101
ways to avoid it.

> Dr. Charles Kroger: Adrian, we can sit here singing show tunes to each
> other, or we can talk about your sex life.
>
> Adrian Monk: [singing] If ever I would leave you . . .

- They love rules. Rules make the world a safe place with boundaries and
fences and control. *Obedience* and *discipline* are often two of their favorite
words in the Bible, particularly when they use them on someone else.
(Blind spots in their own flaws are abundant.)

> Adrian Monk: A stop sign is not a suggestion!
>
> Sharona Fleming: Yes it is!

- When given a choice between glass half-full and glass half-empty, they
pick half-empty nearly every time.

> Adrian Monk: Hope is the worst.

Though there is humor to be found in every brain imbalance at times
(we all need a good laugh at ourselves on a regular basis—it's great for our
mental health), OCD in the extreme is not at all funny in the prime time of
reality. One of the most humorous and touching movies to come along in
years surrounding the subject of OCD is *As Good as It Gets*. (I just noticed
this film debuted in 1997. Has it really been over ten years? *Wow!* Babies
born when this movie came out are already playing video games, chewing
gum, and talking back to their parents. Amazing how time flies.)

Jack Nicholson's character, a grumpy, OCD-inflicted but oddly lovable
man named Melvin, struggles between the comfort of continuing his controlling rituals and the desire to experience true love with a real human being, a
wonderful woman named Carol (played by Helen Hunt)—who has both
flaws and germs. Melvin works up the courage to take Carol on a date to a
restaurant, but she is understandably guarded as Melvin has so often used his
gift of blurt to hurt her in the past. Though the dinner has a rocky start (thanks
to Melvin's gift of blurt), he reaches deep within and tells her that because of

her presence in his life and what she means to him, he is taking medication to help with his OCD.

During that poignant scene, Melvin utters that heart-wrenching, beautiful line, "You make me want to be a better man"—destined to become one of the most popular movie quotes of all time. Carol's taking a risk to reach out to Melvin—along with the risk he is taking to give medication a try—means the difference in two lonely people staying lonely and two lonely people finding a home in each other's hearts.

Cingulate types need someone who believes in them, sees the best in them, and helps them want to be better, more loving, and more emotionally giving people; they need someone who lovingly and with good humor "calls them on their stuff." ("Darling, I love you, but I am not on a witness stand. This is not a debate. I don't want to be graded on my points of logic. We're just having a cheeseburger at Wendy's and a little shallow, pleasant conversation. See if you can try to take off the judge's robe and slip into something more Tommy Bahama-ish . . .")

Even when someone with an overactive cingulate is on medication or working a program, the change will take time. The person who has struggled with a lifetime of negative thinking or rigid thoughts will need a friend or mate who has a lot of patience and empathy, someone who can use humor liberally to help him lighten up and who can speak soothing words to unwind him when his brain gets wound up.

Every Melvin needs a Carol, but, of course, every Carol needs a Melvin who is doing all he can for his sake, and hers, to get better.

This thought segues beautifully to the next section, the part of every chapter I like the best: how to get *better*, already!

CALMING THE CIRCULAR GERBIL WHEEL SYNDROME

Nutrition

There are two ways that food can increase serotonin levels (serotonin is a neurotransmitter needed to help let the gerbil take a break from the mental wheel). Carbohydrate-containing foods such as pastas, potatoes, bread, pastries, pretzels, candy, and popcorn increase L-tryptophan levels (the natural amino acid building block for serotonin) in the blood, resulting in more L-tryptophan available to enter the brain where it is converted to serotonin. The calming effect of serotonin can often be felt in thirty minutes or less by eating these foods. Cerebral serotonin levels can also be raised by eating foods rich in tryptophan, such as chicken, turkey, salmon, beef, peanut butter, eggs, green peas, potatoes, and milk.

Many people unknowingly trigger cognitive inflexibility or mood problems by eating diets that are low in L-tryptophan. For example, high-protein, low-carbohydrate diets recommended for low dopamine states (related to prefrontal cortex underactivity) often make cingulate problems worse.

Foods	Effect	Mood
Pastas, potatoes, bread, pastries, pretzels, candy, popcorn	Increase serotonin	Helps balance cingulate activity temporarily . . . eventually will crave more, and mood swings will increase
Chicken, turkey, salmon, beef, peanut butter, eggs, green peas, potatoes, milk	Increase serotonin	More effective in helping the cingulate; less obsessive and more cognitive flexibility
High-protein, low-carb diet	Decreases serotonin	Increased negative reactiveness

Supplements

Low serotonin levels and increased cingulate activity are often associated with worrying, moodiness, emotional rigidity, and irritability. St. John's wort, L-tryptophan, and 5-HTP are helpful for cingulate gyrus overactivity. (Note: Don't use any two or more of these supplements together at one time. Choose one, and see how it does alone first. This is a good rule of thumb for adding any supplements to your diet: one at a time, starting with the lowest dosage.)

St. John's wort seems to be best at increasing serotonin availability in the brain. Dr. Amen usually suggests a starting dosage of St. John's wort at 300 mg a day for children, 300 mg twice a day for teens, and 600 mg in the morning and 300 mg at night for adults. He sometimes encourages adults to talk to their doctor about going as high as 1800 mg. The bottle should say that it contains 0.3 percent hypericin, which is believed to be the active ingredient of St. John's wort.

I have SPECT studies done before and after showing that St. John's wort has helped to decrease cingulate gyrus overactivity. It clearly decreases cingulate gyrus hyperactivity for many patients. It also helps with moodiness and shifting attention trouble. Unfortunately, I have also seen it decrease prefrontal cortex activity. One of the women in the study said, "I'm happier, but I'm more of a dingbat." When cingulate symptoms are present with ADD symptoms (such as feeling kookier than usual), it's important to use St. John's wort with a stimulating substance like L-tyrosine or a stimulant such as Adderall. It has been reported that St. John's wort increases sun sensitivity (you could get sunburned more easily and, therefore, need to be careful outdoors). Also, don't use it without first stabilizing the temporal lobes if temporal lobe symptoms are present. (There is a specific order we use in calming the brain when it has multiple issues. See appendix B for more information.)

L-tryptophan (the amino acid building block for serotonin) and 5-HTP (also a serotonin building block) are other ways of increasing cerebral serotonin. L-tryptophan is a naturally occurring amino acid found in milk, meat, and eggs. One of the problems with dietary L-tryptophan is that a significant portion of it does not enter the brain. It is used to make proteins and vitamin B3. This necessitates taking large amounts of tryptophan.

A step closer in the serotonin production pathway, 5-HTP is also more widely available than L-tryptophan and is more easily absorbed by the brain. Seventy percent of 5-HTP is taken up into the brain—as opposed to only 3 percent of L-tryptophan—and is about five to ten times more powerful than L-tryptophan. A number of double-blind studies have shown that 5-HTP is as effective as antidepressant medication, boosting serotonin levels in the brain and helping to calm cingulate gyrus hyperactivity (greasing the cingulate, if you will, to help with shifting attention). See the following chart for recommended dosage levels. Take 5-HTP and L-tryptophan on an empty stomach. (The most common side effect of 5-HTP is an upset stomach, but it is usually very mild. Start slowly and work your way up slowly.)

There have also been some recent studies with Inositol, from the B vitamin family, which you can get from a health-food store. In doses of 12 to 20 mg a day, it has been shown to decrease moodiness, depression, and overfocus issues.

Do not take St. John's wort, L-tryptophan, or 5-HTP with prescribed antidepressants unless you are doing so at the recommendation of your physician and under his close supervision.

Neurotransmitter and Brain Subsystem	Recommended Supplements

Low serotonin levels and increased cingulate activity are often associated with worrying, moodiness, emotional rigidity, and irritability.	St. John's wort:
	  Dr. Amen's suggested starting dosage:
	  • Children: 300 mg per day
	  • Teens: 300 mg 2 times per day
	  • Adults: 300 mg in the a.m., 600 mg in the p.m.

High serotonin levels can result in feeling spacier, being more easily distracted, and so on.	Adding L-tyrosine to St. John's wort will help increase dopamine in the prefrontal cortex so a person can be more focused and less distracted.

Serotonin is the neurotransmitter that helps balance the cingulate.	L-tryptophan:
	  An amino acid that naturally occurs in meat and eggs; improves sleep, decreases aggressiveness, and improves mood control
	  Downside: one needs to take large amounts to have an impact on the brain
	5-HTP:
	  5 to 10 times more powerful than L-tryptophan and can be as effective as antidepressant medication
	  Dr. Amen's suggested dose:
	  • Adults: 50 to 300 mg a day
	  • Children: should start at half-dose
	Take 5-HTP and L-tryptophan on an empty stomach (in fact, most amino acids work best on an empty stomach, taken with water)
	  Warning: Do not take 5-HTP, St. John's wort, or L-tryptophan with an antidepressant unless supervised closely by an MD

Medication

It is important to note that a person with an overactive cingulate is often made worse by the stimulant medications, especially if the cingulate is not first calmed by a serotonin-boosting protocol. The Circular Gerbil Wheel from hell can go into hyperspeed when using such stimulant medications as Ritalin, Adderall, Focalin, Vyvanse, and Concerta. The problem is not inattention, as with ADD, but overattention. When you give these people a stimulant medication, they are prone to focus *more* on the thoughts they get stuck on. The best medications for this problem tend to be the antiobsessive antidepressants, which increase the neurotransmitter serotonin in the brain. I have nicknamed them *anti-stuck medications*. At the time of this writing there are ten medications that are commonly used to increase serotonin in the brain. These medications include Effexor (venlafaxine), Prozac (fluoxetine), Paxil (paroxetine), Zoloft (sertraline), Anafranil (clomipramine), Desyrel (trazodone), Celexa (citalopram), Remeron (mirtazapine), and Luvox (fluvoxamine).

SOOTHING THOUGHTS FOR THE STUCK BRAIN

- Just let it go, baby.
- I don't have to be right.
- It's better to be loving than to always be right.
- I don't have to fix other people.
- Inner Hippie-Speak: "Peace, man." "It's all good." "Chill, dude."
- I don't have to be perfect.
- I'm perfectly flawed, like the rest of humanity.
- God loves me, flaws and all.
- Don't worry . . . be happy!
- My favorite saying from speaking in Australia on two different occasions: "No worries, mate."

FOR OCD

- This is a compulsion, just a thought. I do not have to believe or serve my stuck thoughts. For now I can distract myself by walking or watching TV or taking a hot bath and come back to this issue later.

- I can call Marla and ask her to talk me off of this negative loop and give me a new perspective.
- I can write the pros and cons on a piece of paper and get them out of my mind.

SCRIPTURE TO SOOTHE THE RUMINATING SOUL

God is sheer mercy and grace;
  not easily angered, he's rich in love.
He doesn't endlessly nag and scold,
  nor hold grudges forever.
He doesn't treat us as our sins deserve,
  nor pay us back in full for our wrongs.
As high as heaven is over the earth,
  so strong is his love to those who fear him.
And as far as sunrise is from sunset,
  he has separated us from our sins.
As parents feel for their children,
  God feels for those who fear him.
He knows us inside and out,
  keeps in mind that we're made of mud. (Ps. 8–14 MSG)

LETTING GO PRAYERS

The Serenity Prayer is perhaps the most famous prayer next to the Lord's Prayer because it is effective. Beloved of twelve-step groups and beyond, it is what many call their *flare prayer*—the prayer they send up to heaven when overwhelmed:

God, grant me the serenity
to accept the things I cannot change,
the courage to change the things I can,
and the wisdom to know the difference.
—Reinhold Niebuhr

The following prayer from an anonymous seventeenth-century nun never ceases to bring a grin. Could there be a more honest, perfect prayer for those who want to give up being right every time in order to practice being more loving?

Lord, Thou knowest better than I know myself, that I am growing older
and will someday be old.
Keep me from the fatal habit of thinking I must say something
on every subject and on every occasion.
Release me from craving to straighten out everybody's affairs.
Make me thoughtful but not moody; helpful but not bossy.
With my vast store of wisdom, it seems a pity not to use it all,
but Thou knowest, Lord, that I want a few friends at the end.
Keep my mind free from the recital of endless details;
give me wings to get to the point. Seal my lips on my aches and pains.
They are increasing, and love of rehearsing them is becoming sweeter as the
years go by. I dare not ask for grace enough to enjoy the tales of others' pains,
but help me to endure them with patience.
I dare not ask for improved memory,
but for a growing humility and a lessening cocksureness
when my memory seems to clash with the memories of others.
Teach me the glorious lesson that occasionally I may be mistaken.
Keep me reasonably sweet;
I do not want to be a saint—some of them are so hard to live with—but a
sour old person is one of the crowning works of the devil.
Give me the ability to see good things in unexpected places,
and talents in unexpected people.
And, give me, O Lord, the grace to tell them so. Amen.

COUNT YOUR BLESSINGS THERAPY

When I work with cingulate-minded people, I have them do what is a common practice in many twelve-step programs (which I think are some of the best places to retrain your brain): when you realize that you are obsessing on all that's wrong in life, in others, or within yourself, sit down and write for ten minutes, listing all the things for which you are grateful. You may even want to keep a gratitude journal near your bedside to write in when negative thoughts keep you from sleep.

Some of you may remember the words of that old hymn from your childhood: "Count your blessings, name them one by one, and it will surprise you what the Lord has done."[2] Often nowadays, the old-fashioned, simple remedies for negativity that happy little grandmas have been offering us for years are being backed up by the latest and greatest research on happiness. (After you do this exercise, you might want to go give your grandma a hug and tell her she was right.)

Some research has shown that it is impossible to be grateful and loving while also being fearful or angry. Gratitude acts like a middle linebacker in your head, tackling negativity and worry before they can ruin your day.

LETTING GO OF GRUDGES

Cingulate-minded people can sometimes be the most resentful people in the world. And yet Jesus encourages us not to judge, to let go of anger, to not let the sun go down on our anger. If we know someone has something against us, we are to work toward peace and reconciliation.

Forgiveness and letting go of grudges, however, is especially difficult for the person with the overactive cingulate. Have you ever made an attempt to resolve an issue with a cingulate-minded person? Not only are they usually reluctant to forgive, but they will bring up past grievances from twenty-four hours ago, two weeks ago, two years ago, twenty years ago . . . on and on it goes.

Here's an exercise to help let go of resentment:

1. Write out the resentment.
2. How long have you held on to how you were wronged or hurt?
3. How has this resentment helped you? (For some, holding on to a resentment gives them the power they need to set a boundary or to take action. What happens, unfortunately, when a person holds on to a resentment *too long* is that it can give a false sense of empowerment or strength. What benefit do you get from continuing to hold a grudge?)

4. What is your part? Is there something that *you* need to ask forgiveness for?

5. Do you need to ask forgiveness for your lack of forgiveness?

6. Is it possible your resentment is causing more harm than the original offense? What has renting space in your head to bitterness, anger, and thoughts of revenge done to your health of mind, soul, and body? What would your life be like if you let go?

Dr. Frederic Luskin has written a classic book, *Forgive for Good*, that I highly recommend if you are struggling with letting go of a past grievance. Here are some valuable thoughts from his Web site, www.learningtoforgive. com/steps.htm:

Nine Steps to Forgiveness

1. Know exactly how you feel about what happened and be able to articulate what about the situation is not okay. Then, tell a trusted couple of people about your experience.

2. Make a commitment to yourself to do what you have to do to feel better. Forgiveness is for you and not for anyone else.

3. Forgiveness does not necessarily mean reconciliation with the persons who hurt you or condoning their actions. What you are after is to find peace. Forgiveness can be defined as the "peace and understanding that come from blaming that which has hurt you less, taking the life experience less personally, and changing your grievance story."

4. Get the right perspective on what is happening. Recognize that your primary distress is coming from the hurt feelings, thoughts, and physical upset you are suffering now, not what offended you or hurt you two minutes—or ten years—ago. Forgiveness helps to heal those hurt feelings.

5. At the moment you feel upset, practice a simple stress management technique to soothe your body's fight-or-flight response.

6. Give up expecting things from other people (or your life) that they do not choose to give you. Recognize the "unenforceable rules" you have for your health or how you or other people must behave. Remind yourself that you can hope for health, love, peace, and prosperity, and work hard to get them.

7. Put your energy into looking for another way to get your positive goals met than through the experience that has hurt you. Instead of mentally replaying your hurt, seek out new ways to get what you want.
8. Remember that a life well-lived is your best revenge. Instead of focusing on your wounded feelings, and thereby giving the person who caused you pain power over you, learn to look for the love, beauty, and kindness around you. Forgiveness is about personal power.
9. Amend your grievance story to remind you of the heroic choice to forgive.

The practice of forgiveness has been shown to reduce anger, hurt, depression, and stress, and leads to greater feelings of hope, peace, compassion, and self-confidence. Practicing forgiveness leads to healthy relationships as well as physical health. It also influences our attitude, which opens the heart to kindness, beauty, and love.[3]

QUOTES TO GROW GRATEFUL BY

G. K. Chesterton was a round and jolly English soul from the early twentieth century who brought a keen sense of self-deprecating humor to Christian apologetics and reasoning. His writings are a good balancing tonic for those who love to debate (cingulate types) but need to soften the edges of their arguments with self-deprecation and humor . . . and, as you'll see in the following examples, an attitude of gratitude. Here is some perspective in his own words:

• When we were children we were grateful to those who filled our stockings at Christmas time. Why are we not grateful to God for filling our stockings with legs?
• I would maintain that thanks are the highest form of thought; and that gratitude is happiness doubled by wonder.
• You say grace before meals. All right. But I say grace before the concert and the opera, and grace before the play and pantomime, and grace before I open a book, and grace before sketching, painting, swimming, fencing, boxing, walking, playing, dancing, and grace before I dip the pen in the ink.

Music

Any music that is soothing and calming and puts you in a peaceful, grateful state is wonderful. From soft classical (Pachelbel's *Canon in D* is a favorite) to easy-listening, from mellow jazz to praise music—all can calm your brain. A good friend of mine recently discovered a soothing vocalist who left the commercial Nashville scene and now devotes herself to her family and an orphanage, bringing peace to troubled minds and bodies with her music. There are a lot of beautiful instrumentals and background sounds (rain, ocean waves, birds), and Genie's voice is very soft, almost childlike, like a Celtic singer. (She's been compared to Enya.) Her CD *Whispers* is akin to being surrounded by angels who are whispering words of peace. It is perfect to calm and soothe the troubled minds of adults and kids, particularly in winding down for sleep or letting go of stress or, as one woman calls it, "The perfect bathtub music!" (Order her music for any donation at www.geniemusic.com.)

For keyed-up kids, check out a charming set of short, Christian bedtime story-and-music-based CDs called *Psalty's Sleepytime Helpers* (www.psaltykids.com). A friend of mine used them with her children (who loved them!), and even though they are now grown, they still remember the lullaby that ends each CD, with phrases such as "It's time to snuggle up and get cozy in your bed," and "Dream of happy things, like how much God loves you." What child wouldn't calm down with these words playing their way into dreamland on a nightly basis?

Exercise

Dr. Amen suggests intense aerobic exercise for the cingulate area of the brain, and for most cingulate issues, I would agree. However, one of the sticky wickets with exercise for the obsessive-compulsive personality is that a healthy workout routine can quickly become a radical, overdone, frantic desire to over-exercise (particularly in those with eating disorders and distorted body images). In these cases, we recommend the more *peaceful* forms of physical exercise: walking, swimming, stretches, yoga, or Pilates. There are several Christian-based programs and videos with yoga-like movements for those who want to incorporate worship into their routines. (Check out www.christianyoga.us for DVDs and also a list of classes that may be held near you.)

Cinematherapy

These are sure to make you smile and, perhaps, even enjoy a healing laugh at yourself:

- *As Good as It Gets*. Mentioned before, but if you've not seen it, it is a delightful and touching look into one man's obsessive mind.
- *Moonstruck*. A delightful film about flawed human beings and the power of love to lift them above their own neuroses. Nicholas Cage plays the perfect leading man with cingulate issues. His appearance at the beginning of the movie is classic: he's obsessed with a past hurt and cannot let go (he blames his brother for an accident in the bakery that cut off his hand), but eventually his brooding obsession gives way to a romance with a character played by Cher. Her philosophy of handling hurts and life's messier feelings is to simply "Snap out of it!" And thus, opposites attract, and they grow to love each other "something awful."
- *Cold Comfort Farm*. A quirky, hilarious film about a crazy cast of cingulate, overfocused, brooding characters who live on a run-down farm. One especially awful-looking wild-haired woman occasionally breaks into the movie, eyes wide, voice ominous, pointing and saying, "There's something nasty in the woodshed!" Then, enter one perky can-do cousin who bursts onto the dreary farm like Pollyanna on Prozac and proceeds to dismiss their broodings and ominous obsessions with a wave of her hand and goes about bringing order and sunshine and at least a modicum of sanity into their lives. It's the perfect movie for someone who dreams of fixing their obsessive family members in two hours or less, but remember—it's a fantasy!
- *Enchanted April*. When one nineteenth-century Englishwoman cannot let go and forgive her obnoxious husband, she gathers up an equally miserably married friend and escapes to a villa in Italy to restore her weary mind. In time, the beauty of the surroundings, the friendships that develop, and the gratitude that creep up on them help to give each a perspective on life and

love and open their hearts wider than the characters could have ever imagined. If you are struggling to forgive or are holding on to petty grievances, this is a movie worth finding and renting, even if it takes a little Internet sleuthing to find it.

Bibliotherapy

Self-Help
- *Healing Anxiety and Depression* by Dr. Daniel Amen
- *Brain Lock* by Jeffrey M. Schwartz
- *The Boy Who Couldn't Stop Washing* by Judith L. Rapoport
- *When Once Is Not Enough: Help for the Obsessed* by Gail Steketee
- *Up and Down the Worry Hill: A Children's Book About OCD* by Aureen Pinto Wagner. One million children and adolescents have been diagnosed with OCD. See the recommended booklist at www.brainphysics.com for a longer list.
- *It's Not About the Weight: Attacking Eating Disorders from the Inside Out* by Susan J. Mendelsohn, PsyD. See www.remudaranch.com for a Christian-based eating disorders recovery program. They are doing great work in this field.
- *The Diet Cure* by Julia Ross. She focuses on rebalancing body/brain chemistry as a vital component in overcoming all sorts of weight-related issues—from obesity to anorexia to bulimia. If you prefer a nutritional approach to getting well, you may want to look into Julia Ross's Recovery Systems program at www.dietcure.com/consulta.html.

For Fun and Inspiration

Traveling Mercies by Anne Lamott

I should probably put a disclaimer here to anyone who is offended by the occasional bad word or a character evolving from a very liberal, messed-up mind. But many Christians who have problems with forgiving and accepting themselves as God's beloved, flawed child have found relief in Anne's hilarious and poignant, self-revealing writing. If for no other reason than to discover, "Wow! If Jesus loves her, I think he could probably love me too!" Anne struggles with just about every cingulate issue listed in this book. Where do I begin? Promiscuity, alcohol and drug use, eating disorders, obsessing about flaws—those belonging to others and those that she tries so hard to overcome. And yet her humor leaves you laughing out loud between wiping at tears. Not surprisingly, her journey to faith is messy as well. But God is in the business of loving messy people such as Anne who have, what appears to me, stuck cingulates.

Note in her unusual story of coming to faith how music plays a dramatic part in drawing a reluctant, drugged-out, pregnant, and unmarried Anne into a church and, ultimately, into the arms of Christ. Music is one of the loveliest gifts that God uses to calm and to reach the hearts of his beloved, high-strung children.

These ideas should give you some great places to begin giving your cingulate brain a break from fast-forward, stuck thinking. Now that we've tamed the gerbil, let's move on to calming another area of the brain, the one that houses those giant fear monsters.

CHAPTER EIGHT

The Basal Ganglia:
The Basement of Giant Fears

Lion: [crying] Look at the circles under my eyes,
    I haven't slept in weeks.
Tin Man: Well, why don't you count sheep?
Lion: Oh it's no use; I'm afraid of them.

—FROM *THE WIZARD OF OZ*[1]

Perhaps you've read or heard some version of the following story:

> Linda Burnett, 23, was visiting her in-laws and while there went to a nearby supermarket to pick up some groceries. Several people noticed her sitting in her car with the windows rolled up and with her eyes closed, with both hands behind the back of her head.

> One customer who had been at the store for a while became concerned and walked over to the car. He noticed that Linda's eyes were now open, and she looked very strange. He asked her if she was okay, and Linda replied that she'd been shot in the back of the head and had been holding her brains in for over an hour.

> The man called the paramedics, who broke into the car because the doors were locked and Linda refused to remove her hands from her head. When they finally got in, they found that Linda had a wad of bread dough on the back of her head.

> A Pillsbury biscuit canister had exploded from the heat, making a loud noise that sounded like a gunshot, and the wad of dough hit her in the back

of her head. When she reached back to find out what it was, she felt the dough and thought it was her brains. She initially passed out, but quickly recovered and tried to hold her brains in for over an hour. And, yes, Linda is a blonde.[2]

Fortunately, or unfortunately, the source of this story-turned-urban legend cannot be confirmed as fact. However, I can tell you that a good friend of mine swears that she carried a bruise on her upper chest for a week, inflicted by a can of exploding biscuits as she was carrying the groceries into the house. So this much I know: an exploding can of biscuits *can* be dangerous.

For those among us who've ever had a migraine and wondered if it could be a tumor and perhaps creatively taken that negative thought and imagined it into a full-blown deathbed scene, maybe even gone on to visualize the funeral, complete with hymns and flowers and weeping relatives—well, we could have identified with the poor, frightened, biscuit-brained woman if the story proved to be true. We'd have laughed at her, sure. But only as loudly as we'd have had to laugh at our often-too-easily-frightened selves. For who among us hasn't at one point or another felt somewhat like the woman who thought she'd been mortally wounded by a bullet that turned out to be a Pillsbury biscuit?

Alas, Chicken Little has not left the brain building. She can be activated by both inner and outer circumstances, especially if we've been depleted of good, soothing neurotransmitters either by chronic stress, sudden trauma, or anxious genes. In a state of hypervigilance, every time a cloud passes by or a bird chirps too loudly, your cognitive Chicken Little fears the sky is falling.

Many dear people have suffered much in this life, often from multiple traumas and sometimes in a relatively brief period of time. (I don't know why, but often it does seem that tragedies come in bunches.) They know what it's like to walk around on a beautiful, cloudless day, fearing when the next round of dreaded bad news will fall. Sadly, they are wasting the precious present by filling it up with fears of the future because their mind cannot let go of pain from the past. Even though logic may say, "You are safe," the basal ganglia, that Basement of Giant Fears, continues stomping around, waving its wide-eyed amygdala eyeballs, shouting to our mood system to "prepare for imminent danger!"

Needless to say, it is an exhausting, painful way to live.

The good news, once again, is that no one need suffer for the rest of their days over a traumatic or painful event in their past.

Let's take a look at the differences between a healthy, balanced basal ganglia and an overactive Basement of Giant Fears:

Healthy Basal Ganglia	Overactive Basal Ganglia
Sets the body's idle to a relatively peaceful, relaxed setting as the default mood	Irritable; the body idles on anxiety or fear as the default, underlying mood
Controls smooth movement	Anxious; panics
Sets anxiety level	Hypervigilant (being always on the alert, waiting for the other shoe to drop); sometimes micromanaging to keep sense of control
Modulates motivation	Avoids conflict
Mediates pleasure	Tense, often accompanied with headaches, neck or back pain
Ability to perceive, detect, move toward, prefer, and anticipate reward	Predicts the worst
Attentive to surroundings; awareness	Devotes excess energy to surveying surroundings, looking for potential disasters

An overactive basal ganglia is often associated with post-traumatic stress (see appendix C). A diamond pattern in a SPECT scan has proven to be a good indicator of trauma. All of the symptoms on the right are from overactivity; however, on the opposite pole, if there is decreased activity in the basal ganglia, it can register as ADD-like symptoms with decreased motivation.

OLD-FASHIONED, GARDEN-VARIETY ANXIETY

Some people are just born with a higher set point for anxiety, and the tendency often runs in families; whether from nature or nurture, we don't completely know. Perhaps some of each. Dr. Amen's mother, who is in her eighties, has one of the most beautiful brains he's ever scanned, but both he and his mom share a higher set point of anxiety with greater basal ganglia activity than optimal. (Remember, there is no such thing as the perfect brain.) Because his mother is so active—playing golf four days a week, deeply involved in life—he believes her genetic predisposition to anxiety has been tempered and controlled by a positive, giving, proactive lifestyle.

Fears come in all sizes: some come and go; some park themselves in your brain for a month or a year and some for decades. Some are based on reality and are normal responses to real threats; some are completely imagined; some are a little bit of both. Some of the terms you may be familiar with that have to do with the basal ganglia running hot are *panic disorders*, *agoraphobia*, *GAD* (generalized anxiety disorder, causing overworry about everyday things), *phobias*, and *PTSD* (post-traumatic stress disorder). Sometimes a one-time trauma (even a small one) can set a person up for being easily triggered in that area once again unless we interrupt the fear pattern. When it comes to facing the giants in our brain's basement, the best therapies all involve some kind of interruption to break up the looping thoughts that feed the monsters in our heads. For example, if you are watching a scary movie, with the typical doomsday music playing and the shadow of the killer moving ever closer to the victim, your entire body goes on hyperalert. But if the scene is interrupted in any way, by someone opening the door and letting light in the theater or munching popcorn and giggling or someone's cell phone playing the "Chicken Dance" song, your fears begin to subside . . . and fast.

I use this technique of pattern interruption to help my clients who are fearful, adjusting my methods to their degree of trauma.

One of my favorite stories of subduing the Basement of Giant Fears involved Ann who, at sixteen years old and driving on a beginner's permit, was known as the safest driver in her family. However, when she failed her driver's test for the second time, her confidence was shaken. The lady who conducted Ann's driving test took her charge from the DMV of the State of California as seriously as Barney Fife took his oath to protect Mayberry. The woman—who we nicknamed *Sarge*—seemed to take pride in the fact that she was known as one of the toughest testers in Orange County. Kids prayed they would not draw her name.

Ann's parents brought her in to see me because she simply could not bring herself to take the test again. Just the thought of walking into the DMV made her chest and throat tighten in paralyzing fear. Her basal ganglia had become so inflamed that her Presidential Control Center had abandoned her brain just when she needed it most—to help her concentrate on her driving test.

To break up this fear, I knew I would need to think creatively. So I turned to Ann's mom and said, "I've got a stealth assignment for you. Go into the DMV and, using your cell phone or a small camera, try to take a picture of Sarge in an unflattering pose. Then print out the picture and draw a Minnie Mouse hat on her head, frame it, and give it to Ann." Then I turned to Ann, "Is your car in our parking lot?" She nodded in the affirmative. "Okay, let's all go out to your car together."

I had Ann sit in the driver's seat, and I sat next to her, where Sarge would have been. (Mom was in the back.) Then I said, "Okay, now close your eyes and picture Sarge's head on top my body, with Minnie Mouse ears." Ann closed her eyes and as soon as she visualized her instructor's head, complete with Mouseketeer ears on top of my six-foot, six-inch body, she started to laugh. Then I told her to exaggerate the picture even more, especially when fears surfaced. "Picture Sarge in a bright pink polka-dotted dress with huge hot pink sunglasses. And if you start to feel anxious, increase the size of the ears, the dress, or the sunglasses in your imagination."

Though my method may sound bizarre, there was a neurologically sound reason behind everything I did. I helped her create a new trigger (that provoked laughter instead of fear), and by sitting in her car, we actually created a new body memory associated with her being in the driver's seat. (A *body memory* is the term we use for how our bodies subconsciously "remember" feelings even if we don't consciously recall an event.) In essence, I was overlaying a new, benign, funny image and attaching it to a fearful one—making it so ridiculous that from this point on, it would be impossible for Ann to picture Sarge without associating her with Minnie. With practice, anyone can lower their fear quota in everyday encounters with stress-producing people by using this simple technique. Be my guest!

"It's important to practice this visualization during boring times at school," I told her, which further broadened her smile. When she left my office that day, you could feel her rising confidence and joy. She felt back in control of her mind and took charge of the giant Sarge stomping around in her head by using creative imagery. In fact, she stopped at Disneyland and purchased a horrid pair of pink Minnie Mouse glasses—then gave them to her instructor after she successfully and confidently passed the test.

PANIC ATTACKS, AGORAPHOBIA, AND GOOD OL' SOUTHERN COOKING

I wish all cases of fear were as easily erased as Ann's. And perhaps they would be with early intervention. In fact, if Ann's parents had not sought help for their daughter's high anxiety, she might have developed a full-blown phobia. Or perhaps this relatively small trauma could have exploded into a feeling of generalized anxiety—that nothing she did would turn out, that it was better not to try or risk. Then she'd be experiencing generalized anxiety disorder, which could escalate into panic attacks or other more serious phobias.

Paula Deen, who is one of the most popular stars of the Food Network, looks like a woman who has always been happy, gregarious, open armed, and ready to tackle life with a grin. With her deep Southern accent and homegrown laughter, it is really hard to imagine Paula being anything other than the life of the party. She owns one of Savannah's most successful restaurants, The Lady & Sons, with lines that wrap around the block most evenings and weekends. At midlife (when most are winding down their activity level), she appeared in the movie *Elizabethtown*, married a sea captain who is the love of her life, and rides herd over her big, beautiful, blended family. If you listen to her for five minutes, you will instantly know two things: One, this woman loves good food drippin' with butter . . . and lots of it. Two, she loves life to the hilt. "Child, you just have no idea how good it is going to get!" is just one of her many upbeat, Paula-isms.

With Paula bringing so much Southern comfort and sunshine into the lives of thousands of viewers, many of her fans were surprised to discover that after a period of multiple life stresses at a young age, Paula's Basement of Giant Fears went on hyperalert. Those fears stomped around telling her that life would never be safe, that those you love most will be taken away, that the only solution is to stay put and lock the doors.

And so she did . . . for nearly two decades! In her charming and vulnerable book *It Ain't All About the Cookin'*, Paula wrote, "I was twenty-three years old. I had two babies under three, a sour marriage, a sixteen-year-old brother, and our momma and poppa were both dead. My spirit was broken. My mind wasn't doing too good either."

Losing her parents at age nineteen began the spiraling down of her former sense of peace and security. The shock of so many multiple losses took its toll, and she began to live in fear that she would die or, worse, that someone she loved would be taken away. During that time in our society, panic attacks and agoraphobia were not talked about much, so Paula never had a name for this awful experience that had turned her from a spunky, outgoing cheerleader into a frightened woman. After her mother died, she stayed home as much as possible and got out only a little, then hurried back home "as though something were chasing me."

Left untreated, things got worse. She was overprotective of her young sons, always fighting the fear that something awful would happen to them. She became a hypochondriac and hyperventilated enough times that she began carrying around a paper bag to breathe into, should she need it. One day (back in the '70s) a caring friend called and alerted Paula to a television program; *The Phil Donahue Show* was doing an entire segment on agoraphobia and panic. Paula learned that about two million Americans, 1 percent of the population, had this disorder. She recognized all too well the symptoms of a panic attack, such as clamminess, shaking, rapid heartbeat, a feeling of not being able to breathe, numbness in arms and hands, nausea, and the feeling that you were going to die or, at the very least, lose all control.[3]

Knowing a name for what she had helped, but it wasn't until Paula Deen turned forty years old that her escape from fear's grip on her life began in earnest. One day she went to the mirror and whispered aloud, "I can't do this anymore, I just can't." Then she said—"like a thunderclap"—the words to the Serenity Prayer hit her in a whole new way. She got its message down to her toes. *Sure, I'm gonna die*, she said to herself. "Everyone I love is gonna die. But God has given me today, and I'm gonna go out and live today. I won't die today."[4] So walking one block at a time, taking one small risk at a time, she got well. And then she opened a restaurant. Then came a TV cooking show. And then she got rich. And then, famous. And she remarried. But I think she would say, even today, that nothing on earth means as much to her as the day she and God got hold of the fear monster within and wrestled it to the ground, one day at a time.

By the time Paula turned forty-one, she realized she'd lived nearly half of her life in agony and anguish, just waiting to die. Finally, she was free from the paralyzing grip of fear. She wrote, "I felt as though I had two birthdays . . . the day I was born . . . and the day I came back to living my days. The day I took control of my life."[5]

Paula is just one example of a woman who was able to get well on the strength of a prayer, the love and encouragement of good friends, and a major "thought exchange" that turned the tide of her life. But it took twenty years to get there.

Whatever it takes, whatever works, I would love to help set you free from the fear that binds you—starting right now, today. Don't wait twenty years. In fact, why wait twenty-four hours?

Who knows? You may be a light under a bushel of fear, just waiting to become the world's next star.

WHEN TRAUMA LEAVES FINGERPRINTS

Related to fear and anxiety is a condition we call post-traumatic stress disorder—a lingering anxiety often provoked by certain triggers that remind the brain and body of past trauma. Childhood sexual abuse that hasn't been acknowledged and treated is one of the most common issues that rewire the brain to a hypervigilant state. Whatever its cause (an accident, shocking news, war, or abuse of any kind), PTSD limits our ability to exhale, to relax and enjoy life without waiting for the proverbial rain to fall on life's parade. Helping people with PTSD to find higher levels of happiness in their lives is one of my areas of expertise, and I love it.

Because PTSD shows up in a SPECT scan in several areas of the brain, creating a diamond pattern, I've chosen to give this disorder and its cures a section of its own. (See appendix C for a more detailed discussion.)

QUIETING THE BASEMENT OF GIANT FEARS

Nutrition

- Complex carbs act as tranquilizers by increasing the amount of serotonin—the neurotransmitter that calms—in your brain. Include lots of fruits and whole-grain foods to increase your complex carb intake.
- Tryptophan—a precursor to serotonin—has a calming effect on the body. Turkey and milk contain tryptophan and are soothing to anxious minds.
- Caffeine—as you probably already know—can make you jittery and anxious. Try substituting a calming herbal tea such as St. John's wort or chamomile for your morning java. Green tea also has calming properties that counteract the small amount of caffeine.
- Chronic dehydration—however slight—can cause feelings of anxiety. Drink plenty of water often. Boring, you say? Add a slice of lemon, orange, strawberry, kiwi, or mint leaves to liven it up.
- Frequent small meals with some protein, some carbs, and some fat in them can help keep blood-sugar levels even. Even a small drop in blood sugar can cause a big rise in anxiety and agitation in many people.[6]

Healthy Dos and Don'ts

Do:

- Take a multivitamin supplement that includes vitamin B and plenty of vitamin B6. Even undetectable malnutrition can lead to feelings of anxiety. In fact, many anxious people can benefit from a vitamin B complex and a magnesium/calcium supplement. (Start with a low dose, and take with meals to avoid stomach upset.)
- Exercise daily. The endorphins produced make you feel relaxed, plus exercise reduces muscle tension and blood pressure.
- Drink plenty of water or other fluids like herbal tea or decaf green or black tea.

Don't:

- Consume alcohol. Sure, a glass of wine can take the edge off, but once it has worn off, there is a likelihood that your level of anxiety will actually increase. Same effect on sleep—you may fall asleep fast, but you may also be wandering the halls at 2:00 a.m., unable to sleep.
- Consume caffeine, which can be found in tea, coffee, many sodas, chocolate, and some energy/sports drinks and foods.[7]

Supplements
- GABA will help calm overactivity in the basal ganglia. Be sure to ask for a pharmaceutical grade. Also, 5-HTP (5-hydroxytryptophan) may help a little to decrease anxiety.
- Inositol is not helpful for acute anxiety attacks, but long-term use may decrease anxiety.
- True Calm is a combination of calming aminoes and may be helpful.

Herbs
- Chamomile (*Matricaria chamomilla*), hop flowers (*Humulus lupulus*), lemon balm (*Melissa officinalis*), passionflower (*Passiflora incarnata*), and valerian (*Valerian officinalis*) have all been used for many years but have not been studied in people with anxiety attacks.
- Kava (*Piper methysticum*) may be helpful for mild anxiety. When buying it, be sure the label on the bottle says the product is standardized to 70 percent kavalactones.
- St. John's wort (*Hypericum perforatum*) has been used for many years.

Complementary Therapies
- Massage can decrease anxiety
- Meditation
- Pets may decrease anxiety

Medication

Though antianxiety drugs such as Xanax are often prescribed for fearful tendencies or PTSD, I am hesitant to suggest them except in the most severe cases, and only for the short-term. (It's probably no surprise that Xanax is one of the favored drugs prescribed by doctors and then resold among teens and college-age students.) It has an effect on the brain similar to that of some street drugs, and after viewing SPECT scans of brains on some of the stronger anti-anxiety meds, we know they are not good for long-term brain health. Plus, they have an addictive side to them, so we don't encourage their use except for short periods of time and when there isn't an alternative that will work better.

Note: This next chart contains Dr. Daniel Amen's general recommendations to physicians. It is for general information only and not a substitute for your doctor's protocol. However, you may want to share this chapter and the following information with your physician if you or a loved one is having anxiety issues. It is for this reason that I am including Dr. Amen's usual dosages. I'd rather err on the side of giving you information you may not use than to leave you groping in the dark for a generic guideline if you or your loved one is suffering from anxiety. I know I am personally grateful when books are as specific as possible and when doctors are generous with what they have found to be successful for them and their patients. Dr. Amen is one of those generous physicians, and for this so many clients and professional colleagues are grateful.

Medication	Overview and Dosage
Neurontin	Generic name for this medication is *gabapentin*. Preferred medication if no symptoms of manic or bipolar are present. Begin at lowest dose possible, usually 100 mg, 3 times a day. Have had patients who had to start at 50 mg, 3 times a day, taking capsule and using half of it.
Gabitril	Highly effective for anxiety. Start with 2 mg tablets. Take ½ to 1 tablet nightly for 3 to 5 days, then increase to ½ to 1 tablet 2 times daily. Gradually increase until symptom management is reached.
Topamax	Starting dose usually 25 mg at night, and after 3 to 5 days, morning dose is added. Can be increased 25 mg at a time to a maximum of 100 mg, twice daily. For some people, there is a side effect of weight loss. Seems to help with sugar cravings. There are increasing numbers of research articles that point toward the use of Topamax with eating disorders. Watch for memory impairment.
Xanax	Xanax is often prescribed for panic attacks. If a person is a recovering alcoholic or there is alcoholism in the family history, attempt to use Xanax on a short-term basis since there is a risk of addiction. Many times Xanax, Klonopin, or Ativan are given with Prozac, Lexapro, Effexor, or Cymbalta. These medications, for some people, can increase basal ganglia activity while helping with depression. Many times Xanax can be reduced or eliminated if Neurontin or Gabitril are used to help calm basal ganglia overactivity. If Xanax is used on a long-term basis, it can have a side effect of depression and memory problems with some people. Make sure any elderly people in your life are carefully evaluated if using Xanax on a routine basis.

Medication	Overview and Dosage
Xyrexa and Risperidal	Xyrexa and Risperidal are sometimes given in small doses to help with panic and anxiety. These medications will often be used if a person is going through a bout of insomnia. These medications are part of a class called *novel antipsychotics* and are also helpful with people who struggle with bipolar or schizophrenia. In small doses, they can help with panic or sleep. They work as a dopamine inhibitor. If you use them to sleep and find it is a struggle to get going in the morning, or your brain does not "wake up" until 10 or 11 a.m, it could be the Xyrexa or Resperidal causing that to happen. We need dopamine in the frontal cortex in the morning to feel motivated to even get out of bed. If you are having trouble waking up, tell your prescribing MD or your therapist.

STOMPING ON ANTS

Dr. Amen often speaks of automatic negative thoughts or ANTs. I have found that when people have high anxiety, they really do need to retrain their brain. The Scriptures speak of "taking every thought captive" (2 Cor. 2:5 NASB) and "the renewing of your mind" (Rom. 12:2). One way to do this is to exchange our worries for God's reassurances. Another is to become a bystander to your thoughts—questioning their validity and asking yourself, *Is there another way to think about the same situation that might be more true? More kind? More uplifting and positive?*

Here are some ANTs categories that Dr. Amen has found can be a real drain and strain on your brain:

- *Mind reading*: Predicting you know that another person is thinking something negative about you without that person telling you. In all our combined years of counseling others, we still cannot read another person's mind. Neither can you.
- *Fortune telling*: Predicting a bad outcome to a situation before it has occurred. Your mind makes happen what it sees. Unconsciously, predicting failure will often cause failure. You may assume a person won't like

you, and because you've already put up a protective shell, they very well may not like you.

- *"Always" or "Never" thinking*: This is where you think in words such as *always, never, every time,* or *everyone.* These thoughts are overgeneralizations that can alter behavior. If you assume that your mate or your kids will never change or can never change, you actually lock them into a mold from which they cannot escape (at least in your mind).
- *Guilt beatings*: Being overrun by thoughts of "I should have done . . ." "I'm bad because . . ." "I must do better at . . ." "I have to . . ." Guilt is powerful at making us feel bad. It is a lousy motivator of behavior.
- *Talk-back-to-yourself therapy*: Another recommendation is to simply talk back to your mind the way a sassy teen might talk back to an adult. In this case, it is okay. Tell your ANTs to take a hike, and invite APTs (automatic positive thoughts) in, instead.

QUOTES TO CHASE THE FEAR AWAY

- "I gave you life so you could *live* it!" —mother to daughter, *My Big Fat Greek Wedding*
- And the day came when the risk to remain tight in a bud was more painful than the risk it took to blossom. —Anaïs Nin
- Pushing through fear is less frightening than living with the underlying fear that comes from a feeling of helplessness. —Susan Jeffers, author, *Feel the Fear . . . and Do It Anyway*
- Normal fear protects us; abnormal fear paralyzes us. Normal fear motivates us to improve our individual and collective welfare; abnormal fear constantly poisons and distorts our inner lives. Our problem is not to be rid of fear but rather to harness and master it. —Dr. Martin Luther King Jr.
- Here's one of the very few generalizations I believe unconditionally: There is not one useful thing we do that we don't do better when we're relaxed.[8] —Martha Beck

VISUALIZATION

With yet another nod to vivid and funny life coach Martha Beck, here's a wonderful picture of what relaxation looks like. Martha describes her beagle, Cookie, as he is "writhing on his back in the grass, emitting small grunts of pleasure"—in abandoned, uninhibited delight. Beck adds, "I know people who've spent thousands of dollars on sex therapy trying to do that." Meanwhile, Cole (her Lab) chases a Frisbee, and Martha notices that he actually seems to relax before leaping, rather than tightening his muscles. If dogs could speak, I feel sure they'd say, "You humans sure need to chill."[9] And they'd be correct almost every time.

SOOTHING SCRIPTURES

I love the way that Eugene Peterson has paraphrased this wonderful passage on love and fear from 1 John. When love has the run of our Brain House, when we relax into the truth that God loves us—couldn't love us any more or less no matter what—fear cannot inch its way into our minds.

> God is love. When we take up permanent residence in a life of love, we live in God and God lives in us. This way, love has the run of the house, becomes at home and mature in us, so that we're free of worry on Judgment Day—our standing in the world is identical with Christ's. There is no room in love for fear. Well-formed love banishes fear. Since fear is crippling, a fearful life—fear of death, fear of judgment—is one not yet fully formed in love. (4:17–18 MSG)

A great verse to sleep on, and I love the poetic quality of the King James version in this next scripture:

> I will both lay me down in peace, and sleep: for thou, LORD, only makest me dwell in safety. (Ps. 4:8 KJV)

A great go-to verse when you are worried. Praying with gratitude has been shown to stop anxious thoughts in their tracks:

Don't worry about anything; instead, pray about everything. Tell God what you need, and thank him for all he has done. (Phil. 4:6 NLT)

Picture yourself as God's beloved sheep or lamb and pray through the Twenty-third Psalm, imagining that Christ, your Shepherd, is guarding, guiding, and loving you all the way:

> GOD, my shepherd! I don't need a thing.
> You have bedded me down in lush meadows,
>> you find me quiet pools to drink from.
> True to your word,
>> you let me catch my breath
>> and send me in the right direction.
> Even when the way goes through
>> Death Valley,
> I'm not afraid
>> when you walk at my side.
> Your trusty shepherd's crook
>> makes me feel secure.
> You serve me a six-course dinner
>> right in front of my enemies.
> You revive my drooping head;
>> my cup brims with blessing.
> Your beauty and love chase after me
>> every day of my life.
> I'm back home in the house of GOD
>> for the rest of my life. (MSG)

Music

What's your happy, peaceful go-to music? Often it is the same music that we found calming as a child or a teenager. Go back down memory lane and pull some of the best music from your happy memory files. It could be Elvis singing "Follow That Dream" or "Amazing Grace." Or maybe it's James Taylor singing "Shower the People You Love with Love." Or a hymn, such as "What a Friend We Have in Jesus" or "It Is Well with My Soul." Go back as far as your memory lets you, and try to remember lullabies that your mother may have sung to you. Collect a list of happy, peaceful songs from your past, and fill your iPod with them or make a CD of them.

Sometimes I'll think of a song I'd like to hear again and go to YouTube, type in the song and the artist, and get to watch him or her perform it. *Like a blast from the past!* Check out Perry Como singing, "And I Love You So"—on *Sesame Street.* A classic love song made especially fun by the lovable Big Bird's appearance at the end. And really, does anybody sing as effortlessly—as peacefully—as Perry did? Okay, Bing Crosby singing "White Christmas," Dean Martin singing "That's Amore," and Andy Williams singing "Moon River" come awfully close.

Challenge me and see how many great, peaceful crooners and their songs you can find. Or look up some of the new ones like Michael Bublé or Norah Jones. Crooning is back *in*, baby!

Exercise

Just about any kind of movement is great to calm your fears. Walking in the sunshine is especially nice. Because basal ganglia folks like to start nice and easy, begin with a dance or exercise class that doesn't challenge you too much. Then as you master one level, work toward the next in slow and easy increments. Even if you are doing a treadmill for the first time, start with a short, doable distance and pace. When that feels great, move on.

Use this one-bite-at-a-time technique with anything you'd like to do but that feels overwhelming. Yoga-like, slow-movement exercise has been found to be helpful in calming anxiety.

Aromatherapy

Think of your most pleasant memories and try to recall the scents surrounding them. Making cinnamon rolls with your beloved grandmother? The smell of apples from a day in the country? These smells, too, will produce a surge of happiness in your brain.

Many stores offer aromatherapy scents specifically created to help with anxiety, or try a DIY recipe from www.aromatherapyheals.com. If you feel a panic attack coming on or anxious feelings are beginning to overwhelm, certain aromatherapy recipes are particularly useful in treating such symptoms. Try the following blend of essential oils: 1 part neroli (orange blossom), 1 part marjoram, and 1 part bergamot. An alternative is: 1 part sandalwood, 2 parts bergamot, and 3 parts lavender. (Bergamot is derived from the peel of a bergamot orange and gives Earl Grey tea its distinctive flavor and aroma. So to keep antianxiety aromatherapy supersimple, try sipping a warm cup of Earl Grey or orange blossom tea. Herbal teas do double duty: the smells *and* the tastes affect our moods. Take a stroll down your herbal tea aisle at your grocery store, and pick a few preparations formulated to calm and ease tension.)

Cinematherapy

To soothe your anxious heart, I recommend the following movies:

- *Chicken Run.* Cartoon, fine-feathered version of *The Great Escape* is a delightful movie for adults and kids about finding the courage to leave the box. A hen with a dream, named Ginger, courageously inspires the chickens to fly the coop.
- *My Big Fat Greek Wedding. Ahh*, Toula Portokalos. The ultimate makeover character (surrounded by a family of ultimate characters) who dares to risk blossoming outside the traditional circle because it has become more frightening to her soul to avoid doing so. Her reward is getting to fall in love with herself and with a wonderful man who honors her heart. Plus, the laughs in this movie will stomp on a few fearful giants.
- *The Wizard of Oz.* There are so many psychological layers beneath this classic movie. Since basal ganglia folks are in need of courage, the character of the Cowardly Lion is especially heartwarming. But the greatest lesson of all is that behind the fearsome giant Wizard, there was just an ordinary man with a big ego. Behind many of the giant fears stomping around in our

brain's Basement are really just ordinary people with inflated egos who enjoy playacting their personal fairy tales of power on the vulnerable.

- *Titanic.* With multiple stories within the main story, the movie version is a testament to courage on many levels: the courage to be yourself when society wants you to fit a mold; the courage to risk loving; the courage to risk dying so a beloved can live; and finally, the courage to go on in the face of great loss and live a life that honors those who gave you the chance to live it fully. A line from the hauntingly beautiful song "My Heart Will Go On" describes the courage and passion that can be gleaned from a major loss. Even though someone you love may die, the love between you goes on and on forever. And if you choose to honor them with the rest of your life, by squeezing as much joy out of each precious moment as you can, your heart will go on as well.

Support Village

Just in case you are feeling alone in the anxiety vortex, here is a list of some famous people—found on anxietycentre.com—who have pushed beyond their basal ganglia's fear (and corresponding depression and phobias) to enrich their lives and the lives of others with their gifts:

Abraham Lincoln (U.S. president)	Cher (singer, actress)
Alanis Morisette (singer)	Courtney Love (singer, actress)
Alfred Lord Tennyson (poet)	David Bowie (singer)
Anne Tyler (author)	Dick Clark (television personality)
Anthony Hopkins (actor)	Donny Osmond (actor)
Aretha Franklin (singer)	Earl Campbell (Heisman Trophy winner)
Barbara Bush (former U.S. first lady)	Edie Falco (actress)
Barbara Gordon (filmmaker)	Edvard Munch (artist)
Barbra Streisand (singer)	Emily Dickinson (poet)
Burt Reynolds (actor)	Eric Clapton (musician)
Carly Simon (singer)	Goldie Hawn (actress)
Charles Schulz (cartoonist)	Isaac Asimov (author)
Charlotte Brontë (author)	James Garner (actor)

Jim Eisenreich (baseball player)

Joan Rivers (actress)

John Candy (comedian)

John Madden (NFL play-by-play announcer)

John Steinbeck (author)

Johnny Depp (actor)

Kim Basinger (actress)

Marie Osmond (entertainer)

Michael Crichton (writer)

Michael English (gospel singer)

Naomi Judd (singer)

Nicolas Cage (actor)

Nicole Kidman (actress)

Nikola Tesla (inventor)

Oprah Winfrey (talk show host)

Pete Harnisch (baseball player)

Ray Charles (musician)

Robert Burns (poet)

Robert McFarlane (former national security advisor)

Robin Quivers (radio host)

Sally Field (actress)

Sam Shepard (playwright)

Shecky Greene (comedian)

Sheryl Crow (musician)

Sigmund Freud (psychiatrist)

Sir Isaac Newton (scientist)

Sir Laurence Olivier (actor)

Sissy Spacek (actress)

Tom Snyder (television host)

Tony Dow (actor/director)

W. B. Yeats (poet)

Willard Scott (weatherman)[10]

There now . . . don't you feel less alone already? Here are some other sources of support:

- *Dale Carnegie Course: Effective Communications and Human Relations.* This is a classic course that has really proven to be timeless. Many people who battle with fear of speaking or need a boost of confidence have found these courses to be life-changing (see www.dalecarnegie.com).
- *Prayer or Bible Study Group.* Finding (or forming) a small group for the purpose of prayer and/or studying the Bible can be a great antianxiety help. The big church scene is often highly intimidating to the anxious, but getting your feet wet in a small group situation may prove to be your favorite form of "doing church." My only caution: if the personalities in the group or the topic chosen are more anxiety-provoking than calming, look for another that fits you better, or form your own home group with people who help you feel relaxed and affirmed. Many people feel safer when hosting a group in their own home, so volunteer to do this if it's your cup of tea.

- *Continuing Education.* Most cities offer fun, insightful, continuing education courses in confidence, speaking, communication, and conquering phobias. Sometimes they are called *Fun Ed* classes. Most are at amazingly affordable prices and usually are short-term courses offered at convenient times. These are excellent ways to dip your toe into learning something new and shaking up your Basement of Giant Fears. Ask a friend to go with you. Even something as simple as taking a cooking class can be a wonderful, absorbing, and fun diversion.

- *Girl Spa Day.* Many women enjoying taking a friend (or two or three) and going to a spa for a day to de-stress and relax. Go online and google "hot springs" or "spa days" or "therapeutic massages" and put together a day for pure relaxation. It is an investment in your mental health.

- *Overcomer's Outreach.* Christian-based support for a variety of issues. Anxiety often leads to dependence on drugs or alcohol. I helped start this twelve-step model in churches, and there may be a group meeting in your area that is perfect for you. Check www.overcomersoutreach.org.

- *Online.* A Web site devoted to helping people with a variety of anxiety disorders is www.anxietycentre.com. It's backed by twenty-one years of experience and has support from the Better Business Bureau.

- Since many people are too fearful to go outside or experience public support, the Internet is one way to begin your *connecting* experience with others who have a variety of anxiety issues. One site to visit is www.healthyplace.com/communities/anxiety/index.asp.

- I really liked the following checklist (found at HealthyPlace.com) with some wonderful antianxiety goals:

My Symptoms of Inner Peace
1. Tendency to think and act spontaneously rather than from fear based on past experience.
2. An unmistakable ability to enjoy each moment.
3. Loss of interest in judging other people.
4. Loss of interest in judging self.
5. Loss of interest in interpreting the actions of others.
6. Loss of interest in conflict.
7. Loss of ability to worry (a very serious symptom).

8. Frequent, overwhelming episodes of appreciation.
9. Contented feelings of connectedness with others and with nature.
10. Frequent attacks of smiling through the eyes and heart.
11. Increasing tendency to let things happen rather than make them happen.
12. Increased susceptibility to love extended from others as well as the uncontrollable urge to extend it.

Wouldn't it be nice to achieve all of those qualities?

Bibliotherapy

Self Help

- *Feel the Fear . . . and Do It Anyway* by Susan Jeffers. A classic. Many read this book and then reread it as a true courage booster to calm anxiety when they are about to take a risk.
- *Fearless: Building a Faith that Overcomes Your Fear* by Cheri Fuller. One reader described the book well in these review comments posted on Amazon.com: "Cheri draws on a storehouse of personal experiences about her own fears. She'll have you laughing and crying over her stories about fears that paralyze you vs. those that tie knots in your stomach. I can't think of a fear she doesn't cover: from car phobias to health issues, public speaking, panic attacks, disaster, rejection, snakes, etc. You'll find victory, freedom, and success as you read about solutions found in biblical truths, practical applications, and Scripture. I think my favorite parts of the book were those in which she gave insightful explanations about the causes of different phobias. I've already recommended this book to many friends and will continue to do so. It is phenomenal."
- *Healing Anxiety and Depression* by Dr. Daniel Amen. A practical approach to healing the brain's anxiety and low-mood areas. He discusses the seven types of anxiety and depression and goes into greater detail on these areas. One of the best parts of this book is the detail he goes into on both medication and supplemental helps, along with behavior changes. Highly recommended for further reading if you or someone you love are struggling with any of the following:

1. Pure anxiety
2. Pure depression
3. Mixed anxiety and depression
4. Overfocused anxiety/depression
5. Cyclic anxiety/depression
6. Angry anxiety/depression
7. Unfocused anxiety/depression

Great Reads with Redemptive Messages

- *Ellen Foster* by Kaye Gibbons. The perfect weekend read. This feisty little girl escapes a dark family and does so with spunk and an overcomer's outlook. You can't read this without feeling more courageous.
- *Leaving the Saints* by Martha Beck. A flawless, mystery-memoir written by a witty author about her escape from a frightening, rigid, religious cult–like community and a family secret of abuse. It's a page-turner that should come with a warning: don't start reading this book if you don't have the next day or two to finish it because you will not want to put it down. She's now one of America's most well-known and beloved life coaches.

Fun Reads to Bolster Courage in Kids

- *Pippi Longstocking* (the movies are great too) by Astrid Lindgren. She's every fearful child's dream of a fairy god-cousin. No, you don't want your child acting like Pippi, but this kind-hearted, crazy character allows a child's imagination to run away and play . . . and be braver than brave.[11]
- *James and the Giant Peach* by Roald Dahl. Kids love to read how the much-maligned boy named James escapes his terrible relatives and hooks up with fantastical new friends. If you enjoy reading aloud to your school-age kids and using lots of voices and drama, you'll all love this. Roald Dahl, who had some traumatic childhood experiences, spent much of his adult life writing fantasies about escaping from mean people into a world of warmth and joy. He is also laugh-out-loud funny, which makes kids love his writing.
- And of course, the classic tale: *Chicken Little*. An English fable whose original author is unknown. You can find a dozen illustrated versions of it in any major bookstore's children's section.

CHAPTER NINE

The Deep Limbic System:
The Depressed Low-Mood Space

Fits of depression come over most of us. Usually cheerful
as we may be, we must at intervals be cast down. The strong
are not always vigorous, the wise may not always be ready, the
brave not always courageous and the joyous not always happy.

—CHARLES SPURGEON

"**B**aby, you were born smiling!" Daisy's father used to tell her, in his deep, warm Georgia accent. In fact, Daisy grew up with a nickname: Sunshine Child. Happiness seemed her birthright, and her assigned "earth job" seemed to be to generally shine her light and make the world a brighter place. Daisy did this with almost effortless ease most of her life. Though she had the normal ups and downs and stresses that eventually come with marriage, a freelance career, and four kids, most of the time she felt energized by life's challenges. She'd have down days like everyone, but she was always able to right herself with a nap or a chocolate fix or a stimulating conversation with a friend or a good read . . . or every Southern woman's cure for the blues: a trip to the beauty salon for a big hair fluff and a pedicure.

IT'S RAINING ON THE INSIDE

Until, that is, the year from hell arrived at her front door, uninvited and unwanted. It began when her dad—the man who Daisy described as "always

140

sitting on the front row to cheer and applaud my life"—was diagnosed with cancer. Then her husband, Todd, lost his job. They were forced to relocate where Todd could find employment, far away from friends, family, and church. Still grieving, she could not find the energy to reach out to form new friendships and connections. The multiple stressors in Daisy's formerly cheerful life initiated a slow and agonizing descent into a heavy fog of sadness that simply would not lift. There weren't enough Dove chocolate bars in the world to stop the flow of tears. When her dad died, the grief was almost paralyzing. Daisy felt orphaned upon life's stage; the front-row center seat where she'd always counted on seeing her father, clapping and cheering, was achingly empty.

Five months later, as Daisy was walking along with her four-year-old son, still wrapped in a mental fog that left her feeling eerily half-present most of the time, her little boy looked up at her and asked sorrowfully, "Mommy, why don't you smile anymore?"

Oh, the perception of a child.

The question penetrated the fog of pain long enough for Daisy to see that her continued sadness, her depletion of joy, was affecting the ones she loved the most. For her own sake, and for her children's and husband's sake, she had to find her way out of this pit and back onto the sunnier side of the street.

"Honey," she answered tenderly and truthfully, "I do not know where my smile is hiding. But I promise you this. I'm going to try to find it again. Okay?"

Her son's face lit up, and in his smile, Daisy saw herself as she used to be—when joy was her friend and happiness her umbrella and when the world made sense at least most of the time. Daisy allowed herself the space and time to weep when a wave of sorrow hit her, but with renewed motivation, she also began letting the sunshine back into her life. She got dressed and put her makeup on no matter how much she felt like staying in her PJs all day; she focused on better nutrition and added some amino acid supplements to her vitamin routine; then she joined a worship/dance class at a local church. Before long she had a few more good days than bad, and the endorphins from the exercise along with the uplifting praise music helped her feel good enough to ask one of the women from her class out to lunch. She'd always carry the memory of her father in her heart, but more and more, as the weeks passed, she was able to focus on the good times they shared without falling apart with the agony of missing him.

The depression that Daisy experienced is known as situational depression or reactive depression (also known as adjustment disorder with depressed mood, if you are feeling fancy). These include sad or depressive symptoms that develop in response to a specific stressful situation or event, usually a loss such as a death, divorce, breakup, or loss of a job (especially for men, whose identities, more often than women's, are wrapped up in their careers). These symptoms occur within three months of the stressor and last no longer than six months after the stressor (or its consequences) has ended. (Although with a major grief such as the loss of a mate or a child or a close family member, these symptoms can last longer.)

Though this type of grief-related depression causes significant distress and impairs usual functioning (ability to focus and respond to life with your usual joy and enthusiasm), generally with the passage of time, you do eventually feel better, stronger, and happier. True grief comes in waves with some peaceful respite in between the sobs. Recovery from grief is a lot like the coming of spring: you get a few more warm days than cold ones until your life is mostly about warm, positive feelings again.

However, the above symptoms—though heartbreaking—do not meet the criteria for major depressive disorder, which hangs on for months or years without improvement. A clinical depression, in fact, often worsens, and continues for excessively long periods of time. A major depression can be *initiated* by loss, but someone who simply cannot move through normal grief recovery is often chemically predisposed to depression.

WHEN GRIEF TURNS DANGEROUS

Jim came into my office to get some help for his post-traumatic stress disorder (PTSD), left over from his tours in Vietnam. He was a delightful man with a good heart and a true hero. In the first session I said to him, "I want to thank you for your service to our country. You were shamed while you were serving and shamed when you came home. I apologize for that. Thank you for your service."

Tears flowed down his face as he shared one of many stories that would cause intense fear or pain to seemingly come out of nowhere. He once drove by a hospital not too far from my office and had a panic attack. When we looked more deeply into what caused his panic, we found he associated the hospital with his being wounded in Vietnam. After being seriously injured in battle, he was flown to a ship to receive surgery. However, Jim's wounds were so severe that in the emergency triage system, he was placed in the "dead man's bunk," one of many bunks reserved for the soldiers who were not expected to survive. In fact, the medical staff thought he was dead until a nurse spotted signs of life. With immediate surgery, he made it. And though he had PTSD (which was helped tremendously by our therapy together), he went on to live a happy and productive life.

He was married to Penny, and they were a wonderful Christian couple, completely in love. Both had survived painful marriages, so they especially cherished one another.

Then tragedy struck. Jim was self-employed and had flown his own plane to make a sales call in Colorado. He was a safe and capable pilot, so no one understood what could have happened. He had taken off, but his plane did not arrive home at the time designated by his flight plan. Though it took months to find the plane in the snow-covered Rockies, eventually a Civil Air Patrol volunteer, going over tape provided by the FAA, was able to locate where his plane had crashed into the side of the mountain. Probably a rogue wind had caught the plane and thrown it off course, killing a man who had survived some of the worst fighting in Vietnam. On the day of the funeral, Penny was presented the folded flag of our country from a Marine in full dress.

It would be nice if stories like this ended with: "then she grieved a while and went on to live happily ever after." But losing Jim set off a series of dynamic and painful memories. He had been the only man Penny had ever felt safe with and now, bereft of him, memories of earlier wounds surfaced and plunged her into a deep emotional abyss. Eventually, Penny became severely depressed with thoughts of suicide. Her physician started her on an antidepressant that did not seem to help; in fact, her depression only worsened. I suggested that she go to the Amen Clinic of Behavioral Medicine in Fairfield, California. She had a SPECT concentration study, and Dr. Amen recommended a different antidepressant. The change in medications was amazing. Soon, the unbearably dark clouds of depression began to lift. Feeling more inner strength, Penny was able to build a new life and work her way through the grief.

When you have truly loved someone, that loss never goes away; but in time, when a poignant memory surfaces, it does not have to take you to the depths of despair. The change in medication helped Penny grieve for her husband in normal ways without falling into such a pit of darkness that, to her, it made sense to end her life.

A PEEK UNDER THE DEEP LIMBIC HOOD

When the limbic system is working well, you are experiencing:

- Feelings of hope, even during difficult times
- Restorative sleep
- Strong self-esteem
- Enjoyment of pleasurable, fun activities where you feel like laughing at a joke or smiling at the simplest experience
- Desire to be with people
- Enjoyment of hugs and being close
- Optimism

When the limbic system is not working well, then the following symptoms may occur:

- Difficulty being grateful for all of the good that God has done in your life
- Irritation at things that usually do not bother you
- Desire to be alone or to socially isolate
- Experiences that used to be fun are no longer of interest (they seem to take too much effort)
- Difficulty going to sleep or staying asleep
- Waking up in the morning and needing everything you've got just to move out of bed
- A lack of motivation to do self-care
- Frequent feelings of hopelessness, helplessness, or excessive guilt; no

matter how much you pray, or remind yourself of various scriptural truths, you still feel guilty
- Extreme mood changes during PMS
- Low energy
- Lack of sexual interest to the extent that it's rare to have a sexual thought
- Loss of appetite
- Weight loss or weight gain

What scan after scan shows is that when the limbic system is overactive, it correlates with depression and negativity. Healthy pleasures such as love-making take a backseat to mere emotional survival. When I see an overactive limbic system, I will often say to the client, "You probably haven't had a passionate thought in a long time." Inevitably they'll say, "How did you know that, Doc?" And I'll respond, "When the limbic is hot, you're not." Your spouse, friends, or children can be loving toward you and it will not sink in or touch you. In other words, it is difficult to experience the fruits of the spirit—such as love, peace, patience, and *joy*.

CLINICAL DEPRESSION

Though we take all low moods seriously and treat them appropriately, when we see someone who is in a deep, clinical depression, we act as quickly as a surgeon would act with a patient who is having symptoms of a heart attack— clinical depression kills thousands of wonderful people who take their own lives in order to avoid the debilitating pain of living. In almost all cases of a severe depression, we need to use the best, targeted medicines available to get the patients out of being a danger to themselves. There's a point where medicine is simply God's mercy to mankind. Once stabilized, we can look at other alternative therapies that support or, perhaps, someday will replace medication.

Definition of Clinical Depression
A depressive disorder is a syndrome (group of symptoms) that reflects a sad mood exceeding normal sadness or grief. More specifically, the sadness of

depression is characterized by a greater intensity and duration, and by more severe symptoms and functional disabilities, than is normal. Depression symptoms are characterized not only by negative thoughts, moods, and behaviors but also by specific changes in bodily functions (for example, irregular eating, sleeping, crying spells, and decreased libido). At this point the entire nervous system in the brain has changed so much that it causes physical conditions, including physical pain.

Here's a side-by-side comparison of grief and depression:[1]

Characteristics of Grief	Characteristics of Depression
Situational; a normal response to deep and specific loss	General feeling of sorrow about everything; a numbness to most or all pleasures
Physical stress-related symptoms that come and go in waves	Chronic physical pain; vulnerable to disease
Ability to envision a happier future	Future looks entirely bleak
Death wishes come and go but not acted upon	Suicide is not only contemplated but explored as a viable option
Pockets of pleasure	Consistent hopelessness
Can talk about feelings and laugh at times, even through tears	Negative feelings are constant and abiding
Grief comes in waves	Often a blank or expressionless look along with a negative self-image
Finds support and love from others or is able to rely on inner faith and strength	Unable to enjoy life anymore
Temporary need for medication to cope with a tragedy or major upset	Often needs medication or therapy or both

The following are brain scans of a woman who has a combination of depression (limbic system) and anxiety (basal ganglia). She needs both areas of her brain treated medically because although a stimulant like caffeine can be a temporary mood booster to the limbic area, it can exacerbate anxiety in the basal ganglia. The brain—and causes of depression—can be complicated. Thus, the most accurate way to treat any sort of long-term absence of joy is by looking under the hood of your head and seeing what's going on.

THE BASAL GANGLIA When it is lit up on the left side, anxiety is often expressed outwardly in irritability. On the right side, anxiety is more internal.

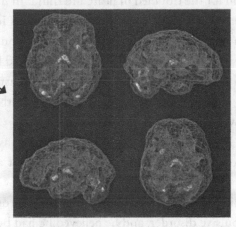

THE DEEP LIMBIC SYSTEM When it is overactive, the SPECT indicates a combination of anxiety and sadness or depressed feelings.

(Top left: underside, active view)
(Top right: side angle, active view; front of brain on right)
(Bottom left: side angle, active view; front of brain on left)
(Bottom right: top-down, active view)

WHEN FALSE RELIGION MAKES THINGS WORSE

Perhaps you've struggled with depression but have put on a fake smile because your religious tradition demanded that a good Christian must have that *joy, joy, joy, joy down in your heart*, and there it has to stay. "God," they said, "deserves nothing less after all He's done for you." But you are tired of performing from an empty soul.

Lest you think that brain imbalances are of new and passing interest or confined to the realm of psychology—a far cry from theology—I'd like to turn back the pages of time, say five hundred or so years, to the era of Martin Luther, the leader of the Reformation who nailed ninety-five thesis statements to a castle door in Wittenberg, Germany. The most inflammatory of his thesis points was that he believed the Bible to speak of a salvation by God's grace and not by our works. This "free gift of forgiveness," as you may recall, won him no favors with the pope since no petty sum of gold flowed into the church from the selling of papers that would supposedly wipe out mortal sins.

Author Tony Headley, professor of counseling at Asbury Theological Seminary and a licensed psychologist, wrote a wonderful article about Luther and his compassion for the troubled of heart and mind. In it he described how as a pastor, Luther often bumped up against parishioners in emotional pain. "Luther's writings reveal his knowledge of various emotional difficulties. For example, in August 1536 he interceded for a woman named Mrs. Kreuzbinder, whom he deemed insane. He described her as being 'accustomed to rage and sometimes angrily chasing her neighbor with a spear.'" (Perhaps temporal lobe issues, which we will talk about in the next chapter.)

"In addition, Luther's wife, Kate, struggled with pervasive and persistent worry indicative of generalized anxiety disorder." (Was it a basal ganglia on high alert?)

"Prince Joachim of Anhalt, to whom Luther often wrote, exhibited signs of obsessive-compulsive disorder, and he believed he had betrayed and cruci- fied Christ." (Maybe a hot cingulate gyrus.)

"Conrad Cordatus, a pastor and frequent guest at Luther's table, exhib- ited signs of hypochondriasis, a disorder involving preoccupation with fears of having a serious disease." (A combination of cingulate and basal ganglia issues, perhaps.)

Besides observing mental difficulties in others, Luther had a compelling reason to affirm their reality. Luther himself suffered from many bouts of depression. He used a variety of adjectives to describe his inner experience: melancholy, heaviness, depression, dejection of spirit, being downcast, sad, and downhearted. He suffered in this area for much of his life and often revealed these struggles in his works. Evidently he did not think it a shameful problem to be hidden but a human condition to be addressed with compas- sion. In fact, his insight and the antidotes for depression were actually quite wise, especially considering the limitations of medication and of the brain studies at that time. Luther recommended a balance of spiritual, cognitive, physical, emotional, and social balms to rebalance a sorrowful soul.

Luther also knew that depression could sometimes turn deadly, like when a downcast soul became weary of life and preoccupied with death. To help ensure one depressed parishioner's safety, Luther instructed his wife: 1) Ensure that his surroundings are not so quiet that he sinks into his own thoughts. 2) Do not leave him alone for a single moment. (Luther believed that solitude is poison for such a person.) 3) Leave nothing around with which he might harm himself.

Sound advice by any clinical standard!

Luther also emphasized the fact that God created healthy pleasure for human enjoyment because he'd observed (accurately) that many Christians avoided pleasurable activities, thinking them sinful. Not exactly a philosophy of life to put a smile on your face and a spring in your step. Luther reminded his flock that "proper and honorable pleasure . . . is pleasing to God."[2]

DEPRESSION: THE EQUAL OPPORTUNITY DESTABILIZER

About 20 million people are depressed during any one year. It affects people from all walks of life and ethnic backgrounds: young and old, rich and poor, men and women, celebrities and . . . saints. Though some of the faithful would protest this, many have been persuaded that a really good Christian should believe that a) since Christ is always sufficient for any soul, b) they should live in a state of joy without any chemical or psychological help. One well-known conservative Christian pastor who doesn't think that psychology or medicine has a place in emotional healing asserted (to those who continue to struggle with depression, anxiety, and other ailments): "Scripture hasn't failed them—they've failed Scripture."

In response to this sort of superspiritual rhetoric, I can only say, "That's the craziest thing I've ever heard!" What planet are some of these preachers coming from? I do know this: my office is probably filled with their parishioners, who are desperate for some compassion and hanging on to their faith by a thread. Especially after having a heap o' guilt placed on top of their already-flagging spirits.

Much was made recently of Mother Teresa's confession to have struggled with her faith. "I am told God lives in me—and yet the reality of darkness and coldness and emptiness is so great that nothing touches my soul," she wrote at one point. Mother Teresa was a mortal being, and thus not immune to doubts and fears. At times the horrors she saw in Calcutta must have overwhelmed her limbic system, reminding her of such a hell that she even questioned the existence of God and heaven at vulnerable times.

When our limbic system takes a hit—either from personal grief, tragedy, or a chemical imbalance—often our faith takes a hit as well. Not usually the reality of what we believe to be *logically* true, but the *feeling* of God's closeness can seem far away just when you wish him to be the nearest.

Though Martin Luther penned the great, affirming, declarative hymn of faith "A Mighty Fortress Is Our God" in 1527, he wrote: "For more than a week I was close to the gates of death and hell. I trembled in all my members. Christ was wholly lost." According to Luther's famous biographer, Roland Bainton, Luther found himself "subject to recurrent periods of exaltation and depression of spirit." Luther himself had written that "the content of the depressions was always the same, the loss of faith that God is good and that he is good to me."[3] So he knew, firsthand, that we cannot always believe our thoughts, for our thoughts often lie to us when our chemistry is off balance. And yet, his PFC knowledge didn't protect his overactive limbic system from the awful feeling of abandonment.

The famous preacher Charles Spurgeon struggled so severely with depression that he was forced to be absent from his pulpit for two to three months a year. In 1866 he told his congregation of his struggle: "I am the subject of depressions of spirit so fearful that I hope none of you ever get to such extremes of wretchedness as I go [through]." He explained that during these depressions, "Every mental and spiritual labor . . . had to be carried on under protest of spirit."

THE GOD OF ALL COMPASSION, WHO UNDERSTANDS

Christ himself felt abandoned on the cross, and yet in reality, God was probably never closer to him. His human and godly emotions were tested to their absolute limit in his hours of agony.

Jesus understands what it is like to be "overwhelmed with sorrow to the point of death" (Matt. 26:38) and to have his friends, who he needed so badly in those hours of sorrowful anticipation, fall asleep, unaware of his pain. Although Jesus was often joyful, he was also "a man of sorrows, acquainted with deepest grief" (Isa. 53:3 NLT). So never think that he doesn't understand your pain.

Old Testament saints like Moses, Elijah, Job, and Jeremiah suffered from depression, often to the point of being suicidal. Elijah's miraculous victory over the prophets of Baal in 1 Kings 18 is followed in the next chapter with Elijah being despondent and trembling with fear: "And he was afraid and arose and ran for his life . . . and sat down under a juniper tree; and he requested for himself that he might die" (1 Kings 19:3–4 NASB).

Though preachers and some less-than-understanding Christians have often poked fun at Elijah's rollercoastering emotions, God gave the prophet a tender and practical response: "And the angel of the LORD came again a second time and touched him and said, 'Arise, eat, because the journey is too great for you'" (19:7 NASB). Far from being critical, God comforted his weary child. Comforting his kids is the business God is in, even when, during a "dark night of the soul" (or chemical brain imbalance), you may not feel him there. God never promised a sparrow would not fall to the ground, or that his children would never suffer, but he did promise his presence. Most often, God's presence shows up in my life in the form of another kindhearted and compassionate person.

Paul wrote, "We were afflicted on every side; conflicts without, fears within. But God, who comforts the depressed, comforted us by the coming of Titus" (2 Cor. 7:5–6 NASB). Don't you love that? "But God . . . who comforts the depressed, comforted us. . . ." How? By sending Titus to be "God-with-skin-on" to weary and anxiety-riddled saints. Perhaps because Paul had been there himself, he asked the church of Thessalonica to "encourage the faint-hearted, help the weak, be patient with all men" (1 Thess. 5:14).

"Consider this thought experiment," writes Dwight Carlson, who has been a Christian for fifty years, a physician for twenty-nine, and a psychiatrist for fifteen. "Give me the most saintly person you know. If I were to administer certain medications of the right dosage, such as amphetamine, thyroid hormone, or insulin, I could virtually guarantee that I could make this saint anxious with at least one of these agents. Would such chemically induced anxiety be explained as a spiritual sin? What if the person's own body had an abnormal amount of thyroid hormone or insulin and produced nervousness? I have seen patients in this precise predicament."[4] If you could see my limbic system right now, it would be standing up and giving Dr. Carlson a standing ovation for this powerful, compassionate argument on its behalf!

BLOWING THE DARK CLOUDS AWAY:
HOW TO HELP LIFT DEPRESSION

Nutrition

To know what sort of diet is helpful for a particular type of depression, it is important to know what kind of depressive symptoms a person is experiencing. If you are feeling lethargic, then you probably need a diet and perhaps supplements that will help stimulate your brain's production of dopamine, the stimulating neurotransmitter. If your depression is more anxiety based or is a low mood that is stuck in a negative-thinking loop, then you will probably be most helped by a diet that increases serotonin, the calming neurotransmitter. Author Julia Ross suggests that low endorphins make people highly sensitive—they don't just cry at sad movies but at commercials with soft music, even if those commercials are about toilet paper. They feel thin-skinned. Some people need calming foods before bed, and others need energy-producing foods during the day.

For all types of depression, consume the joy foods discussed in chapter 5. In addition, it is important to:

• Eat regularly. You are robbing your body of good mood nutrients when you skip a meal, even breakfast.
• Eat three good meals daily, plus healthy snacks. Include some protein in every snack: use nut butter on a banana; sprinkle almonds or walnuts on yogurt or in a small bowl of nutritious cereal; eat apple slices with string cheese. Doing this will keep your blood sugar steady and your energy up.
• Try to get at least 20 grams of protein per meal but include plenty of fruits and veggies so your digestive system can handle it well. Here are a few ways to get in your 20 or more grams of protein:

- 3 eggs
- 3 ounces of tuna
- 8 ounces of cottage cheese
- 1½ cups of beans
- 3 to 4 ounces (a palm full) of meat; try to have fish (salmon is best) at least two times a week, more if possible

If you suspect that you are low in serotonin (need more calming foods in your diet), incorporate more tryptophan-rich protein into your diet. Some of the world's best sources of tryptophan-rich protein are turkey, cheese (Cheddar and Parmesan), chicken, beef, shrimp, pork, fish, seeds (sesame and sunflower), eggs, milk, yogurt, cottage cheese, chickpeas, and peanuts. In addition to these protein-based sources, other good sources of tryptophan are chocolate, oats, bananas, mangoes, dried dates, rice, and potatoes.

A good rule of thumb is that the more energy you need, the more you should stick with mostly fish, meat, cottage cheese, or eggs to get the big protein bang in your food. As the day winds down, you may want to make your last snack be a bowl of cereal with milk and a banana or some rice pudding (try warmed yogurt with brown rice and chopped dates). The lactose in milk and the natural sugar in bananas and dates will make you calm and sleepy.

Supplements

All of the supplement recommendations that follow are adapted or taken from *The Mood Cure* by Julia Ross. I highly recommend that you purchase this book and read it for yourself; it is entertaining, readable, and doable. One benefit of trying supplements for low to moderate depressive symptoms is that if they work, many people only have to take them for a few months to restore their body's balance. If you have the time and patience to try amino acid or herbal supplementation—and you aren't in too much emotional pain—it could really be worth your while.

Note: You may have a combination of symptoms, and if so, you may treat them with appropriate supplements for each symptom. For example, you may need energy for your daytime depression but a calming supplement to help anxiety at night.

- For all

    1 to 3 capsules of fish oil. Fish oil has been a near-miracle supplement for many who suffer from depression, especially from bipolar disorder and its less intense cousin, cyclothymia.

- For depression with lethargy

    Need: Focus and energy

    Recommendation: L-tyrosine (500 mg), 1 to 4 capsules, up to 3 times a day. Try one capsule before you increase your dose, and cut back if you feel agitated. And/or L-phenylalanine (200 to 500 mg), 1 to 4 capsules in the morning and midmorning; 1 to 3 capsules at midafternoon.

    If this recommendation does not do the trick, you can add or substitute the following and see if they work better with your body: SAMe (400 mg), 2 at midmorning and 2 at midafternoon. Grapeseed extract (100 mg), 1 at breakfast and 1 at lunch.

- For depression with anxiety

    Need: Calming

    Recommendation: 5-HTP (50 mg), 1 to 3 capsules at midafternoon and 1 to 3 capsules at bedtime. Start with 50 mg, and if you don't get relief within an hour, increase to 2 capsules. If needed, add a third dose in about an hour. You've established the dose that works for you. If you awaken at night and can't get back to sleep, you may also take 1 to 2 more capsules.

    Alternatives: a) Tryptophan (500 mg), 1 to 3 at midafternoon and 1 to 3 at bedtime. (For a very few people, tryptophan works better than 5-HTP; the vast majority do better on 5-HTP.) b) St. John's wort (300 mg), 1 to 3 at lunch, 1 to 3 at dinner, and 1 at bedtime. c) SAMe (400 mg), 2 at breakfast and 2 at lunch. (If you get no improvement after one bottle, discontinue.)

    For Sleep: Melatonin (1 to 6 mg), at bedtime.

- For depression with sensitivity

    Need: Comforting

    Recommendation: DLPA (500 mg), 1 to 2 capsules, 3 times a day. Free-form amino-acid blend (700 to 800 mg), 1 to 2 capsules, morning and midmorning. (You probably won't need the complete amino-acid blend after the first month if you're eating plenty of protein three times a day.)

- For depression with stress

    Need: Relaxing

Recommendation: GABA (100 to 500 mg), 1 to 3 times a day, at or before your high-stress times.

Alternative: Try a combination of GABA with the aminos taurine and glycosine or insitol (such as GABA Calm by Source Naturals, True Calm by Now Foods, or Amino Relaxers by Country Life).

Under stress and adrenal overload, it is common to fight cravings as well.

Recommendation: for excessive sweet and starch cravings, try glutamine 500 (1500 mg) at early morning, midmorning, midafternoon, and bedtime if you tend to wake up hungry in the night. Or try chromium (200 mcg), 3 times per day with meals and at bedtime.[5]

Medication

Dr. Amen's SPECT research also indicates several different types of depression, which he divides into seven types. A list of these depression types follows along with the common medical protocols that are used to balance them. For more thorough information, check his excellent Web site at www.amenclinic.com (where he also lists helpful supplements as an alternative).

- Type 1. Pure Anxiety

  Symptoms: Sufferers with this type feel stirred up, anxious, or nervous.

  SPECT: Increased activity in the basal ganglia, seen on both the concentration and baseline studies.

  Medications: Buspar, short-term use of benzodiazepines.

- Type 2. Pure Depression

  Symptoms: This type is associated with primary depressive symptoms that range from chronic mild sadness (termed *dysthymia*) to the devastating illness of major depression. The hallmark symptoms of pure depression include a persistent sad or negative mood; a loss of interest in usually pleasurable activities; periods of crying; frequent feelings of guilt, helplessness, hopelessness, or worthlessness; sleep and appetite changes (too much or too little); low energy levels; suicidal thoughts or attempts; and low self-esteem.

  SPECT: Markedly increased activity in the deep limbic area at rest and during concentration. Decreased activity in the prefrontal cortex at rest that improves with concentration. Deactivation of the prefrontal cortex at rest and improvement with concentration is a finding that is very commonly, but not always, present.

Medications: Stimulating antidepressants such as Wellbutrin.

- Type 3. Mixed Anxiety and Depression

  Symptoms: Sufferers of this type have a combination of both pure anxiety symptoms and pure depressive symptoms.

  SPECT: Excessive activity in the brain's basal ganglia and deep limbic system.

  Medications: Antidepressants with antianxiety qualities, such as desipramine.

- Type 4. Overfocused Anxiety and Depression

  Symptoms: These people have trouble shifting attention and tend to get locked into negative thoughts or behaviors.

  SPECT: Increased cingulate gyrus activity and increased basal ganglia and/or deep limbic activity at rest and during concentration.

  Medications: SSRI antidepressants.

- Type 5. Temporal Lobe Anxiety and Depression

  Symptoms: When there are problems in this part of the brain, people struggle with temper outbursts; memory problems; mood instability; visual or auditory illusions; and dark, frightening, or evil thoughts. People with this type tend to misinterpret comments as negative when they are not, have trouble reading social situations, and appear to have mild paranoia. There may be a family history of these problems, or they can be triggered by a brain injury.

  SPECT: Increased or decreased activity in the temporal lobes and increased basal ganglia and/or deep limbic activity at rest and during concentration.

  Medications: Antiseizure medications.

- Type 6. Cyclic Anxiety and Depression

  Symptoms: Cyclic disorders, such as bipolar disorder, cyclothymia, and premenstrual tension syndrome, along with panic attacks, fit in this category because they are episodic and unpredictable. The hallmark of this type is its cyclical nature.

  SPECT: Not surprisingly, SPECT scans vary with the phase of the illness or the point in the patient's cycle. For example, when someone is in a manic phase of a bipolar illness, there is increased deep limbic activity and what we call *patchy uptake*—which means there are multiple hot spots of overactivity throughout the brain. When this same person is in a depressed state, there is overactivity in the limbic area but not the patchy look of hot spots all over the scan.

Medications: Antiseizure medications or lithium for bipolar disorder; full-spectrum lights for seasonal affective disorder.

• Type 7. Low Anxiety and Depression

Symptoms: This type complains of being inattentive, distracted, bored, off task, and impulsive. This type may also be the result of some form of toxic exposure or brain infection, such as chronic fatigue syndrome, a near-drowning accident, or other insults to the brain.

SPECT: Decreased activity in the prefrontal cortex at rest and during concentration along with increased basal ganglia and/or deep limbic activity; sometimes overall decreased activity.

Medications: Wellbutrin, Provigil, stimulant medications (such as Adderall, Concerta, Ritalin, or Dexedrine).

Knowing your type is essential to getting the right help for yourself.

LET THERE BE LIGHT! (SEASONAL AFFECTIVE DISORDER)

More than 25 percent of Americans suffer from a special sensitivity to the natural decrease in sunlight during fall and winter in a condition called SAD (seasonal affective disorder). For many lower-serotonin people, late afternoon brings on the sad hours. If you are able to get to a window, open up your curtains first thing in the morning and let the sunshine in! It will help your emotional outlook on the day and also help you sleep better at night.

Getting some natural sunlight will be a big boost. Even on a cloudy day, you'll get 10,000 times more lux (the standard unit of illumination) outdoors than you'll get indoors. There are special therapeutic lamps that you can sit under for several minutes a day if needed. You can read and talk and work under the light as long as the light reaches your pupils.

Note: Bright lights can also trigger irritable or manic moods. If major mood swings or bipolar moods are a condition for you, avoid these lamps.

You can buy full-spectrum lamps in a variety of models, or just purchase the bulbs from a health or hardware store. ParaLite, Verilux, Happy Eyes, and Ott-Lite are a sampling of the brand names for which you can search.

THE BABY BLUES (POSTPARTUM DEPRESSION)

Many new mothers are totally taken aback by feelings of sorrow after what should be the happiest time of their life—when they've just had a baby. The reasons for postpartum depression are numerous, but just remember that hormones (which are running rampant during and after pregnancy) affect your brain, which affects your mood. You may actually not feel sad until a few weeks after having the baby and the feeling may disappear soon, or it may hang on. One mother who went off antidepressants during pregnancy and childbirth did just fine—until she stopped breastfeeding, and then the tears began to flow. Apparently the feel-good hormone oxytocin, produced during lactation, had protected her mood. But she needed help and fast when she could not stop crying after three days.

The treatment for postpartum is similar for all normal depressions, but you'll just need to make sure that your doctor knows that you are breastfeeding before trying supplements or medication. Bonding with other moms who've been there is a huge help. See www.postpartum.net to find help and a support group in your area.

PMS OR PRE-MONSTER SYNDROME

Not all women experience a drop in mood during PMS, but enough do that just the mention of it makes many women weep and grown men tremble. Because of its cyclical nature (when you think about it, PMS is a bit like being bipolar), we usually only need to use supplements or medications for the period of time most affected by the rise and fall of hormones. However, some women prefer to just stay on supplements or medication throughout their cycle because the symptoms are so severe and often a cause of marriage problems.

Here's a list of what you may expect to observe in a woman's monthly cycle as it relates to her mood, adapted from *Women and Stress* by Jean Lush. I recommend that husbands and wives staple this to the back of their calendar in order to prepare for PMS by lessening stress and increasing self-soothing activities:

Emotional Phases of a Woman's Cycle

First Week (after period)
- Estrogen levels rising
- Self-directed, disciplined
- Outgoing
- Task-oriented and focused
- Reasonable
- Optimistic

Second Week
- Estrogen levels off and declines slightly
- Blue skies—good, warm, summer-like feelings; happy, hopeful, easy-going
- Sense of well-being and inner strength
- Less assertive, more realistic goals than first week
- Peaceful, not bothered by small irritations, enjoys loveliness of environment
- Creative with positive energy
- Feels reasonable and tolerant of self and others
- Ovulation (approximately ten days following end of period)
- Estrogen rising again, progesterone rising
- Passive and introverted or patiently accepting and open-minded
- Content, nurturing feelings
- Especially amorous and interested in lovemaking
- Might have odd cravings (as in pregnancy)

Third Week
- Rising estrogen and sharp rise in progesterone
- Subject to variable feelings: some good, some bad; up and down
- Moody and gloomy—sense of feeling doomed, apprehensive without reason
- Slowing down—disliking pressure, feeling immobilized, doubting self

- Discouraged, less friendly and outgoing
- Losing sense of well-being, longing for more peaceful life
- Impatient with others, losing interest in goals and plans, bored
- Lacking coordination and clarity of thought (PMS *fog*)

Fourth Week (premenstrual)

- Estrogen and progesterone levels fall
- Very reactive, irritable, touchy, nervous, unable to concentrate
- Moody, unstable, quarrelsome; unpredictable outbursts of emotions
- Sensitive to noise, prone to food binges, craves sweets or spices
- Childlike, unreasonable
- Lack of self-confidence, loss of interest in hobbies and tasks, melancholy, withdrawn, awkward, shaky[6]

YOUR PERSONAL HAPPY LIST

Everybody needs a go-to list of self-soothing, healthy pleasures. Write down twenty things that you simply enjoy, with or without a good reason attached. One friend tells me that walking into a Target store with all its white and red and bright colors gives her a mood boost. Others love a trip with the pooch to the dog park. Some love nothing more than a bag full of books and a cozy couch or porch swing. Another person gets a kick out of tinkering with a car, another from watering flowers. Let's see, there's . . .

- Walking in the rain—or listening to it hit a tin roof
- A hot bubble bath
- A foot rub
- A guilt-free nap
- An afternoon of golfing
- Going to a professional sporting event
- Hitting the movie theater with a tub full of popcorn and a film-loving friend

Now, you take over. Keep this list handy when you need to do something to keep from sinking into prolonged sadness.

SCRIPTURE

The Psalms are penned by a songwriter/poet who swings from a state of absolute despair to euphoria so many times that it can make your head ache, but David always, eventually, finds his emotional equilibrium again by reminding himself of who God is, that God cares, and that God is there.

Most people who have been depressed are comforted by reading David's up-and-down, bipolar-like journey with God. If God called David a man after his own heart after voicing his real feelings—good, bad, and ugly—you can trust that God can handle any real emotion you want to throw at him.

A white-tailed deer drinks from the creek
I want to drink God,
    deep draughts of God.
I'm thirsty for God-alive.
I wonder, "Will I ever make it—
    arrive and drink in God's presence?"
I'm on a diet of tears—
    tears for breakfast, tears for supper.
All day long
    people knock at my door,
Pestering,
    "Where is this God of yours?"
These are the things I go over and over,
    emptying out the pockets of my life.
I was always at the head of the worshiping crowd,
    right out in front,
Leading them all,
    eager to arrive and worship,
Shouting praises, singing thanksgiving—
    celebrating, all of us, God's feast!
Why are you down in the dumps, dear soul?
    Why are you crying the blues?
Fix my eyes on God—
    soon I'll be praising again.

He puts a smile on my face.
    He's my God.
When my soul is in the dumps, I rehearse
    everything I know of you,
From Jordan depths to Hermon heights,
    including Mount Mizar.
Chaos calls to chaos,
    to the tune of whitewater rapids.
Your breaking surf, your thundering breakers
    crash and crush me.
Then GOD promises to love me all day,
    sing songs all through the night!
    My life is God's prayer.
Sometimes I ask God, my rock-solid God,
    "Why did you let me down?
Why am I walking around in tears,
    harassed by enemies?"
They're out for the kill, these
    tormentors with their obscenities,
Taunting day after day,
    "Where is this God of yours?"
Why are you down in the dumps, dear soul?
    Why are you crying the blues?
Fix my eyes on God—
    soon I'll be praising again.
He puts a smile on my face.
    He's my God. (Ps. 42 MSG)

PRAYER

Sometimes I like to turn to hymns to help me pray when I am at a loss for words. One old, beautiful, and comforting hymn is "Abide with Me," and it can be used as a simple prayer when your heart hurts too much to make sense to yourself and you just need God to throw his comforting arms around you. *Abide* is a word we don't use much anymore, but it literally means "to settle in and make your home with me." A lovely image at 3:00 a.m. when you are crying tears in your ears, wondering where God is. He's abiding, with you.

> Abide with me, fast falls the eventide
> The darkness deepens, Lord with me abide
> When other helpers fail, and comforts flee
> Help of the helpless, oh, abide with me.

St. Julian of Norwich's prayer has been a calming balm to many a furrow-browed saint. "All shall be well, and all shall be well, and all manner of things shall be well."

Music

A song that touches my heart in times of sorrow is by the late Rich Mullins, who was a master at creating simple lyrics that tug straight at the heart. The song is called "Bound to Come Some Trouble" and speaks of the need to "hold on to Jesus, hold on tight"—because "he's been there, and knows what it's like." The lyrics speak of how other people use well-meaning platitudes to try to cheer you up, "but it just ain't enough when you need something to hold on to . . ."[7]

Little did Mullins know how many people would need the comfort in that song when he was suddenly killed on the way to a benefit concert while riding with a buddy in a jeep that flipped over on an Illinois highway in 1997. His buddy was badly injured but survived. The songwriter left us all with a gift, the legacy of his music to comfort and inspire our hearts. You can hear the whole song at www.last.fm/music/Rich+Mullins/_/Bound+to+Come+Some+Trouble. I hope it blesses and comforts your heart.

Now, switching gears, I've got a crazy assignment for you. Write down all the songs that make you smile and laugh. No matter how goofy—even if it is "Dancing Queen" by Abba, "Don't Worry, Be Happy" by Bobby McFerrin, "The Lion Sleeps Tonight," "Dancing in the Streets," James Brown's "I Feel

Good," or "Do Wah Diddy." Well, I think I'd better stop before I really embarrass myself.

But I want you to make a list of the silliest, most singable songs that make you just want to get up and dance or chill out and smile for a while. Then pack them into your iPod or make a CD and call it *Antidepressant Playlist*. Need some help? Just google "happiest songs" and you'll find others who've already started their personal lists.

Exercise

By now, unless you've skipped all the other chapters and landed on this one randomly, you know that regular aerobic exercise of any kind (walking, rowing your boat, skiing, dancing the rumba) is as successful at reducing mild to moderate depression as an antidepressant drug. Unless you are in a deep clinical depression, there's little harm—and much to be gained (with the exception of pounds)—by putting on your sneakers and movin' around. If you can couple exercise with your prerecorded happy songs, you are bound to get a boost. (I know what some of you are thinking: *why not just dust off my old Richard Simmons* Sweatin' to the Oldies *videos?* Hey, whatever turns you on and gets you smiling and moving is great by me. Though I hope you won't mind if I buzz out of that activity and opt for a game of hoops with some sweaty, balding, but *manly* middle-aged guys instead. I still have *some* pride.)

Aromatherapy

- Clary Sage Essential Oil. Used in treating insomnia, anxiety, and depression.
- Basil Essential Oil. Used to lift fatigue, anxiety, and depression.
- Rose Essential Oil. Great on the entire nervous system and disorders.
- Sandalwood Essential Oil. Sedative properties are good for treating depression and tension.
- Lavender Essential Oil. Used for nervous system disorders such as depression,

headache, hypertension, insomnia, migraine, nervous tension, and stress. Also known as an aphrodisiac.
- Jasmine Essential Oil. Increases the beta waves in the PFC, which gives you a more alert and responsive state of mind.[8]

Note: Growing the above herbs and flowers and breathing in their fragrance can have a threefold positive effect: fresh herbs for your cooking, a lovely potted plant, and the scent makes you feel better too. You can float the petals of fresh or dried roses or lavender or jasmine blossoms in a tub for a relaxing and aromatic treat.

Cinematherapy

- *Life Is Beautiful.* The use of humor and creativity in the worst of circumstances (a Nazi concentration camp) shows one brave father's determination to protect his son from horror as best he could. There are times when denial is a gift from God, helping us to survive the worst of a traumatic situation by escaping into fantasy.
- *Steel Magnolias.* Women bonding to help each other through tragedy. Best quote: "Laughter through tears is my favorite emotion."
- *City Slickers.* Men overcoming a midlife malaise and crisis together. A man's *Steel Magnolias*.
- *Under the Tuscan Sun.* Beautiful film about starting life over again after divorce, with all the messiness of the journey during the "crazy year" following the breakup of a marriage.
- *Babette's Feast.* If you are at all into foreign films, this is a classic and a joy to watch, particularly if you are feeling blue. Babette, an immigrant French woman with a mysterious past (as a famous chef) arrives into the plain vanilla lives of a Norwegian village, peopled with many stout and cranky Christians. It's a wonderful reminder of how the simplest things, such as a good meal prepared with love, and the company of friends, can lift a downcast soul and turn it happily heavenward again.
- *It's a Wonderful Life.* Just when you think the solution is to end it all, a chubby angel named Clarence shows up to prove this is just the end of one chapter of your life with a newer and better one to follow.

- *Patch Adams*. Demonstrates the use of humor therapy in the medical and psychological field. Also shows that one can overcome a deep personal loss by focusing on the life you have left to live and using the compassion born from sorrow to heal yourself and others.
- *Shadowlands*. A poignant story of C. S. Lewis's midlife romance when he was surprised by a woman named Joy. I love the way no-nonsense Joy overlooks all Lewis's high-sounding sermons on love and lures this reluctant bachelor deep into the stream of experiential love, even with its sidekick—the agony of potential loss—standing ever close. Even though Lewis and Joy learn that she will not live long, they choose love; they choose joy as long as God grants them time.

Lewis's book *A Grief Observed* has comforted many a believer because of his frank, unflinching look at loss and all the doubts that flooded his soul in the wake of his beloved's death. Death and grief make stumbling children of us all for a while, for our intellect and reason don't save our emotional heart from aching.

Here's one of my favorite Lewis quotes:

> To love at all is to be vulnerable. Love anything, and your heart will certainly be wrung and possibly broken. If you want to make sure of keeping it intact, you must give your heart to no one, not even to an animal. Wrap it carefully round with hobbies and little luxuries; avoid all entanglements; lock it up safe in the casket or coffin of your selfishness. But in that casket—safe, dark, motionless, airless—it will change. It will not be broken; it will become unbreakable, impenetrable, irredeemable.[9]

Ultimately it really is better to have loved and lost than never to have loved at all. It just takes moving through the grief process to realize the truth of it.

Support Village

Here are a few of the rich, the famous, the . . . depressed, fellow sufferers who've found their way up from down:

Actors/Entertainers

- Mike Wallace—News journalist and correspondent of *60 Minutes*. He was diagnosed with clinical depression in 1984 (after being sued for libel). Wallace has experienced severe depressive episodes but has overcome them with therapy and antidepressant medication.
- Jim Carrey—Starred in movies such as *Ace Ventura: Pet Detective, The Mask, The Truman Show*, and *Eternal Sunshine of the Spotless Mind*. On *60 Minutes* (November 2004), Carrey openly discussed his history of depression and being on Prozac.
- Drew Barrymore—This sunny, happy actor, in films such as *The Wedding Singer* and *E.T. the Extra-Terrestrial*, and director/producer of *Charlie's Angels* and *Ever After* has a depression history that includes a suicide attempt and being hospitalized. Life, indeed, can get better!
- Dick Clark—Host of *New Year's Rockin' Eve* and *American Bandstand*, Clark was interviewed about his experience with depression in the book *On the Edge of Darkness* by Kathy Cronkite.

Musicians/Singers/Songwriters/Composers

- Sting (Gordon Sumner)—Former lead singer and bassist of the rock group the Police and a successful solo artist. While writing his memoir, *Broken Music*, Sting fell into a depression that lasted for two years.
- Billy Joel—Musician, singer, songwriter. Some of his well-known hits include "Piano Man," "Just the Way You Are," "It's Still Rock & Roll to Me," and "My Life." In the 1970s, Joel experienced serious depression and admitted himself into a hospital for treatment after attempting to end his life by drinking furniture polish.
- Sheryl Crow—Singer and musician with hits such as "All I Wanna Do" and "Every Day Is a Winding Road." In an interview with *Ladies' Home Journal* (April 2003) Crow discussed having chronic depression since she was a child. In the late 1980s, Crow had a period of depression after touring with Michael Jackson. Her depression was helped by antidepressants and therapy.
- Tammy Wynette—Country singer, Country Music Hall of Fame inductee, most famous for her song "Stand by Your Man." Wynette received ECT (electroconvulsive therapy) for her depression.
- Marie Osmond—Country singer and starred in *The Donny and Marie*

Show. Osmond describes her bout with postpartum depression in her book *Behind the Smile*.

Athletes

- Terry Bradshaw—Former NFL quarterback for the Pittsburgh Steelers. In the late 1990s, Bradshaw was diagnosed with clinical depression and began taking antidepressants (Paxil). (Bradshaw also had panic attacks after games.)
- Ty Cobb—Professional baseball player for the Detroit Tigers and Philadelphia A's and Baseball Hall of Fame member. Cobb was hospitalized for depression during his first year with the Tigers.

Writers/Poets

- Art Buchwald—Writer and humorist known for his column in *The Washington Post*. Buchwald was hospitalized for depression in 1963. He has talked openly about his depression (for instance, as a guest on *Larry King Live*) and the need for treatment and decreasing stigma.
- John Keats—Nineteenth-century English romantic poet most famous for his series of "Odes." Keats experienced periods of severe depression.
- William Faulkner—Winner of the Nobel Prize in literature (1949) whose novels include *The Sound and the Fury, As I Lay Dying*, and *Absalom, Absalom!* Faulkner struggled with depression (and alcoholism).
- Leo Tolstoy—Writer of novels such as *War and Peace* and *Anna Karenina*. Tolstoy started to experience depression while writing the latter book.
- Others include Lord Byron, F. Scott Fitzgerald, Edgar Allen Poe, Charles Dickens, Tennessee Williams, and Ernest Hemingway.

Artists

- Claude Monet—French Impressionist painter of "The Woman in the Green Dress," "Impression, Sunrise," "Water Lily Pond." Monet entered a depressive episode after the death of his wife, Alice Hoschedé.
- Georgia O'Keeffe—Prominent American painter, beginning in the 1920s (died in 1986 when she was ninety-eight). After her husband's affair, O'Keeffe became depressed and was hospitalized for a short period of time.
- Others artists include Vincent van Gogh and Michelangelo.

Political/Public Figures

- Princess Diana—The late wife of Charles, Prince of Wales, and greatly involved in AIDS charity work. Princess Di suffered depression from her transition in becoming Princess of Wales and from marital problems. She also experienced postpartum depression after her first son was born.
- Abraham Lincoln—Sixteenth president of the United States. President Lincoln's first major episode of depression began in his twenties, and he struggled with this illness for the remainder of his life (in addition to anxiety attacks).
- Tipper Gore—Wife of Vice President Al Gore. In 1989, Tipper experienced depression after her son's near-fatal car accident. She was officially diagnosed with clinical depression two years later and fully recovered with medication and therapy. (Also, Tipper's mother was chronically depressed, was on antidepressants, and was hospitalized twice.)
- Kitty Dukakis—Wife of former presidential candidate and Massachusetts governor Michael Dukakis. Dukakis has a history of severe depression and hospitalizations and began ECT in 2001. She has stated that ECT helped her taper off antidepressants and improved her work in therapy. Dukakis has written about her experience in the book *Shock: The Healing Power of Electroconvulsive Therapy*.
- Calvin Coolidge—Thirtieth president of the United States. Coolidge fell into a deep depression after the death of his son.
- Others include Barbara Bush, Theodore Roosevelt, Winston Churchill, and Richard Nixon.

Bibliotherapy

Spiritual Encouragement

Classic Christian books on radical grace, such as *The Ragamuffin Gospel: Good News for the Bedraggled, Beat-Up or Worn Out* by Brennan Manning and *The Sacred Romance: Growing Closer to the Heart of God* by Brent Curtis and John Eldredge, have helped many believers realize that they are not alone—that all of humanity struggles, and still God loves us and pursues our hearts.

Bipolar Disorder

Patty Duke was a child star who was secretly abused for years. She is also the author of *My Name Is Anna: The Autobiography of Patty Duke* and *A Brilliant Madness: Living with Manic Depressive Illness.* An unstable-but-brilliant actress turned honest and lovely spokeswoman for bipolar disorder, Duke manages to weave a dramatic story while also educating us on what it is like to live with the "brilliant madness." If you get a chance to view the Biography Channel's story of Patty Duke, I highly recommend it. It is a beautiful experience to see the life of someone who was once at the edge of death and who is now living so peacefully, happily, and authentically. And using her recovery from pain as a platform to help others.

Depression

- *Why I Jumped: My True Story of Postpartum Depression, Dramatic Rescue & Return to Hope* by Tina Zahn and Wanda Dyson. A page-turning story of a Christian wife and mother who was rescued in midair as she was jumping off a bridge. The jump was caught on videotape and aired on *Oprah*. This book is not only a dramatic read, but I appreciate how the author points to various symptoms and identifies where the right interventions might have spared her from her desperate attempt to end her life (www.whyIjumped.com). She also speaks poignantly to victims of sexual abuse.
- *Down Came the Rain: My Journey through Postpartum Depression* by Brooke Shields. Even the *beautiful* people are not spared from depression. Shields was the first celebrity to open up about this issue, for which many women are thankful (in spite of Tom Cruise's much-publicized comments—toxic religion, in any form, does strange things to human compassion).
- *Good Grief* by Granger E. Westburg. A small volume but a perennial bestseller because it is so helpful for those moving through the stages of loss. Truly a classic.
- *New Light on Depression: Help, Hope, and Answers for the Depressed and Those Who Love Them* by David B. Biebel and Harold George Koenig. A wonderful blend of medical and biblical approaches to depression. A comforting and valuable resource.
- *Healing Anxiety and Depression* by Dr. Daniel Amen. When it comes to

healing any combination of anxiety and depression with a targeted treatment plan, Dr. Amen's suggestions are tops.

Yes, lots of God's children have sung the blues. If you are suffering on the inside today, know you are not alone. I hope you've found this chapter to be a verbal care package along with some hope and practical encouragement from my heart to yours. None of us gets out of this life without some tears and some pain, and that's all right. But I don't want you to cry one more tear than is absolutely necessary for your journey back to joy.

CHAPTER TEN

The Temporal Lobes:
The Temper Lofts

Temper tantrums, however fun they may be to throw,
rarely solve whatever problem is causing them.

—LEMONY SNICKET

Perhaps you've seen the movie *Patton* or read General George Patton's biography. It's in the library under "Most Fascinating and Volatile Leaders in American History." On the one hand, Patton probably helped us win WWII; on the other hand, he was a loose cannon who appeared to have often demoralized others just as much as he inspired them. He was extremely religious, praying several times a day. (In Patton's case, prayer seemed more of a compulsion than a joy, a ritual of duty to ensure victory rather than the intimate communion with God that most believers enjoy.) But he also peppered most of his conversation and many of his speeches with extremely foul language. His grandiosity seemed to know no bounds, yet his childhood history reveals a boy with much insecurity. He had reading problems (probably dyslexia) and a legacy of big, patriarchal military shoes to fill. (His father and grandfather were military heroes before him.)

In 1943 General Patton's most famous and costly outburst of temper nearly cost him his military career and the glory he so desperately sought with his title. (He fancied himself a modern-day Napoleon.) On this particular day in August, Patton visited the 93rd Evacuation Hospital to see if there were any soldiers claiming to be suffering from combat fatigue. He found Private Paul G. Bennett, an artilleryman with the 13th Field Artillery Brigade. When asked what the problem was, Bennett replied, "It's my nerves, I can't stand the shelling anymore." Patton exploded with a parade of expletives and severely berated the young man, whom he felt was a whining coward. "You're a disgrace to the Army," he continued, "and you're going back to the front to fight, although that's too good for you. You ought to be lined up against a wall and shot. In fact, I ought to shoot you myself right now . . . !" With this, Patton pulled his pistol from its holster and waved it in front of Bennett's face. After putting his pistol away, he hit the man twice in the head with his fist. The hospital commander then intervened and got in between the two men. (Rather than focusing on the enemy out there, Patton's lack of empathy and insight caused him to turn on many of his own men.)

The man's doctor sent a report of the incident to General Dwight Eisenhower. The story was also passed to the four newsmen attached to the 7th Army. Although Patton had committed a court-martial offense by striking an enlisted man, the reporters agreed not to publish the story because Eisenhower feared it might undo the war's progress. Quentin Reynolds of *Collier's Weekly* agreed to keep quiet but argued that there were "at least 50,000 American soldiers on Sicily who would shoot Patton if they had the chance." (Eventually, however, the story broke.)[1]

General Eisenhower responded to the incident in a letter to Patton on August 5, 1943, saying:

> I am aware that firm and drastic measures were at times necessary, but it did not excuse brutality, abuse of the sick, nor exhibition of uncontrollable temper in front of subordinates. If this is true, then I must so seriously question your good judgment and your self-discipline as to raise serious doubt in my mind as to your future usefulness.
>
> No letter that I have been called upon to write in my military career has caused me the mental anguish of this one, not only because of my deep personal friendship for you but because of admiration for your military qualities; but I assure you that such conduct will not be tolerated in this theater no matter who the offender may be.

After the war ended, General Omar Bradley wrote about Patton's character in less-than-glowing terms:

Why does he use profanity? Certainly he thinks of himself as a destined war leader. Whenever he addressed men he lapsed into violent, obscene language. He always talked down to his troops. When Patton talked to officers and men in the field, his language was studded with profanity and obscenity. I was shocked. He liked to be spectacular; he wanted men to talk about him and to think of him. "I'd rather be looked at than overlooked." Yet when Patton was hosting at the dinner table, his conversation was erudite and he was well-read, intellectual and cultured. Patton was two persons: a Jekyll and Hyde. He was living a role he had set for himself twenty or thirty years before. An amazing figure!

I would have relieved him instantly (after the incident at the 93rd Evacuation Hospital) and would have had nothing more to do with him. He was colorful but he was impetuous, full of temper, bluster, inclined to treat the troops and subordinates as morons. His whole concept of command was opposite to mine. He was primarily a showman. The show always seemed to come first.[2]

Now, keep in mind all that you've just read about General Patton, and then look at the following list of typical problems with the temporal lobes:

- Frequent feelings of nervousness or anxiety (Patton was beside himself when not engaged in a "good war")
- Short fuse or periods of extreme irritability
- Periods of rage with little provocation
- Irritability tends to build, then explodes, then recedes; often tired after a rage (Patton tended to be contrite after a rage)
- Extreme religiosity

People often wonder how a man with such deep religious convictions could rise from his knees in prayer and immediately dive into a fit of anger, his language filled with expletives. Most of us know a deacon or pastor or very religious person whose similar behaviors cause us to scratch our heads in bewilderment. Visions of martyrdom and grandiosity sometimes play into a person's religious outlook where you can sense them imagining themselves surrounded by a blaze of messianic glory. (You could probably go to your television set right now, flip a few channels, and find a case in point.) And yet from what we know of Christ—who was "gentle and humble in heart" (Matt. 11:29)—emotionally balanced and discerning people of faith can see that something religiously *toxic* is at work.

Patton-like preachers and legalistic parishioners, in our experiences, tend to have imbalanced brain scans (often in the temporal lobe or cingulate areas). Yet because of the forcefulness of their anger and surety of their own misguided convictions, many people (often those with hyperactive Basements of Giant Fears) unwittingly fall prey to spiritual tyrants. We are never doing the body of Christ a favor by overlooking an outburst of anger by the pastor or layleader and dismissing it because of stress. When that happens we've just received a snapshot of what life is like for his spouse, children, and coworkers. When we overlook leadership anger, we are giving a silent sanction to it occurring again.

To help with further understanding: someone who has imbalanced temporal lobe issues often senses internal experiences that *feel* supernatural, including voices and even ghostly figures and visions that can be both frightening and empowering. The temporal lobes are also involved in epileptic seizures—sometimes accompanied by feelings of an intense spiritual nature—and schizophrenia, in which people hear voices and have imaginary conversations (demonstrated in the life of Nobel Prize winner John Nash, which was portrayed in the movie *A Beautiful Mind*). Most major mental disorders are related (farther along the mental health scale) to more minor brain issues; they are just more exaggerated in full-blown brain problems. In one case, a minor temporal lobe problem could leave someone with a few illusions of grandeur, believing they are more special or chosen (like a bumper sticker I saw that said "Jesus loves you. But he loves me *most*."). On the other end of the scale is full-blown schizophrenia, in which the person really believes he *is* the Messiah. Just as someone with a basal ganglia problem might feel a bit more anxious than others, another person may be absolutely trapped in the prison of his own fear—unable to leave home.

When the temporal lobes are working correctly and balanced appropriately, a person's spiritual experience is positive, enlightening, touching, and transforming in all the ways that Christ spoke about. Researchers have made much of the *God Spot* in the brain, and though some use this information to say, "See! Experiencing God is a brain thing, not a supernatural thing!" I would say quite the opposite. I would say, "Isn't it amazing that when God created man and woman in Eden, with fully functional human brains, he also created their brains with the capacity to sense his presence, to commune with him, and to enjoy a spiritual experience of peace and joy?" It is not unusual for an atheist or agnostic or even an angry fundamentalist zealot to get his temporal lobes working correctly and find that he begins to believe in God. And not just in God but in a *good* God who, like a good father, guides our lives with love and discipline in perfect balance. Unfortunately, religious abuse, like other forms of anger, has hurt the cause of Christ more than helped it.

The temporal lobes house a wide variety of functions. It's like the beatnik part of the brain as well as the Temper Lofts—because music, spirituality, literature, rhythm, language, tones, and memory are processed here. Here's a list of the healthy versus unhealthy functions of the temporal lobes:

HEALTHY TEMPORAL LOBE FUNCTIONS

- Understand/use language
- Auditory learning
- Retrieval of words
- Emotional stability
- Facilitating long-term memory
- Reading (left side)
- Read faces
- Read social cues (right side)
- Verbal intonation
- Rhythm, music
- Visual learning
- Spiritual experience

UNHEALTHY TEMPORAL LOBE PROBLEMS

- Memory difficulty
- Auditory and visual processing problems

- Trouble finding the right word
- Mood instability
- Anxiety for little or no reason
- Headaches or abdominal pain, hard to diagnose
- Trouble reading facial expressions or social cues
- Dark, evil, awful, or hopeless thoughts
- Aggression toward self or others
- Learning problems
- Illusions (shadows, visual or auditory distortions)
- Overfocused on religious ideas

PROBLEMS WITH LOW ACTIVITY
IN THE TEMPORAL LOBES

- Head injury
- Anxiety amnesia
- Left side—aggression, dyslexia
- Right side—trouble with social cues
- Dissociation
- Temporal epilepsy
- Serious depression with dark or suicidal thoughts

(Problems show up as dents in the surface scans and look like tie-dyed bread dough.)

PROBLEMS WITH HIGH ACTIVITY
IN THE TEMPORAL LOBES

- Epilepsy
- Religiosity
- Increased intuition or sensory perception

(Problems show up as overlit areas of the brain in the active scan.)

In marriage counseling, I have found the following chart to be a simple way to show what temporal lobe problems look like in a day-to-day relationship:

Healthy Temporal Lobes	Unstable Temporal Lobes
Person processes tone of voice consistent with the other person's intentions	Person will genuinely hear the other person as angry or critical when they are not
Accurately processes facial expressions	Tendency to overinterpret or underinterpret facial expressions; difficulty reading social cues
Manages anger, irritability, or frustration	Anger can quickly escalate out of control. There is the feeling of "walking on pins and needles" for those who live or work with someone with TL imbalances
Enjoys experience of rhythms, music, dance, and so on	Does not feel or experience music, dance, or rhythm as deeply as others
Able to access short-term memory and long-term memory under times of stress	Under stress has difficulty accessing memory whether it is short-term or long-term
May feel depressed, irritated, or hopeless but can work through it	Frustration, depression, irritation can turn into thoughts of harming self and others

STICKS AND STONES AND HARMFUL WORDS

Perhaps one of the most prevalent yet hidden "sins" in Christian homes today is verbal abuse. Yes, sexual abuse and physical abuse are found in Christian homes and leave terrible scars, but I am grateful that both of these issues have received great media coverage and that good therapy and pastoral counseling—in general—have risen to address these issues.

Sexual and physical abuse leave both physical and emotional scars. The evidence of these crimes can be found, recorded, and shown in a court of law—and guilt in either crime will result in a legal sentencing of some kind.

As a therapist, however, I can tell you that some of the most painful and lasting scars cannot be seen by the naked eye. And the offender is not generally prosecutable in a court of law for this particular crime. However, the scars that come from being cussed at, belittled, negated, frightened, threatened, or abandoned or from being called profane names or ridiculed for years by family members, a spouse, or peers (usually as a child or teen) can last forever if not addressed. And because others don't see them, the impact of words on the soul may never be fully recognized. However, because of working with post-traumatic memories and SPECT scans, I can tell you that the effects of long-term verbal, emotional, or mental abuse can be seen (usually in a diamond pattern as seen in PTSD-affected clients) and that sticks and stones may break bones, but names can hurt you just as deeply. Often *more* deeply. What is the most common culprit of such explosive and vindictive language? Our little twin friends: the temporal lobes.

Verbal Abuse: The Characteristics
- Always referring to the opinions of others as irrelevant and wrong
- Inconsideration of a person's feelings
- Using verbal abusiveness jokingly
- Refusing to listen to others
- Using accusations and blame to manipulate and control others
- Being judgmental and critical of others
- Belittling the concerns of others
- Consistently undermining a person's confidence
- Threatening to do physical harm
- Name-calling
- Purposeful cancelations of appointments or agreements
- Making difficult or impossible demands on others
- Denial of perpetrating the abuse
- Causing fear in people through outbursts of rage

Signs of Verbal Abuse Exhibited by the Abuser
- Ignoring, ridiculing, disrespecting, and criticizing others consistently
- Using manipulative words
- Purposefully humiliating others
- Accusing others falsely for the purpose of manipulating a person's decision making
- Manipulating people so they eventually submit to undesirable behavior

- Making others feel unwanted and unloved
- Threatening to leave the family destitute
- Placing the blame and cause of the abuse onto others
- Isolating a person from some type of support system, whether friends or family

GOOD NEWS FOR THE ANGRY AND THE ABUSED

Any sort of aggressive, controlling, and abusive talk in a home will eventually rip the people within to emotional shreds. So that's the really, really bad news.

But this is a book on *joy,* right?

So how about a little good news to cheer us all up? Correcting aggressive, bullying, and raging behavior is one of the areas where we see *the most amazing, fast, and complete turnarounds,* especially with an accurate SPECT scan and targeted medication. Supplementation may help as well, but usually by the time someone has been referred to our office for anger problems, the relief they and their families need comes most quickly from medication. Once their brain is calmed, therapy and alternative nutritional and supplemental support can begin in earnest. Unbridled raging is one of those issues we consider an emergency because it is usually only a matter of time before a verbally abusive person turns physically violent. Another beautiful thing about the SPECT scan is that we can show the client, in living color, exactly what his brain looks like, where it is misfiring, and how we can help. This is a huge motivator for the client, as almost everyone wants to have the best possible brain function they can have in order to enjoy life and relationships.

Just in case you missed it, let me repeat a statistic I shared early on in the book. In the first year that I performed SPECT scans, I treated thirty couples wherein one of the spouses had an anger problem. I had all of them scanned and asked them to follow up on every recommendation that Dr. Amen made in order to balance their mood. With a balanced brain, we could then dive into marital counseling. *Twenty-nine* of those couples remained married, and the only couple who divorced had a spouse who refused to follow Dr. Amen's suggested protocol to balance raging emotions.

THE HALF-LIFE OF THERAPY

Do I believe in anger management counseling? Marriage counseling when there are anger issues? Absolutely. But I know the half-life of an anger management counseling session is minimal if the brain issues have not been addressed first. What do I mean by that? Drugs have what is known as a *half-life*—the amount of time that the drug will stay in your body until it is out of your system. For example, Prozac has a long half-life; even when you stop taking it, the effects stay in your body for several weeks. Not so with Adderall or Ritalin. They stay for a few hours, and then their effects are gone.

I've noticed a half-life issue in counseling. With some couples—usually those who have fairly balanced brains but are tackling some difficult life issues—a lot can be accomplished in therapy, and the effects of what we discussed in the session seem to take root and last. We therapists love these couples. They are like sponges who soak up information and apply it to their lives, find success and love, and then write you a note to tell you what a brilliant marriage counselor you are. Then I can pat myself on the back and bask in the wonder of this rewarding profession.

Then there is the *other type* of couple. When they come into your office you can feel the tension. (In fact, I can almost hear the lonesome whistle and the ominous music from *High Noon* playing in the background.) They may sit in chairs that are close to each other, but every inch of their body is leaning as far away from their mate as humanly possible. I will do all I can to help them relax, then employ every counseling skill I know of to help them reconnect. Sometimes miracles happen before my eyes. They'll hold hands and apologize; perhaps, we'll all end in prayer as they recommit their marriage to God and to each other. It's all just so warm-fuzzy and marvelous. Until five minutes later, when I happen to look out the window and into the parking lot below my office and see Mr. and Mrs. Lovey-Dovey, red-faced and yelling words at each other that would embarrass a raunchy stand-up comic. The half-life of my therapeutic intervention lasted less time than a dose of Ritalin.

What happened? There was more than a lack of communication or a particularly complicated issue at hand; generally, at least one mate (and sometimes both) have hair-trigger anger problems resulting from a brain imbalance.

THREE KINDS OF ANGER

Often, aggressive behavior—including easily provoked anger and rage, along with verbal or physical abuse—is a temporal lobe problem. However, there is no way to know this for sure without a SPECT scan. In order to treat the issues with pinpoint accuracy, I almost always prefer that a client bite the bullet and get a scan, particularly if there was a brain injury of any kind in his past. Because the temporal lobes are housed in a little cup made of boney ridges in the skull, they are especially prone to injury in a trauma to the head. The tofu-like temporal lobes (which, in the side view of the brain, look like the thumb of a boxer's glove) hit the boney ridge and can easily suffer damage.

Amen Clinic's research has shown that these three different types of anger and violence all require different treatments:

- Impulsive violence (low prefrontal cortex): sudden and rash explosions; their "thinker" has left the building, and their emotions are suddenly in charge.
- Compulsive violence (high cingulate gyrus): this person gets stuck on a negative thought, cannot be dissuaded by their internal logic, and grows angrier by the moment.
- Random or senseless violence, accompanied by dark thoughts: this sort of rage often comes with a deep sense of gloom, injustice, and self-righteousness if it is expressed in aggressive ways.

Knowing which type or combination of types is essential to getting the right help.

The SPECT scan can show if one or more of the areas are affected, and then we can treat each area in a prescribed order. We always begin by balancing out the temporal lobes with appropriate medication if this area shows up on a scan as being under- or overactive. If we try to balance the cingulate first with an SSRI, temporal lobe problems can actually become worse. A doctor may prescribe antidepressants to those who complain of having dark or violent thoughts, and these are the people you hear about in the news who "took Prozac and then committed suicide." Tragically, this happens in too many cases. If we suspect there is any possibility of a temporal lobe problem when doing the Amen Brain System Checklist, we do not recommend an SSRI until we are sure that the temporal lobes have been balanced first (often with an antiseizure medication—but more on that later).

The joyful news is that when these brain abnormalities are properly treated, there is often significant improvement, and it doesn't generally take very long to see and feel it.

I LOVE A HAPPY ENDING!

By age seven, little Alissa was close to two years behind in school. Two years earlier, she had been diagnosed with childhood arthritis. Vioxx was the only anti-inflammatory that would bring her relief. (Little did anyone know that Vioxx would soon be removed from the market because of its harmful side effects, increasing risk of strokes and heart attacks.)

In addition to the arthritis, Alissa would have panic attacks to such a degree that it was difficult for her to leave the house. She was also prone to outbursts of anger that were a sight to behold. With the combination of joint pain, panic, and temper outbursts, it was difficult for her to go to recess at school.

Going to an amusement park or an outing as a family was a struggle because her family never knew what might happen. Alissa's parents struggled with guilt and shame because they could not control their own child, whose puzzling emotions were off the charts.

Very few friends came over to play with Alissa because of her physical limitations but mostly because of her emotional instability.

Their church was highly supportive of a popular Christian parenting program at that time that defined anger as "a rebellious and defiant spirit." Graduates of this program received a "whacker" to be used to administer discipline (taking the proverb to "spare the rod . . . spoil the child" out of context).

Fortunately, Alissa's parents were willing to withstand the pressure and advice of their well-meaning church friends and began to search for possible underlying reasons for their daughter's out-of-control behavior. They contacted me, and I referred them for a SPECT brain imaging scan. Alissa's scan showed what we call a *ring of fire*. In fact, when I saw the scan, I felt so much compassion for this little girl that I got tears in my eyes. Note that in the SPECT scan below on the left, there is activity around the entire outside of the brain encompassing the temporal lobes, and also there's too much activity in the cingulate gyrus and basal ganglia. What do you get when you cross a Circular Gerbil Wheel with the Temper Lofts and Basement of Giant Fears? A furious, frightened gerbil who can't stop the madness.

Before   After

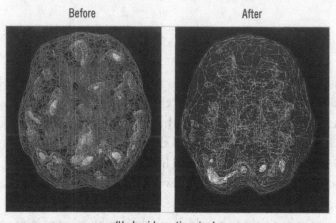

(Underside, active view)

I encouraged Alissa's parents to contact Dr. Renee Thomas (see www.kidsneedusnow.org), who has a clinic in Boston. The family went to the clinic, and the entire family went on the Zone Diet, popularized by Dr. Barry Sears (similar to what I recommend for the joy diet with an emphasis on adequate protein with every meal and snacks as a key component). In addition, we gradually worked Alissa up to two tablespoons of a pharmaceutical grade of fish oil per day. (You can find great flavors of fish oil for kids where the taste is disguised. They love it.)

Alissa's mother decreased the Vioxx 50 percent with no return of the joint pain. Besides being calming to the brain, omega-3s are powerful anti-inflammatories. One month later, her mother took Alissa completely off the anti-inflammatory with no return of pain, and Alissa also had control of her mood swings.

Three years later, we took another scan, and Alissa now has a much-improved brain. All this change from fish oil alone! Truly amazing. Some neurologists believe that when they find this ring-of-fire pattern in children, it can bloom into bipolar disorder later in life. Treated early, with high-quality, pharmaceutical-grade fish oil, this condition may be avoided. Scientists are also discovering that omega-3 fish oil can work as well as medication in some cases of adults with bipolar (manic-depressive) disorder.

By the way, Alissa is now reading at college level. With her brain stabilized, she can cope with her learning disabilities and has great mood management—a miracle that took five years to accomplish.

HOW TO CALM THE RAGING WITHIN

Nutrition

Follow the joy diet in chapter 5, being sure to include plenty of protein.

Supplements

- GABA
- Valerian
- Omega-3 fish oil
- Alpha lipoic acid
- Vitamin A and vitamin C as antioxidants
- Phosphatidalserine
- Ginkgo biloba
- Low-dose ibuprofen

Medication (if appropriate)

- Antiseizure meds for mood instability and temper problems: Depakote, Neurontin, Gabitril, Lamictal, Trileptal, and Topamax.
- Lithium, Depakote, Trileptal, and Tegretol are helpful with bipolar disorder.
- Neurontin and Lyrica are helpful for anxiety and useful for pain management.
- Gabitril is helpful for anxiety.
- Memory-enhancing meds, such as Namenda, Aricept, Exelon, or Reminyl, for more serious memory problems. These medications are helpful for those whose memory problems are related to trauma and are often used with Alzheimer's and various forms of dementia.

HAPPY MEMORIES

Since it is so easy for someone with temporal lobe issues to have darker memories, it is especially helpful to purposefully create a Happy Memories photo album or scrapbook. For others, this may be a fun hobby, but for those with anger issues, creating and reviewing positive memories should be a daily mental heath practice. By viewing pictures of positive times (or magazine pictures cut out as reminders) and regularly flipping through the collection, deeper neuron highways to happiness can be made. Starting a journal of happy memories to read and reread or saving encouraging cards or letters can also help. The late Barbara Johnson created an entire Joy Room in her home so when she walked into the room, she saw all her favorite things: gifts, notes of encouragement, silly cartoons, and stuffed animals—anything that made her smile.

BIOFEEDBACK

Using biofeedback techniques is an effective way to learn to calm your emotions and the temporal lobes. Basically, your fingers are connected by special wires to a computer software program screen that trains you, visually, to see and recognize when your body is relaxed. Eventually you learn to automatically relax your body's internal systems on your own without the computer.

To find a certified practitioner in your area via the Internet, go to www. BCIA.org. You may also purchase a home-based biofeedback relaxation program. One resource can be found at www.biofeedbackzone.com.

ANGER MANAGEMENT

There are many fine anger management programs around the country, but most counselors will tell you that abusive men tend to have to be court-ordered to take the classes. Still, if you or your mate struggles with anger and is willing to take the class voluntarily, you'll be welcomed by a group of folks (and a counselor) who understands. These support groups—focused on honesty, compassion, and getting better—are enormously valuable.

One highly successful compassion-based boot camp for both angry abusers and their partners can be viewed at www.compassionpower.com. Dr. Steven Stosny has appeared on several talk shows and is the author of *Love Without Hurt*. What's unique about his book is that the author speaks to both sides of the abusive relationship and, using an approach to increase empathy and compassion, helps retrain angry brains and those who love them.

I need to add that in my clinical experience, I have found that patients will have a greater likelihood of success with Dr. Stosny's boot camp, anger management, and biofeedback processes if the temporal lobes are treated first. If you utilize these programs yet find that outbursts of anger are still an issue, do not hesitate to get a SPECT scan or have your prescribing MD try a mood stabilizer.

SELF-SOOTHING

Breathing slowly and regularly, in and out ten times, can also calm overactive temporal lobes. Mark Twain once said, "When angry, count four; when very angry, swear." (Perhaps he should have kept counting until ten.)

You might consider getting a fish tank or water fountain, and stare into it until you begin to feel your muscles relax. Sitting outside in the sun can also be calming—and porch swings that echo the rocking chairs of our childhoods can be soothing to our systems.

Keep a squishy ball in your desk or dresser drawer at home and squeeze and release it until the tension within subsides.

Keep a CD or iPod or a radio set on a station that plays soothing music nearby. (There are many CDs created especially to relieve stress.) Go into your *happy music* world until your body relaxes in rhythm to the calming sounds. True confession: probably because of my ADD (or being a child of the '60s and '70s), I like high-energy music, even loud rock 'n' roll, and find that sometimes those wild guitar sounds really do soothe my soul. To each his own!

Use progressive relaxation from chapter 5 also. Or lie down in a tub of warm water or on a soft bed, and imagine a warm spot in your chest. Let that warm spot slowly grow wider and wider, spreading peaceful feelings to your entire body.

SCRIPTURES

- "Go ahead and be angry. You do well to be angry—but don't use your anger as fuel for revenge. And don't stay angry. Don't go to bed angry. Don't give the Devil that kind of foothold in your life" (Eph. 4:26 MSG). This is a wonderful verse on anger: it happens! But it is what we do with our anger that matters most.
- One anger management tool is to get in the habit of seeking first to understand and listen before asking to be understood and listened to. This is a great verse and simple to remember: "Understand this, my dear brothers and sisters: You must all be quick to listen, slow to speak, and slow to get angry" (James 1:19 NLT).
- *God Calling* is a classic devotional written many years ago. It and *Come Away My Beloved* (another classic devotional) are written as if God is speaking to you. If you have a hard time hearing God's voice as a loving Father in your head, these devotionals help capture the way the Lord speaks to his children. Used on a daily basis for a year, you may be able to hear God's loving tone more easily.

VISUAL PRAYER: RELEASING ANGER

Try this prayerful exercise when you are feeling angry:

Imagine you are at the beach, watching waves come and go with the tide. Close your eyes and imagine the *swish . . . swish . . . swish* of the sea lapping the shore—perhaps the sound of gulls, the feel of the sun on your face. Let the feeling of warmth and calm envelop you.

Visualize the scene in the Bible when Jesus commanded the raging sea to be calm, saying, "Peace, be still" (Mark 4: 36–39 KJV).

Now, let a situation that has caused you anger come to mind. Picture your emotions, tossing and turning the boat of your mind. Then imagine Jesus standing over the rough seas of your mind and saying, "Peace, child. Be still." Let the anger subside and allow His peace to envelop you. Remind yourself that all is well. Jesus is in control.

Just as the tide takes the waves out to sea, let what has upset you drift away. Allow God to take your anger and carry it beyond the horizon until it disappears. Then return to that wonderful place of peace: the beach, the *swish* of the waves washing your mind clean. Feel the sun on your face. Breathe deeply. Rest in Him.

QUOTES TO QUIET AN ANGRY MIND

- For every minute you are angry, you lose sixty seconds of happiness.
  —Author unknown
- People who fly into a rage always make a bad landing. —Will Rogers
- Resentment is like taking poison and waiting for the other person to die.
  —Malachy McCourt
- Anger is short-lived madness. —Horace
- Anger blows out the lamp of the mind. —Robert G. Ingersoll
- I don't have to attend every argument I'm invited to.
  —Author unknown
- Anger is a bad counselor. —French proverb
- To carry a grudge is like being stung to death by one bee.
  —William H. Walton
- When a man sends you an impudent letter, sit right down and give it back to him with interest ten times compounded, and then throw both letters in the wastebasket. —Elbert Hubbard [3]

Music

In the good ol' days before TV and MTV, families used to gather 'round the old upright piano and sing together for simple entertainment. Even in the '60s and '70s, someone could nearly always play some simple folk songs on a guitar and gather a singing crowd on the front porch. Actually, this generation has found its own kind of sing-along fun with karaoke and dueling piano bars. But for regular weekly singing that lifts your soul and soothes your temporal lobes, the communal singing experience is only a few blocks away at a church of your choice.

Dr. Amen writes, "Song is often associated with spiritual experience. When I was in college, I attended Calvary Chapel, a large church in Southern California. The music was magical. Listening to the choir was not just a pleasant listening experience; it was a wondrous experience that resonated through every cell in my body. The music uplifted both the soul and mood of the congregation. The pastor said the music was 'blessed by God Himself.' Several of my friends were choir members. I often saw them become transformed when they started to sing. Shy people would become more extroverted, more alive. People in the congregation became more involved in the service during congregational singing. The church community glistened with the contagious joy of the music."[4]

So next time you find yourself *singin' in the rain*, remember that you are also *tuning up your brain*.

A Biblical Musical Story

King Saul (from Old Testament times) was said to have suffered from an evil or, more specifically, a "tormenting" spirit that would come over him (1 Sam. 16:14–15) When these episodes occurred, Saul would turn into a raving maniac. But he found that when David played his harp, his mind would settle and he'd be at peace. From a brain point of view, David's soothing music calmed Saul's overactive temporal lobes. Music does indeed "calm the savage beast." Eventually, however, as much as David loved and wanted to comfort King Saul in his torment, the harpist had to flee for his life: Saul's jealousy and rage simply became too much. After dodging the king's spear a couple of times during his private concerts, David had no choice but to save his own life. (This is a great picture of what so often happens when someone lives with and loves a rageaholic. There's a natural desire to calm and comfort someone who has totally lost it since it is often easy to tell that the angry person is inwardly tormented, often by the lies in their own head. But eventually, rage tends to progress to abuse, and the abused person—like David—has no choice but to flee to protect his own life.)

Exercise

Any kind of physical movement, but especially aerobic workouts, can help burn off angry negative emotions. Before you explode, excuse yourself from a tense scene and just say, "I'll be back in a few minutes." Then walk as hard as you can out the door and anywhere you can until you begin to breathe normally and the volcano of emotion has been released with physical movement. If you find yourself about to blow up at a child, put the child in a safe place—a crib or the bedroom with the door closed—and pace around the house until you are calmed down.

- Next time you're mad, try dancing out your anger. —Sweetpea Tyler
- The best remedy for a short temper is a long walk. —Jacqueline Schiff [5]

Cinematherapy

- *What's Love Got to Do with It?* The story of Ike and Tina Turner's volatile marriage and its eventual dissolution. Realistic story of how abuse begins verbally and often ends up with physical abuse and the loss of a marriage. R-E-S-P-E-C-T is what both men and women need from each other to enjoy a satisfying marriage.
- *Analyze This.* A lighthearted comedy about a therapist played by the ever-funny Billy Crystal who gets involved in helping a member of the Mafia, played by Robert De Niro, who needs to learn to control his temper. Not anything deeply healing here, except humor—which all of us need.
- *Where the Heart Is.* Novalee, the main character in this tender movie, is seventeen and pregnant. She has never had a real home. When her musician boyfriend dumps her at Wal-Mart, she hides in the store, keeping track of all the items she uses in case she ever gets the chance to pay it back. She is discovered in her hideout just as she is giving birth and awakens in a hospital bed to find that she has gained instant celebrity status in the small town as the mother of "The Wal-Mart Baby."

  Over the next few years, she creates a makeshift family from a group of eccentric friends and realizes her own strength. The theme of women overcoming abusive men and finding others who'll value their hearts is powerful for any woman caught in the grip of an angry or abandoning man.
- *Good Will Hunting.* Not always an easy film to watch (and the language is raw), but the healing relationship between therapist and client is worth the discomfort some of the scenes evoke. When Will is unable to connect

emotionally, the root of his pain is slowly uncovered in the safety of the therapeutic relationship: he was terribly abused by an angry foster parent. The joy of seeing Will's life open up to include a future and a loving relationship is worth the periodic moments of pain in getting there. A masterful movie of ultimate hope.

Bibliotherapy

Self Help

- *Boundaries in Marriage* by Dr. Henry Cloud and Dr. John Townsend
- *Love Without Hurt: Turn Your Resentful, Angry, or Emotionally Abusive Relationship into a Compassionate, Loving One* by Steven Stosny
- *The Anger Trap: Free Yourself from the Frustrations That Sabotage Your Life* by Les Carter

Memoir

Finding Home: An Imperfect Path to Faith and Family by Jim Daly and Bob DeMoss. A living testament to the fact that with intervention and mentoring, people can rise above the angry adults in their past to become happy, loving marriage partners and parents.

Poetry

The Singer/The Song/The Finale (The Singer Trilogy 1–3) by Calvin Miller, a Christian classic of epic poetry—now over thirty years old—was written by one of Christendom's finest artistic, poetic, and lyrical minds. If you lean toward poetry and story and words spoken in rhythm, this is a wondrous read for the temporal lobes. Dr. Miller's work continues to inspire each new generation that discovers these books.

Joy Everlasting

CHAPTER ELEVEN

An Apostle on Joy: The *Real* Secret

When I see you again, you'll be full of joy,
and it will be a joy no one can rob from you.

—JESUS (JOHN 16:22 MSG)

Unless you are from another country, planet, or galaxy, you've probably heard of the best-selling book *The Secret*—five million copies sold and counting at the time of this writing. But about two thousand years ago, another writer claimed to have found *the secret*. His name was Paul though, at one time, his name was Saul. Saul, as you may recall, once spent his days persecuting and killing Christians until one day, in a blinding light, Christ himself showed up and asked Saul a question he couldn't ignore: "Why are you persecuting me?"

Needless to say, Saul was never the same, and to mark the end of one life and the beginning of a new one, he changed his name to Paul. Then he spent the rest of his life following Christ and proclaiming God's love. This involved preaching and making friends, traveling and growing spiritually. It also involved floggings, imprisonment, shipwreck, and finding himself, with some regularity, knocking at death's door.

Paul wrote a letter about the secret to the church at Philippi (a small town in what is now Turkey) while under house arrest in Rome. He wanted to thank the Philippians for a gift they'd sent via Epaphroditus, who also stayed awhile to minister and encourage Paul during his imprisonment. Paul poured out his heart to the church people in this letter, for they had been supportive and caring toward him, and he felt the same toward them.

We all need encouragement, and Paul reassured his friends in Philippi that he was confident God would complete the good (literally, "excellent, joyful, and happy") work in them that he had begun. The central theme of this letter was to inspire his friends to embrace joy, come what may. Toward the end of this heartfelt thank-you, the aging apostle wrote, "I have learned the secret . . ."

The secret to what? Inquiring minds want to know.

"The secret," Paul writes, "of being content" (4:12).

LAID-BACK JOY

Contentment is a wonderful word, related to joy and happiness. By the way, in Scripture, *joy* usually means a sense of internal delight; *happiness* is the recognition of how blessed we are. They are very much intertwined, and so I've not made a big deal of differentiating the terms. Both bring a smile and are related to feelings that are connected to an inner attitude of gratitude. In fact, I think of contentment as being happiness and joy's peaceful, relaxing, satisfied cousin. Contentment contains the habit of being grateful for every possible thing there is to be thankful for, in any and every situation. It doesn't happen to someone overnight, and it certainly doesn't happen to everyone. In fact, how many people do you know who you could describe as being joyfully content as a state of mind most of the time?

Contentment, even for the esteemed apostle under discussion, was "learned"; it was a process. And to be truly content involves some proactive training of the brain. G. K. Chesterton said, "True contentment is a thing as active as agriculture. It is the power of getting out of any situation all that there is in it. It is arduous, and it is rare."

Unlike the blinding light of his conversion, learning to live in laid-back joy didn't come instantaneously to Paul. It happened slowly, bit by bit, experience by experience, as the apostle grappled with the messiness and mystery of life as it is, and not life as we all wish it were. God never left Paul's side, but lovingly, compassionately tutored his pupil in what really mattered, in what men and women could live without (and live with) and still be profoundly at peace, even joyful.

I long to know this secret too. I want to know how to sustain a peaceful sense of abiding joy when fear threatens to rattle my world. I know, at middle age, that life is uncertain, and though I cherish and believe good things will unfold in the years that lie ahead, I also know that with those years will come pain, discouragement, and the death of loved ones. I want to know Paul's secret for myself, but I also want it so that I, too, can pass it on to those I love; to others who are stuck in pain and want a way to move on.

I do not need a perfect world; I need perfect peace.

So do our children. They don't require that we give them perfect lives or a perfect world, as much as we'd love to grant these to our kids. They need solid secrets to internal joy and peace when their worlds are rocked, and rocked they will be, for such is life. If life were perfect, it wouldn't be life; it would be heaven.

Paul found this kind of permanent state of relaxed joy in a very real and often harsh world. Realizing this peace was a sacred treasure, he had a scribe put ink to parchment and used his well-worn life to pass along the secret map to the place of contentment.

Eastern gurus may describe someone who lives in such a state of contentment as having found bliss. Psychologists might say they are self-actualized. Paul simply called himself a joyful servant of a worthy, loving, and faithful Lord. Though he was at one time harsh, judgmental, and pious, in the small letter he wrote to the Philippians we see a man who, like the famed Velveteen Rabbit, was loved and rubbed to a state of being spiritually real, relaxed, and at ease. Even in jail, awaiting his death, he uses some form of the exuberant word *joy* sixteen times.

Not only did Paul claim to have found the secret to contentment, but he stated that he had found the secret to contentment in any circumstance. A bliss without boundaries! "I have learned to be content whatever the circumstances. I know what it is to be in need, and I know what it is to have plenty. I have learned the secret of being content in any and every situation, whether well fed or hungry, whether living in plenty or in want" (Phil. 4:11–12).

How does Paul pull this off? He says he can be happy no matter what because "I can do everything through him who gives me strength" (v. 13).

Cool. Very cool.

Let me put this another way. Paul is saying, "I have learned over my years of experience and God's guiding hand that the real secret to contentment (laid-back joy)—no matter what—is that I know I am never alone in anything life throws at me. I have Christ living in and through me, giving me strength to face situations one at a time, day by day, as they come to pass. Because I know this is true, from the top of my old bald head down to my wrinkled toes, I live in a state of total inner relaxation, complete with an outer smile."

In fact, almost humorously, Paul has an inner debate with himself at one point in this joyful letter: Would it be better to keep on living or better to die? Alas, there are days when I can identify with Paul's struggle although probably for different reasons. When I am longing for heaven, it is often because I've allowed myself to get miserable on earth. Then I have to talk to myself (kindly) and say, "Earl, buddy, you know your temporal lobes are not the best. How's your nutrition been today? Did you eat something that is giving you a bad glycemic reaction? Did you forget to take your fish oil today?"

It is sad that the joy and contentment of Christ within me, beside me, above me, and below me are hindered when I don't responsibly care for my brain and heart. When I am taking care of my heart and brain, then I am touched by Christ, who is right here with me as I write these words. It is at this very same moment in space and time, right beside and with you, dear reader, that he is wanting to love you and guide you to the best of what is here on earth for you.

Paul struggles, though, with the stay-or-go question because he sees such a wealth of benefits on both sides of heaven. The apostle has arrived at such a place of perfect peace and joy that he would be ecstatic to live a while longer or to go on home to be with Christ. It's all good.

Can I just interject that this is one exceptionally emotionally balanced man?

You may be thinking, as I am, that it would have been amazing to have spent a couple of hours with Paul at this point in his life, just gleaning every drop of wisdom he had to offer before his days on earth were done. Thankfully, this letter to the Philippians is a pretty good substitute for that dream dinner date, at least until the day when I can sit down on a heavenly porch swing and shoot the breeze with Paul, one on one. Wouldn't that be something? To sit with a man whom God used to write letters of care, love, and instruction to his hurting children? An author whose God-inspired work reaches across time, space, and centuries to encourage me even today as I read his words and find renewed hope for the hours ahead of me this morning?

I highly recommend that you take time to read through this little book of Philippians as the whipped cream on top of your journey to joy, and maybe do it a few times this month. You will discover treasure after treasure, secret after secret to living a deeply satisfying life. I have found six little *secrets to joy* that stand out for me, both as a Bible student and a therapist with a high interest in brain health. However, don't stop with my gleanings; dig for more gold in your own personal study.

SECRET TO JOY #1: REFRAME YOUR CHAINS

Now I want you to know, brothers, that what has happened to me has really served to advance the gospel. As a result, it has become clear throughout the whole palace guard and to everyone else that I am in chains for Christ. Because of my chains, most of the brothers in the Lord have been encouraged to speak the word of God more courageously and fearlessly. (Phil. 1:12–14)

In the book of Acts, we read the story of a time that Paul and Silas were put in chains in a prison (Acts 16:24–26). They sang hymns and prayed and— voilà!—their chains fell off! The same sort of thing happened to the disciple Peter. Don't you just love it when God answers our prayers this way? We pray, he changes the circumstances . . . our chains fall off, and we're happy and free.

This is by far my favorite way to receive answers to my heartfelt prayers!

But here in the book of Philippians, Paul is in chains again. I cannot help wondering if he tried singing every hymn he'd ever learned, in every key, seeking to find that magical combination of prayer and singing that worked to make chains fall off. But alas, this time God didn't remove the chains. This time, Paul's deliverance would come from a miracle of the inner kind. God would help him see his chains in a new light, to reframe his particular circumstantial pain. (Remember that real joy, with contentment, involves retraining your brain.)

So Paul looks around himself but with a new attitude of gratitude. He searches for the blessings in the mess. It doesn't take long for him to find one. "Because of my chains . . ." he says, good things are happening. For one, he has a captive audience of guards with whom he can share his life's message: the good news of God's love.

What are your chains today? Don't know? Fill in this blank. "If _____ would only happen, I could be happy." Whatever goes in the blank is your chain of pain.

Then ask yourself an honest follow-up: *What is my part in keeping these familiar chains?* What are you choosing to believe that could be a falsehood? What options are you missing or avoiding?

Rather than postpone joy until your circumstances change, do a treasure hunt in your current set of circumstances. Find the nuggets of joy and blessings in your life as it is. Truly, truly: the happiest people are the most grateful ones; the most joyful brains have learned to reframe their pain.

Beached Wails

Becky, my friend and collaborator on this project, told me about an unexpected turn of events on a family vacation. "It was a vacation long anticipated, a week at the beach where we planned to be soaking up the sun's warm rays, bobbing in the bright blue surf. What we got instead was seven days of nonstop rain."

As any honest thinker knows, life is what happens to you when you are making other plans. Then Becky thought, *I am postponing joy by waiting for the sun to come out. I am telling myself and my family that we will be happy when the rain goes away and the sun comes out.* The rain had become her chain.

Becky continued: "After about the third day of checking the waterscape for a glimpse of sun, like some shipwrecked sailor in search of rescue, I had to accept the possibility that our outside circumstances might not change. This acceptance ushered in an epiphany: I was powerless to stop the rain, but I still had the power to shift my brain.

"So I began to look (and look *hard*) for the natural beauty God *did* give us and to make the most of the time we had. Remember that Crosby, Stills, Nash, and Young song from the 1970s, "Love the One You're With"? Well, I decided that I might not have the weather I wanted, honey, but I was determined to love this day, with this rainy weather I'd been given. With the resolve of a soldier with fresh orders, I opened the front door, held my dripping head high, sloshed to the car, and drove to the store where I purchased all manner of happy ingredients for an indoor beach party: yellow sunshine balloons, a blue ocean cake with mini beach umbrellas, cheesy Bingo cards, a Beach Boys CD, and Elvis's *Blue Hawaii* video."

Needless to say, Becky's *rainy day party* proved to be a hit. She and her kids learned a valuable lesson that day: sometimes the sun shines from the outside in, but sometimes you have to let it shine from the inside out.

I want to close this thought with quotes from two people who had every reason to let joy die because of the chains that bound them: Helen Keller, who lost the ability to see and hear at nineteen months; and Viktor Frankl, a psychiatrist who survived the horrors of a Nazi concentration camp. Both reframed their chains by training their minds to look for whatever good could be found and be thankful for it.

Happiness cannot come from without. It must come from within. It is not what we see and touch, or that which others do for us, which makes us happy; it is that which we think and feel and do, first for the other fellow and then for ourselves. —Helen Keller

We who lived in concentration camps can remember the men who walked through the huts comforting others, giving away their last piece of bread. They may have been few in number, but they offer sufficient proof that everything can be taken from a man but one thing: the last of the human freedoms; to choose one's attitude in any given set of circumstances, to choose one's own way.[1] —Viktor Frankl

SECRET TO JOY #2: SHRINK IRRITANTS

It is true that some preach Christ out of envy and rivalry, but others out of goodwill. The latter do so in love, knowing that I am put here for the defense of the gospel. The former preach Christ out of selfish ambition, not sincerely, supposing that they can stir up trouble for me while I am in chains. But what does it matter? The important thing is that in every way, whether from false motives or true, Christ is preached. And because of this I rejoice. (Phil. 1:15)

Paul had irregular people in his life who loved to say terrible things about him in order to stir up trouble; they preached Jesus alright, but it was out of purely selfish motives.

And then there were those wonderful friends who served Jesus out of love and treated Paul as a beloved brother.

Life gives most of us a mixed batch of relatives and friends, but the vast majority of us get at least one *irregular* person to deal with, one irritating, depressing, hurtful, or illogical person. You really only have two (healthy) choices in dealing with irrational, difficult people:

1. Do all you can to humbly deal with your part of the problem, to reconcile as much as you can.
2. If you've done all you know to do to accept responsibility and to be Christlike, and the person is still behaving like a dysfunctional jerk, you must—for your own sanity—shrink their influence in your life.

I have found a couple of mental, visual pictures to be very helpful to me when I need to tune down or tune out a negative voice in my life. (Sometimes these voices even pop up from the past and sit on my shoulder whispering judgments and false accusations.)

First, take an imaginary look at negative people and try to see them as if they are simply overgrown toddlers in need of a nap. (You may recall the story of the teen girl mentally putting Mickey Mouse ears on the scary driving instructor from the basal ganglia chapter. This is a similar concept.) While they are ranting and raving or gossiping or avoiding, just mentally shrink them to about two or three years old in your mind because this is usually about the level they are functioning on, and it helps not to take their insults personally. Let their comments roll off your back in the same way a duck lets water roll off its feathers. Realistically, their comments may affect you for a period of time (you are human, and even irrational criticism hurts), but by putting boundaries around your heart, backing off, and logically assessing the truth of the situation, their comments will not get under your skin and linger long-term. With practice in shrinking their influence, you will shake off hurtful comments from hurting people in less and less time. You'll go from months of stewing, to days of mulling, to hours of brooding . . . and eventually, they'll only cause you a few uncomfortable minutes.

From a brain perspective, here is what happens. When you shift from focusing on a negative scene in your mind to one that is truer, more joyful, and more peaceful (using your Presidential Control powers and taking custody of your own mind), the rest of your brain and even your body follow suit. Adrenalin starts to slow up; your heart stops racing; your brain increases its supply of calming serotonin; and GABA also starts to soothe the nerves. Pretty soon, you'll feel some life kicking back in as dopamine (the motivating neurotransmitter) begins to flow, clearing your mind. The intense focus is off this one hurtful loop, and it's now as though the curtain rises on "The Rest of Your Wonderful Life" (the life you couldn't see when blinded by stressors).

In spiritual terms, the Holy Spirit is responding to your step of faith, permeating and filling you body and soul with the truth of God's love, strength, and power. To me, science and spirituality go hand in glove: God created our brains and our bodies to respond positively and in healing ways.

Another mental image to use when you are feeling overwhelmed by a negative experience or person is to visualize the handy-dandy *minimize* button on your computer screen. You can imagine your irritating Aunt Agnes who never loses an opportunity to give you a piece of her mind (which she really can't afford to lose)—and then just hit the minimize button on your mind's computer and shrink her to a tiny box. If you like, you can also mentally turn off the volume.

Once you are no longer overwhelmed by people's negative input, you may find yourself able to be more and more mentally generous as Paul was with others who were saying bad things about him but who, as he pointed out, were still preaching Christ. He found something to be genuinely joyful about even though his opponents' motives were skewed.

One research study found that the happiest people on earth had learned the art of not looking around at others; they were so focused on their goals that they honestly didn't feel they had the time or need to join in the comparison game. I love Paul's words here. "What does it matter?" Paul was playing to an audience of One, brushing off nasty rumors as if they were gnats. He was way too involved in meaningful work to get sidetracked by small stuff.

Before I end this point, I want to put on my Dr. Henslin hat for a minute. Many of the irregular people in your life can have amazing turnarounds if they are willing to get treatment. (Of course, I know that this is a big *if* for many of you, but it is worth mentioning.) One of my close friends grew up in a religious family, but it was a mixture of legalistic religion and fear-based discipline. Today, the sort of discipline that my friend experienced as a child would be called child abuse. His father, in a rage, would beat him with a stick, over and over, until my friend could hardly walk at times.

One day at lunch, my friend confessed his years of hurt and frustration with his father. "My mother is a long-suffering codependent, so Dad's angry and critical behavior just continues to escalate unchecked. They are in their eighties now. Probably just best to accept what is and move on with my life. But it is hard. When my children are on the phone, they work hard to quickly get him off so they can talk to their grandmother. All of them have commented that if their grandmother passes away first, they would probably never talk to their grandfather again."

"It's never too late for a brain scan," I said. "Let's see if we can find a creative way to talk your dad into getting one. My guess is that what we find will help you to forgive him and, if he's willing to get help, allow him to be the man he wants to be."

To make a long story brief, we got my friend's elderly father to agree to a scan. When we got the SPECT printout, we found an injury in his temporal lobe, the Temper Lofts. He'd forgotten that when he was a kid, he'd been playing baseball and, standing too close to the batter, received a thud to the head that knocked him out for a while. An enormous goose egg popped up, but in those days, no one took kids to the doctor for that. However, looking back, the now-aging man recalled that after that point in time, he struggled with dark thoughts—often of a religious nature—and with controlling his temper.

I encouraged his prescribing MD to try an antiseizure medication that is especially helpful in calming the temporal lobes. Within forty-eight hours, my friend called me and said, "Just got off the phone with my dad, Earl, and he said, 'So is this the way other people feel?' For the first time in his life, he felt relaxed and at peace, positive and calm. Then my mom got on the phone."

"What did she say?" I asked, my curiosity high.

"Earl, she couldn't say anything. She just cried." I could hear my friend's voice break with emotion at this point as well. When he was able to speak, he finally said, "All these years our family has lived in fear and pain because of a man whose brain was malfunctioning. It's like a miracle. If only we'd known this fifty years ago!"

It was my privilege to watch my friend turn from anger and distance toward his father to a place of understanding and forgiveness. Even at age eighty and beyond, it is almost *never too late* to improve brain functioning and thus see miraculous improvement in *irregular* relationships.

SECRET TO JOY #3: LETTING GO, LOOKING AHEAD

> But one thing I do: Forgetting what is behind and straining toward what is ahead, I press on toward the goal to win the prize for which God has called me heavenward in Christ Jesus. (Phil. 3:12–14)

We all have done things in our past that could serve as excuses to exit our calling to minister to others. We can easily disqualify ourselves (or let others do it for us) through guilt. (Erma Bombeck aptly described guilt as the gift that keeps on giving.)

Paul had to deal with images of guilt from his past wrongs: he'd participated in the stoning of Stephen; he'd killed Christians, many of whom had to be sons and fathers of those with whom he now worked side by side. But this one thing Paul did: forgetting what was behind, he pressed forward toward finishing whatever God had for him to do in his time left on earth. He knew he could not undo his past; he could only do his best today.

Seeing yourself as a victim means your identity comes from the belief that the past is more powerful than the present. It is the belief that your failures of yesterday are more real than the reality of today. It is the false belief that other people from long ago are responsible for who you are now, either your emotional pain or your inability to grow.

Perhaps the best part of the gospel is the good news that all our sins were thrown into God's sea of forgetfulness because of Christ's love for us and his atoning death. People don't generally grasp this part of the good news until they really, really, really mess up. Then the Christian story that once seemed like a fairy tale from their parents' old, dusty Bible comes alive as the need for a Savior who forgives us and who is the Author of Fresh Starts suddenly takes on new meaning. How many times have I sat in what basically turned out to be the *confessional booth*—as a counselor—and listened to people weep out their sins, their secrets, their "unforgivable" pasts?

I always count it a privilege to be able to say, "As far as the east is from the west, so God casts your sin away from the beloved child you are to him." Then I simply encourage that person to walk in who they are today, "forgetting what is behind" because that is old news.

There's work to be done as we press forward to a higher calling! And we cannot fully sign up for a meaningful life if we are hauling around yesterday's baggage. Paul knew he couldn't do it, and he had some awfully heavy loads to bear if he chose not to give this burden to God.

But because he didn't let his past determine his identity, God was able to shine his light through Paul's life.

In Thornton Wilder's play *The Angel That Troubled the Waters*, there is a physician who is about to finally make it to the water's edge where healing is promised. But an angel blocks him from entering the healing waters, saying, "Draw back, physician; this moment is not for you." The physician is bewildered and devastated until the angel explains: "Without your wound, where would your power be? It is your very remorse that makes your low voice tremble into the hearts of men. The very angels themselves cannot persuade the wretched and blundering children on earth as can one human being broken on the wheels of living. In Love's service only the wounded soldiers can serve. Draw back."[2]

In truth, until most of us have been "broken on the wheels of living," we are not able to be the sort of wounded soldiers so sorely needed in Love's service. So if you do look back at your past, your pain, your sorrow, or your sin, let it be only with the desire to use your past to help others see God's love through your brokenness.

SECRET TO JOY #4: THE REMEDY FOR HIGH ANXIETY

Do not be anxious about anything but in everything, by prayer and petition, with thanksgiving present your requests to God. And the peace of God, which transcends all understanding, will guard your hearts and your minds in Christ Jesus. (Phil. 4:6–7)

The more I understand brain chemistry, the more I appreciate the wisdom in this simple verse. Paul didn't just tell his friends, "Do not be anxious about anything!" Have you ever had someone tell you, "Just don't worry about it"? It's about as useful as a bent house key. In fact, the more I think, *Don't worry about it,* sometimes the larger the problem looms in my mind.

But Paul not only tells us not to worry, he tells us to do something: pray about everything instead! But here's the real secret to anxiety-calming prayer: he encourages us to pray "with thanksgiving." Throughout Paul's letters, he talks about praying with gratitude and usually opens his books with a prayer of thankfulness.

Scientists have discovered that when we are actively blessing others or saying thanks to God for his many gifts to our lives, the neuron path to worry and fear is literally blocked. You can't be grateful and anxious at the same time. Hmm . . . I wonder how Paul knew that?

Becky's mom, Ruthie, called her on Christmas Day this past December. Becky was concerned because her mom had been supersick with a sinus infection and, in fact, so ill that she'd had to miss Christmas Day festivities altogether—including seeing her out-of-town great-grandbaby. Ruthie encouraged Becky's dad, George, to go on and enjoy the festivities, so Ruthie was alone most of the holiday.

When Becky called to check on her mom, she expected to hear Ruthie sound sick and heartbroken and sorrowful. But what she heard was her mother in a state of surprising joy.

"Okay, Mom. What have you been drinking? You into the cough syrup?" Becky teased.

"Becky," Ruthie said, "here's the truth. I've had the most peaceful, joyful day with Jesus. Of course, I was sad that I couldn't be with everyone, so I just decided to pray for each and every member of the family; to lift each of you to him and ask his blessings to pour all over you. And Becky, he was so real and tender and sweet to me. The older I get, the more I feel like the Lord is closer and closer."

Becky laughed. "Mother, I think you are the only woman on earth who could somehow turn spending Christmas Day alone, nursing a sinus infection, into a spiritual party. You remind me of when Paul promised that if we pray and give thanks, we'll experience a peace that doesn't make any logical sense."

"Isn't that the truth? And the rest of that verse—where he promises to guard our hearts and our minds—has also been true for me today. As I turned the day and the worries and my kids, grandkids, and great-grandbabies over to God in prayer, he kept my heart from aching and my mind from stewing. I even think I'm starting to feel better physically."

Becky also says her father is one of the most continually grateful men she has ever known, sometimes calling her just to say, "Isn't God good? Isn't life wonderful, Becky?" She says, "My dad is one of those rare men who enjoys just pausing now and then to talk about the good things that God is doing. I am not sure I've ever met anyone else quite like him. He lives in gratitude."

It's unusual to find one positive, grateful person in a marriage, but George and Ruthie make a dynamic duo of joy even in their senior years. Still deeply in love with each other after fifty-three years of marriage, they are also highly involved in ministry to others and love to laugh and have a good time as well.

People who pause on a regular basis to simply "have a little talk with Jesus" and remember to thank him for their blessings on a regular basis continue to bring joy on this earth until they take their last breath. They know the real secret.

SECRET TO JOY #5: A RICHLY STORED MIND

> Summing it all up, friends, I'd say you'll do best by filling your minds and meditating on things true, noble, reputable, authentic, compelling, gracious—the best, not the worst; the beautiful, not the ugly; things to praise, not things to curse. Put into practice what you learned from me, what you heard and saw and realized. Do that, and God, who makes everything work together, will work you into his most excellent harmonies. (Phil. 4:8–9 MSG)

What is your favorite *joy drink* in the morning? A cup of hot tea? A steaming cup of coffee or cocoa? A glass of fresh orange juice? Whatever your beverage of choice, have you noticed how good that first sip tastes? It's as if all your taste buds are standing at full attention, ready to be watered and nourished.

Most of us know how to savor our first cup of java or Earl Grey by instinct.

We hold the cup and breathe in the aroma. We enjoy the feel of the warmth in our cupped hands. Often we have a favorite mug with a design that pleases our eye. We turn the whole morning drink thing into a little pleasure ritual.

Starbucks understood the human desire to have a pleasurable experience to go along with their morning coffee, and because they understood how to help us "savor our sips," they are a very, very wealthy company. They provide cozy chairs, nice music, friendly greeters, great smells—they turned the simple morning beverage into a full sensory experience of joy.

What if we were to become more than coffee connoisseurs? What if we became aficionados of life, learning to savor more moments? What if we applied the Starbucks full-sensory idea to all of our little everyday rituals? Wouldn't we upsize the joy in our lives a hundredfold? Look again at Paul's list above and ponder how we can practically begin storing our minds with uplifting thoughts. I find most of us can do this when we are in a generally uplifting environment or involved in something meaningful. But what about taking out the trash? How's that supposed to be a praiseworthy task? Walking the dog, or worse . . . cleaning up the dog's mess. Really. How are you supposed to think noble thoughts when you are walking behind your Lab with a pooper scooper?

Here's an idea for you to try. What if you made a list of everything you do in a typical day and then thought of ways to broaden the pleasure from these tasks by searching for what is lovely or admirable or praiseworthy in the mundane? Martha Beck, an enormously creative life coach, suggests that we go through all the tasks and chores that we do each day and rate them from 1 to 10 in terms of the pleasure they bring to our lives.

Let's take, for example, washing the dishes. (I thought I'd start with something easier than cleaning up after a dog.) Let's say it is about a 3 on the pleasure scale to you. Martha suggests that we do one of three things to help put more joy into these mundane things on our to-do list:

1. Bag it (cross it off your list).
2. Barter it (swap washing dishes for folding laundry with someone in your house who gets a buzz out of soapy hands).
3. Better it. This is where you get to be really creative. How could you make dish washing a better experience? One way is to think of your senses

involved with this chore and how you might heighten them in a positive way. For example, you could:

- Choose a scent of soap that you like.
- Buy some soft rubber gloves if you hate the feel of dishwater hands.
- Turn on some fun music or listen to an audiobook or TV. (I know a preacher's wife who turns on Aretha Franklin when she wants to get in a housecleaning mood.)
- Pray or memorize an uplifting scripture. Sing praise songs while you are working.
- Do your work as a gift to God, even if it is changing a diaper or unclogging a sink. Brother Lawrence, a monk who learned to incorporate the presence of God in the mundane, said, "To do great things is not necessary. Today, I turn my little omelet in the pan for the love of God."
- Create a kitchen that is bright and cheerful so that you want to be there.
- Sip a cup of hot tea or a glass of merlot while you work.
- Call an old friend and wash while you talk.

Using this method, you may find that dish washing is suddenly your new favorite chore. Maybe even a 7 or an 8.[3]

I have a friend who is a remarkably even-tempered guy. If the world of men were chairs, he would definitely be a comfy easy chair. But his one area of frustration is driving, and especially being stuck in traffic. His normally sunny mood can disappear as soon as he's behind the wheel if he even *anticipates* that traffic might be slow. (Too many years on L.A. freeways when he lived there in the '80s.)

But using Martha's upsize-the-joy-in-the-mundane suggestion, my friend actually loves driving now, even in traffic. The secret has been bimonthly trips to the library for books on CD. He's a history buff, so now he can listen to the exploits of the 101st Airborne or hear author/historian David McCullough (who has a great reading voice) intone about past presidents— all stories that absolutely transport him to another era as he's driving. "Sometimes, I'll find myself driving slower than normal just so I can hear the rest of a good story." Because my friend's career involves lots of reading, it is a special treat for him to be able to rest his eyes from words on the page and just listen to books on subjects of great personal interest.

As you look for the pure, the lovely, and the excellent things in your life (or seek to add *quality* experiences to the mundane), a unique phenomenon will begin to happen. God will work into your life, bit by bit, a little more harmony and a lot less frustration. Just as dish washing can turn into a time of fun and relaxation, driving can become a laid-back joy. Now. How many ways can you start to savor your day?

"Does anyone ever realize life while they live it? Every, every minute?"
—Emily in Thornton Wilder's *Our Town*

SECRET TO JOY #6: BE DEEP-SPIRITED FRIENDS

If you've gotten anything at all out of following Christ, if his love has made any difference in your life, if being in a community of the Spirit means anything to you, if you have a heart, if you care—then do me a favor: Agree with each other, love each other, be deep-spirited friends. Don't push your way to the front; don't sweet-talk your way to the top. Put yourself aside, and help others get ahead. Don't be obsessed with getting your own advantage. Forget yourselves long enough to lend a helping hand. (Phil. 2:1–4 MSG)

Throughout this book I've discussed the importance of being connected to people as friends or in a community. Few investments pay off in terms of happiness and joy like the investment you make into the lives of people: your family, friends, and community. Paul knew this. Giving altruistically to others has proved to be one of the most consistent elements of happiness in people across the world. The brain science and research that supports this verse could fill up several pages.

When I read the admonition to "be deep-spirited friends," I think of my natural bent toward connecting with others—particularly over a hunger to know more about deeper issues of life and faith, science and personality. Over the years my Curious George personality has overtaken any shyness I might have had about meeting someone whose insights I wanted to glean. So

I have risked asking many people to lunch who might intimidate the average person. But hey, inquiring minds want to know what other interesting minds are thinking. And my prefrontal cortex usually doesn't inhibit me from risking a question that could lead to a connection. By far, the risk I took in getting to know more about Dr. Amen's work has led to one of the most rewarding friendships of my life.

A Modern-Day David and Jonathan

I began this book with a story about myself and Dr. Amen . . . and it only seems fitting to come full circle. David and Jonathan, from the Old Testament, were close friends who stuck with each other through good times and bad. David was doing what God called him to do, but you will remember (from the temporal lobe chapter) that David was attacked by the emotionally unbalanced King Saul, who happened to be Jonathan's father. Jonathan provided real encouragement to David during those times of stress, and vice versa.

Dr. Amen and I met at a time twelve years ago when brain imaging was not welcomed warmly by many professionals: mostly people who just had not had the chance (yet!) that I had been given to learn how to care for the brain and to learn the integral part it plays in every aspect of our lives. My patients were pleased and relieved to know that there was new hope for many of them who'd not been given relief through therapy alone.

Truly God brought Daniel and I together at a time when we both needed encouragement. I discovered a psychiatrist who was breaking new ground and building new paradigms every day and who was eager to share this knowledge. In me, Dr. Amen found someone who really *got it* and began to apply his research in an applicable way. I referred many people to his clinic in northern California and encouraged other professionals to do the same when they came upon cases where I knew a SPECT scan could be of great value. I began to fly to northern California just to spend time sitting with Dr. Amen at the monitor as he taught me about the brain. I got my own brain scanned in 1997, and now, looking back at that scan . . . I am amazed that he took the chance to be my friend! (Of course, he knew that things would improve.)

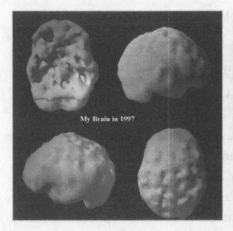 

(Surface views [clockwise from top left]:
underside, right side, left side, top-down)

Several years later, Dr. Amen realized that 25 percent of his referrals were coming from Brea, California, where our offices are located, so he decided to open his second clinic in nearby Newport Beach. With even closer proximity, our professional relationship grew into a David and Jonathan type friendship: two men encouraging and affirming each other as we went through the struggles of birthing a new way of helping people with old problems. During the writing of this manuscript, Dr. Amen had the opportunity to share his groundbreaking work on a highly acclaimed public television program. God is opening doors of new hope and healing for his hurting children throughout the country.

In 2008, Dr. Amen's book *Change Your Brain, Change Your Life* reappeared on the *New York Times* bestsellers list once again, just as it did when first released back in 1999. It is my honor to rejoice with my friend Daniel as he's experiencing such positive public affirmation in the long and hardfought battle of applying brain research to the lives of real men, women, and kids. And he's equally thrilled to encourage my efforts in bringing brain science into the realm of Christian thought. King Solomon said that as iron sharpens iron, so one friend sharpens another. Indeed, both of us have been better sharpened and readied for the work we do in the world by such a deepspirited friendship.

REAL COMMUNITY

I also think of the people I've met in support groups when I needed a safe place to land and to grow. The support group experience of friendship, with the purpose of helping each other to overcome a variety of issues, was so valuable to me that I helped to start a support group ministry specifically for churches. It is called Overcomer's Outreach (www.overcomersoutreach.org) and has expanded to a nationwide ministry. Arthur H. Stainback said, "The value of compassion cannot be over-emphasized. Anyone can criticize. It takes a true believer to be compassionate. No greater burden can be borne by an individual than to know no one cares or understands."[4]

To me, this emphasis on compassion sums up the healing attitudes of most twelve-step groups: an attitude the church could stand to embrace more often.

In being willing to be the sort of friend that Jesus was to others, it helps to remember that most of us are carrying some sort of invisible burden, that we all take our turns on the bottom of life's heap, and that offering the gift of tender-hearted compassion to another human being makes all of heaven smile.

MORE THAN BRAIN MATTER

We've talked so much about the brain in this book: how to care for it, how to make it better, how to use it to glorify God. So it was with special interest that I read about the story of Henri Nouwen's friendship with a young man named Adam, a man who was profoundly and permanently mentally retarded. To a brain guy, this story helps me to remember that the soul is more than the sum of our gray matter, and in the end, God can use those "of very little brain"—as Winnie the Pooh describes himself—to further his kingdom in mysterious ways. It just takes a little supernatural vision and love, and risking reaching out.

Henri Nouwen was a beloved priest, best-selling author, and highly respected scholar among Ivy League schools. Then one day he experienced what he termed "downward mobility" in a major way. He became resident priest at L'Arche, a community of mentally handicapped people and their assistants who try to live in the spirit of the Beatitudes. In his own simple words, Nouwen described his descent from head to heart, from knowledge to kindness, from a lifetime of struggle with perfectionism to finally relaxing into his role as God's beloved the day he entered L'Arche.

Nouwen wrote about his first assignment, working with a twenty-four-year-old young man named Adam, in a slim, posthumously published book entitled *Adam: God's Beloved*. Adam was severely handicapped: he could not walk, speak, or dress himself. In addition, Adam's back was deformed, and he suffered from constant epileptic seizures.

"I was really afraid," Nouwen admitted. "Here I was a university professor. I had never touched anybody very closely . . ." And now, he was presented with Adam, who would require very little intellect and lots of touching, handling, lifting, and pushing to simply get through his *normal* day.

On Nouwen's first morning on duty, he went to Adam's room and began the excruciatingly long and arduous task of getting this man bathed and dressed, his teeth brushed and hair combed so he could be wheeled to breakfast. The one thing Adam could do was lift a spoon to his mouth, so Henri simply watched the young man feed himself. Slowly. Very slowly. "It took about an hour," Nouwen would later report.

You can imagine what a stark contrast this life in slow motion, caring for one profoundly handicapped young man, was to Henri's former fast-forward life in academia. But something happened. Little by little, Henri started to realize something about himself and his relationship to God, something he was learning from caring for Adam. Adam taught Henri that *being* was more important than *doing*. So much of Henri's life, like most of our own lives, was focused on doing things to make others like or approve of him.

As a highly driven and accomplished person, Henri began to grasp, with awe and wonder, that Adam didn't care anything about his successes or degrees or books or speeches. Adam just wanted the kindly priest to be with him. Much the way God simply wants our presence with him. With God, it's always a big *come-as-you-are party*. He just wants us to skip or stumble into his presence with the brains we are struggling with, sit a spell, and remember what matters most. Eventually Henri learned, through Adam, how much God just loved being with him, that God really only wanted one thing from Henri and that was to love him. He didn't need Henri to impress him or prove his worth; God just needed Henri to abide—settle down and make himself at home in his Father's presence.

Adam, like most of the residents at L'Arche, didn't care one whit about intelligent conversation; most were incapable of it. But the one thing they could do was give and receive love. Adam, Nouwen wrote, "was so vulnerable, so weak, so empty, that he became just heart, the heart where God wanted to dwell."[5]

One time Nouwen invited his friend Bill, another of the mentally challenged people from L'Arche, to share a few words at a speaking engagement. News reporters and other people in the audience had come a long way to hear Henri Nouwen, not Bill.

"In order to give Bill support, Nouwen stood next to him on the stage. Bill looked out over the audience, and suddenly all his words failed him. He was overcome. He simply laid his head on Nouwen's shoulders and wept. Much that Nouwen said has passed from the memory of that North Carolina audience; the memory of Bill resting his head on a priest's shoulder has not."[6]

It would be hard for me to find a better example of what Paul meant when he encouraged us to love others, to be deep-spirited friends, to put aside our own needs long enough to lend a helping hand—than Nouwen's friendships with Adam and Bill.

Who would have thought that the path to real joy is to happily, sacrificially, kindly, and deliriously . . . give your life away in the service of Love? (And it doesn't even require a brilliant or perfectly functioning brain!)

The Day I Had My Head Examined

Since the first time I read Dr. Amen's book *Change Your Brain, Change Your Life* with complete fascination (over ten years ago now), I've wondered, *Hmmmm . . . what would my brain SPECT scan look like?*

And then I quickly decided that some things were probably just better left . . . a mystery.

I was that girl in high school who, though a true brunette, was often the butt of blond jokes anyway. I was book-smarts rich but common-sense poor. I might make straight A's, but while accepting my report card from the teacher, I could be wearing mismatched shoes and my shirt inside out and never notice it. After forgetting to bring my gym suit to my seventh grade PE class for nearly two weeks in a row (each day being as astonished at my own forgetfulness as the day before), the junior high school coach held a conference with my mother and told her flatly, "Becky is going to have to really lean on that cute little way about her in order to get through life. Her ability to make me laugh is all that's keeping me from strangling her."

So I took to carrying my honor society card in the wallet of my purse so that I could pull it out in scenarios where my basic intelligence might be called into question. And it worked, as long as I could remember where I last put my wallet . . . and my purse.

But, alas, my junior high gym teacher was right. My sense of humor has saved my forgetful neck in more ways and for more years than I care to count. I actually had a fairly prolific career as a humor writer and speaker, telling stories about the scatterbrained situations I so often found myself in. As my youngest son, then age fifteen, once said to his buddies after hearing me speak for the first time: "Mom basically just tells about the funny or weird stuff that is always happening to her, and people laugh like crazy and actually *pay her for it.*" So using my naturally high sense of optimism, I simply turned my most blaring faults into a cottage industry.

Though it may seem totally out of my normal character to collaborate on a book about the brain, when I was asked to consider writing this project with Dr. Henslin, I fairly leapt at the opportunity! Since reading Dr. Amen's first book so many years ago, I'd become an armchair brainiac. My bedside table nearly always had one or two books about the mind or the brain, which I absorbed like a cingul-hungry sponge. While other women flipped through *People* magazine, I was soaking up *Scientific American Mind.* Equally of interest to me were books on what makes happy people . . . well, *happy.* So when Dr. Henslin proposed writing a book on the brain *and* joy from a Christian perspective, all the pieces clicked. A dream came true. I jumped at the opportunity to learn more about brain imaging and how the brain affects our moods, behavior, relationships, and more. (I have learned that the fastest way to learn something well is to write about it or teach it.) Moreover, because I am not exactly your average science person, I hoped I could help a brilliant mind like Dr. Henslin's communicate life-changing concepts to an even wider audience.

Then Dr. Henslin and Dr. Amen offered me a chance to have my brain scanned as part of the research for this book. At first, I was truly thrilled about that opportunity, but the night before the actual scan was to take place, I found myself feeling surprisingly nervous. The insides of my head would be exposed—naked!—and what if I really didn't have much of a brain? What if it was stuffed with fluff? Or was one of those brains with big potholes instead of healthy blood flow?

One stipulation before the brain test was that I could not have coffee—no stimulants before the scan. I had visions of my husband having to wheel me in to the clinic, stuck in my usual state of morning catatonia until I get my first jolt of java. (I would soon discover why I'd relied on coffee to jump-start my head every day.)

I felt a little foggy the next morning as we drove to the Amen Clinic in beautiful Newport Beach, California. The clinic itself is in an unassuming but nice, private area—nothing intimidating or frightening about it. In fact, there's a pretty garden and fountain in front of the clinic door so you get a shot of calming beauty before entering.

The staff was friendly, and I flipped through maybe half a magazine (I'm a fast reader) before the technician called my name to go back. I sat in a little room where I was soon stationed in front of a computer screen. The tech gave me a little shot of the imaging tracer, which I hardly felt. The needle was tiny and barely noticeable. I felt no effects—or aftereffects—from it at all. Unlike most patients coming to the Amen Clinic, I just took one kind of SPECT scan (since my purpose was more research oriented than a diagnostic need): the concentration test. (I didn't do the resting test.) However, I would still get two different pictures of my brain: the surface scan (or tie-dyed-bread-dough scan that checks blood flow), and the active scan (which can show overactive areas deeper inside the brain).

The concentration test involved eye-hand coordination and concentration, like a video game for grown-ups. Eye-hand coordination has never been my strong suit though I did win third prize once in a three-legged race in third grade. (Sadly, it was the only athletic ribbon I ever won.) At first, I felt as I always do when trying to play a computer game, that my brain had just vacated the building when I needed it most. But eventually, I caught on to the game, and felt I did pretty well (which is just more proof that how we *feel* doesn't necessarily reflect *reality*).

Then it was time for me to lie down on the big machine for the scan. The scanner itself is sort of like a bed with a three-sided triangle (the camera) where your head tucks neatly inside. One thing I really appreciated was that only half of my face went into the scanner, so there wasn't that terrible sense of claustrophobia some people have when they have to go fully into "a tube" for other sorts of medical scans (that you see on *ER* and *Grey's Anatomy*). I couldn't move during the scan, so, of course, my head was duct taped to the bed. Okay, well, that's not exactly true. The technicians gently put some kind of soft belt around my head to remind me not to move. Then they threatened to take my firstborn child if I so much as sneezed. I was given a blankie, which I really appreciated. I get very cold in any kind of doctor's office—whether from nerves or the typical arctic conditions in medical facilities, I don't know.

I decided to spend the fifteen minutes or so doing all the relaxation exercises I could think of while the camera slowly clicked its way around my head, including praying blessings over everyone I loved. (I should point out that all the relaxation I used at that point had no effect on my scan. The picture that showed up on the scan was captured and held in sort of a cerebral *still life* by the imaging tracer, taken during the earlier concentration task.) I actually enjoyed the experience, and because I was thinking such happy thoughts about people I cared about, entrusting them into God's hands, the time went by quickly. I felt totally relaxed at this point, except for the little nagging worry about what my scan would look like and if a brain would actually appear on the photos. My grandmother had Alzheimer's, and in the back of my mind, I suppose, I worried that the forgetfulness I had struggled with since puberty could be a sign of early dementia. (Of course, it would have had to begin at age twelve.)

When I walked into Dr. Amen's office, my husband and Dr. Earl Henslin were also there. Earl (I can call him Earl now) must have known that I was anxious because he said to me, "Becky, the first thing Dr. Amen said when he saw your scan was that you have a beautiful brain."

I thought I might swoon. I have a *beautiful* brain! This, in the world of ditzy people, is bigger than winning the Miss America pageant. I not only *had* a brain; it was beautiful. The surface scan showed even blood flow with pretty pigments of hot pink, blue, yellow, and lime green throughout. I wanted to make a T-shirt out of it and wear it everywhere as both a fashion statement and a "See: I *Told You* I Wasn't Senile!" proclamation to my kids. There was, however, just one wee little dent in my left prefrontal cortex. Dr. Amen took a look at the results of my computer-game-playing stress test, grinned, and without fanfare said, "Oh, you did just awful."

"What does that mean?" I asked, worried.

"It means that you have a superhealthy brain with no signs of dementia in your near future at all. However, you probably have a little inattentive ADD. This means that when you are required to concentrate on a task, the blood tends to leave your prefrontal cortex."

In fact, when I took the Amen Brain System Checklist in this book, it showed that I probably had inattentive ADD symptoms, and now the SPECT backed it up. (This type of person usually wakes up in a fog, begging for caffeine—but they are usually mumbling, so it may be hard to understand their requests in the morning.) "You could take a half dose of Adderall," he said, "to help with focusing." But I decided to try the supplement route. I'm finding it to be very helpful. I take L-tyrosine, an amino acid that works like a stimulant to the brain. I also take a good omega-3 fish oil, L-carnitine, and Co-Q10 along with an amino acid complex called NeuroLink. (The Amen Clinic offers a wide variety of supplements.) I am blessed that my husband, Greg, besides being the dearest man on earth, is also one of the most gifted organizers I've ever met. He is happy to help keep me organized and considers it his spiritual gifting and joy. "I like the challenge," he'll say, and *means* it with all sincerity.

So my forgetfulness doesn't keep me from living a happy, productive life right now. But in case it ever does cause more irritation than either Greg or I can stand, and my cute little way of making people laugh isn't enough anymore to cover the general aggravation of my losing several items per day, it is good to know there is medication available as well as a variety of activities I can do to improve my condition.

Right now you may be asking, "How could a scatterbrained person be a writer? Doesn't that take, like, *concentration*?" Remember that ADD types *can* focus on something they find highly stimulating. In fact, we will actually overfocus on it. Reading new information and writing about it is one of my greatest pleasures. Apparently, it just tickles my prefrontal cortex to no end. So if I am on a project that I love, I'm totally focused on it. Of course, the roof could be falling down around me and fire alarms could be going off, and I wouldn't be aware of it if I'm absorbed in crafting a really good paragraph.

The next scan, the active SPECT scan, showed a lot more red-hot activity than I had expected to see. "Do you have any past traumas that you struggle with?" Dr. Amen asked as he looked over the scan.

So here was the part where I felt emotionally exposed: but thankfully, I was in loving, kind, and professional hands. I have suffered for several years with what Greg and I have called *episodes*—all of them relating to traumatic memories from my previous marriage. I had nightmares for a few years where I would be faced with and trying to escape from a painful memory. Greg would pray for my sleep to be good and sweet. Usually, I was fine during the daytime hours, and my experience of life (particularly since my second marriage) was always joyful and peaceful—unless I was somehow triggered by a person or event that reminded my brain of past pain. And then my body would react by shutting down or trying to flee. It was the oddest thing—even to me, the person it was happening to.

I remember one time I was on the patio in our backyard, and one of our guests began speaking in a belittling tone to his wife. I didn't say a word, but I immediately stood up, went inside the house, and closed and locked the door behind me. Then, still shaking, I walked upstairs robotically and into my bedroom, locking the door. Then I walked into the bathroom, locking *that* door behind me. Then I just sat there and tried to breathe and recover from whatever had just happened to my mind and body.

What happened was that I was triggered by a tone of voice that reminded me of confusing and painful experiences that I had once endured on a fairly regular basis in what felt like a past life. However, my body was reexperiencing what I had wanted to forget and went on autopilot into shut-down-and-get-outta-here mode.

"You have a scan that shows the classic diamond pattern of overactivity in the cingulate, basal ganglia, and limbic associated with PTSD," Dr. Amen said gently. "You've probably got some trauma memories here that are stuck in your brain's neural system."

I felt both sad and relieved. At least there was a name for what had been happening to me: post-traumatic stress. I plan to do some EMDR therapy (which you can read about in the appendix on PTSD). I've heard and read great reports about its ability to repair the brain when it gets stuck like this. And Dr. Amen, who has also gone through EMDR himself when he was in a particularly stressful situation, says that brain scans can show radical improvement after just a few EMDR sessions with a trained professional. This also happens to be one of Dr. Henslin's specialties.

In addition to that, I am also taking some supplements at bedtime that are calming support for PTSD. I've found that taking DLPA (a calming amino) in the evening before bed has really helped my sleep and my dreams to be more peaceful.

In addition to the improvements I have found with daytime focus and nighttime sleep by using supplements, I have also noticed a near-miraculous improvement in the lessening of chronic headaches. I have been especially prone to headaches, and I thought, perhaps, it was the move to a higher altitude (we live in Denver, the Mile-High City). Or the barometric pressure, my hormone cycle, tension, eye strain, the moon's alignment, a bad hair day—just about *anything*—seemed to trigger a headache. I realized one day after starting the DLPA and L-tyrosine supplementation that three weeks had passed without a headache of any kind. Just being headache free alone has significantly increased my personal happiness.

In writing this book with Dr. Henslin, I also realized that my protein intake was shy of what I needed, and since I am prone to low blood sugar, I have focused on getting at least 20 grams of protein at every meal. And Dr. Amen's suggestion to enjoy a bowl of just-defrosted blueberries (about twenty minutes out of the freezer) is a winner. I put a little bit of half-and-half (about a tablespoon) on them, and it is quite the heavenly treat. (If they are tart, a drizzle of real maple syrup is de-lish.) Knowing it is good for my brain and my body is also great.

Now, enough about me. You probably have some more questions: perhaps about SPECT imaging or perhaps you'd like more information about PTSD. Keep reading. Dr. Henslin has more answers.

Common Questions About SPECT Scans

1. Does everyone need a scan? No. Often the Amen Brain System Checklist included in this book can help guide us to the right medications or supplements to try, if needed. We look at the degree of angst and pain that the person is in, the history of what they've tried before, and several other factors. Often we can be of help by using therapy or coaching techniques and suggesting supplements or medications that one's healthcare professional may want to consider.

I am not a medical doctor; I am just a trained therapist who has deeply studied the area of brain imaging and picked up all I could possibly learn from Dr. Amen, the pioneer of this research. So I am only one piece of the total health puzzle. The book *The Tipping Point* talks about a personality called The Connector, and that really fits my personality. I may be able to help you, but if I cannot, I know a good list of healthcare professionals who probably can.

2. When does a person need a SPECT scan? When your situation is complicated and you are not seeing improvement or when there's a suspicion of past brain injury or trauma that could be affecting behavior, a scan would be beneficial. When we suspect the temporal lobes may be a problem, using a SPECT scan really helps us diagnose exactly what's happening and determines the order in which we will treat brain issues. Also, in cases of complicated ADD, we use it where the normal stimulant protocol isn't working or is making things worse. A scan can help us with much better accuracy to help you help yourself.

3. Aren't SPECT scans expensive? In a word, yes, they can be. (At this writing, anywhere from $1,500 to $5,000, depending on how many scans are taken and the protocol needed.) Insurance may cover some of the costs; however, most scanning centers—including the Amen Clinics—require you to pay first and let the insurance company reimburse you. But if you (or your therapist or doctor) suspects you really need a brain scan, there may be ways to help reduce costs or divide payments with a payment plan. Sometimes it does help to ask yourself, "What is it worth for me to know exactly where my brain may be misfiring and exactly how to help it?"

The easiest way to see if our office can help you is to contact us at www.henslinandassoc.com or 1-714-256-HOPE, where we can assess your individual needs and situation and let you know how we can best help within your circumstances.

4. Where can I find a healthcare provider in my area who is familiar with SPECT scans and understands the benefit of Dr. Amen's work? Go to www.amenclinics.com/ac/referrals. You can enter in your location, and a number of healthcare professionals who are familiar with Dr. Amen's approach will pop up.

Here are some more common Q & A's from Dr. Amen's Web site:

1. What is SPECT imaging? Single Photon Emission Computed Tomography imaging, also called brain SPECT imaging, is a nuclear medicine procedure that evaluates cerebral blood flow. SPECT is easy to understand. It evaluates areas of the brain that work well, areas of the brain that work too hard, and areas of the brain that do not work hard enough. The information from the scans, along with a detailed clinical history, helps us understand the underlying brain patterns associated with our patients' problems and helps to pinpoint the right treatment to balance brain function.

2. What is the procedure? You will be placed in a quiet room and a small IV line will be inserted into your arm. For the concentration study, you will take a fifteen-minute computerized test of attention and focus. Three or four minutes into performing the test, the imaging solution will be injected through the IV, and then you will complete the test. For the baseline study, you will be instructed to sit quietly. Several minutes later, the imaging solution will be injected through the IV. After the injection, you will lie on the imaging table, and the SPECT camera will slowly rotate around your head, taking images of brain blood flow. (You are not placed inside a tube.) The time on the table is approximately eighteen minutes.

3. What is the injection, and are there side effects? Since a SPECT scan is a nuclear medicine procedure, it requires the injection of a very small amount of a radioisotope through a small needle inserted into a vein in the arm. The medicine we inject is not a dye; therefore, people typically do not have allergic responses to it.

4. Does the injected substance you use contain iodine? No, it does not. It is not a dye or a contrast agent such as those used in CTs or MRIs. It is a radioactive tracer ("radiotracer" or "tracer"). This is a very important distinction: in CT, the term *dye* or *contrast agent* refers to an injected compound that typically contains iodine and is used to enhance an X-ray or CT image. Severe reactions can occur in some patients who receive these iodine-containing substances. A history of bad reactions to CT dyes, however, does not mean that a patient will have a bad reaction to the tracers we use. Adverse reactions to the radiotracers used at the Amen Clinics are so rare that hospital nuclear medicine departments typically do not stock the drugs given to patients with a history of reactions to iodine-based contrast agents.

The radiotracers injected at the Amen Clinics do contain a substance called *methylene blue*. This substance is a dye but is not the same kind of dye as the iodine-containing X-ray and CT contrast agents. It functions as a preservative and helps the radiotracer stay in its compounded form. There are no serious allergic or adverse effects that we know of associated with the administration of methylene blue.

5. Is there radiation involved, and how safe is it? How safe is it for children? The amount of radiation exposure from one brain SPECT scan is comparable to one-half to two-thirds of a brain CAT (CT) scan (about 0.7 to 1.0 rem). According to the Health Physics Society, the radiation dose of two SPECT scans is well below the cut-off level (10 rem) for any potential or observable health risks. Furthermore, according to the National Institutes of Health, research data does not show children to have any increased cancer risks from low-level radiation.

6. Are there any risks from the radiation you get from a SPECT scan? Minimal risks, if any, may exist. The radiation from a SPECT scan is considered a standard medical procedure. Last year in the United States, there were nearly 20 million nuclear medicine procedures done on children and adults. Please see http://interactive.snm.org/index.cfm?PageID=5574&RPID=10 for a thorough discussion.

7. Do I have to be off medication, and for how long? We prefer to scan patients on as little medication as possible, if not off it completely. We realize this is not always practical depending on your circumstances. Stimulant medications need to be stopped four days prior to the first scan. Any other decrease or removal of medications needs to be done in consultation with your treating physician.

For more information about SPECT and Amen Clinics, go to www.amenclinic. com.

A Different Kind of Diamond Head: Post-Traumatic Stress Disorder

Christy walked into my office in obvious distress and said, "Dr. Henslin, I'm a basket case."

I smiled and said, "Well, I happen to specialize in basket cases. First let's talk about what's in your basket."

As her stories unfolded, it was clear that Christy was living through the recovery of some heavy-duty past emotional traumas, including disturbing dreams—always variations on a memory she wanted nothing more than to forget. Many people experiencing PTSD are puzzled at how they managed to stay together when they were in crisis but fell apart years afterward. Personally, I believe it is because of God's merciful wiring: our brain can only handle so much stress at one time. So for example, when a soldier has to fight in the heat of battle, he cannot afford to stop and think about his fear or even grieve the death of fallen comrades. Soldiers are usually protected, almost numbed, by the flow of chemicals that help them to fight or flee. It isn't until a person is in a truly safe place that the brain will begin the process of trying to deal with pain that was shelved during the actual crisis or emergency.

Perhaps you've experienced a cocoon of calm and focus in an emergency situation, such as coming upon a car wreck. And it was only after the worst had passed that your legs began trembling and perhaps tears flowed. On a minor scale, this is how PTSD feels.

Because Christy's anxiety was so high, I hesitated to recommend psychotherapy until her brain was calmer. In some cases, when a patient's fear is off the charts, therapy can actually trigger more anxiety. Needless to say, that is not our goal.

So with her physician's approval, Christy was put on Gabitril (an antiseizure medication used quite successfully to calm anxiety) that calmed her basal ganglia and temporal lobes (often associated with PTSD); Prozac helped calm the cingulate and her limbic overactivity problems. She was able to relax enough to move forward in the psychotherapy that I normally use in trauma recovery.

One of my areas of expertise is post-traumatic stress, and I see a lot of success using a therapy called EMDR, something I will explain in a later section. After the EMDR was completed, we were also gradually able to get Christy off medications, using some interim supplements, and her second scan showed what we already suspected: her brain had calmed down, and the fear that stalked her day and night had dissipated.

Women or men who have suffered trauma or abuse of any kind (sexual, mental, verbal, or physical) in their past or who continue to live in an abusive or walking-on-eggshells relationship will often have signs of chronic fear in their brains. For example, a woman who lives with a man whose anger is unpredictable will experience an inner terror: she shuts down, freezes, and has difficulty holding on to her own thoughts, feelings, and opinions. She will emotionally isolate to survive and pull farther away from the source of her

anxiety. She may love her husband, but his anger and her fear have made true intimacy an impossibility. A part of her has to remain vigilant, and love and fear cannot flow at the same time. (John the disciple noted, "There is no fear in love; but perfect loves casts out fear" [1 John 4:18 NASB]. Fear has no part in a truly healthy relationship of love.)

Adult children of alcoholics, who had to live in an unpredictably violent home, often have their "fear center" set higher than normal. The younger the psychic injury, the more likely they will

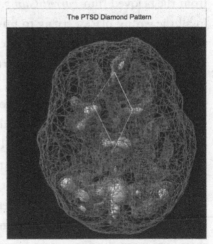

The PTSD Diamond Pattern

(Underside, active view)

experience some delayed form of post-traumatic stress (if left untreated). The brain scan for a person who is harboring trauma shows that several mood centers are activated at once: cingulate, limbic, basal ganglia, and often, temporal lobes. It forms almost a perfect diamond pattern.

I like to see this as God's way of reminding a person that she is a precious jewel who wasn't cherished or completely soothed after trauma at some critical point in her life. With help, the crystal-clear diamond of who she really is—at the core—can come shining through the fire of emotional pain.

Left BG versus Right BG

Interestingly, in cases of general anxiety or post-traumatic stress, we have found that in SPECT scans, the left basal ganglia is more "lit up"—the anxiety appears more as outward irritation (the fight response). When the right side is lit up, it reveals itself more in avoidance behaviors of social situations or potential conflict (flight response).

SEXUAL ABUSE: RESTORING CAPACITY FOR INTIMACY

There are fewer more poignant portrayals of what happens to a young woman when she's been abused by a trusted adult than Jenny, the young girl from the beloved film *Forrest Gump*. She spends a long time looking for love in all the wrong places, trying to numb her pain, and then there's a wonderful scene where she returns to her childhood home—the scene of so many crimes forced on her innocent heart. An adult now, Jenny hurls one stone after another at the house.

"Sometimes there just aren't enough rocks," Forrest says soulfully in the voice-over. Having witnessed the suffering of women as they return to their childhood pain in their memories, I honestly couldn't express it better than Forrest does in this one, poignant line.

Sadly, the most common scenarios of women seeking help with anxiety are women who are trying to recover from a sexual trauma from their childhood or youth. One in four women are sexually assaulted at some point in their lives, according to nearly every staggering statistic available (and many studies say one in three, depending on the definition of sexual abuse). This means in a given crowd of women, every fourth woman will have experienced a sexual trauma of some sort.

Even when a woman is safe from her past abuser(s) and, perhaps, currently married to a wonderful man, she may still suffer at times from overactive basal ganglia. That means she may be more easily triggered by a small slight and find herself in fight mode (overreacting) or flight mode (running away, hiding, looking for emotional cover). She may feel some discomfort in crowds, social situations, or any situation that triggers something related to her past trauma. It could be the smell of cologne or alcohol (or a mixture), a dark basement, or anyone whose appearance or voice reminds her of past pain.

Most women who have been sexually abused need help in this healing process, or they may find themselves pulling away or shutting down when touched or when their husbands want to be intimate. Though a woman's husband isn't frightening or abusing her—and, in fact, she may love him very much—when the basal ganglia is triggered, it is as if her body is involuntarily reliving the memories. One term we use for this phenomenon is *body memory*.

If you have ever experienced your body recoiling from something without your mind comprehending why, if you follow the reason, it will usually be because something is reminding your body of a painful or unpleasant past memory. One woman, whose father was a mean, sexually abusive alcoholic, would recoil even at the sight of a funny, harmless town-drunk character like Mayberry's Otis Campbell from the old *Andy Griffith Show*. To a child whose world turned black every time her father came home with liquor on his breath, there's simply nothing funny about a drunk. Most of us have triggers that can subconsciously bring on low moods, and even if you do not suffer from PTSD, you can probably imagine how someone who was highly traumatized can be more sensitive to triggers that resurrect old feelings of pain.

A sexual trauma to a child or a teenager is stored not only in the low-mood limbic system but also in the hippocampus and amygdala, which are parts of the basal ganglia or the Basement of Giant Fears. The basal ganglia actually stores the muscle experience of pain, pleasure, terror, and shame. When triggered by an outside source or an inner thought, a person's changes in perception, internal emotional state, and activation of survival response (fight-flight-freeze) are automatic. Sometimes these autoresponses really cannot be controlled. Sadly, when a husband approaches his wife, she may feel arousal, but if she's been sexually abused (and hasn't yet been healed of the memories), she'll also feel involuntary emotions of terror or shame. These mental patterns are not just formed in childhood; they can be formed through painful experiences in adult relationships (with an abusive or abandoning boyfriend or husband) and other significant relationships (sibling, parent, or authority figure).

So you can see how—when a body memory is triggered—a woman with past abuse issues may go on emotional autopilot and want to fight or flee (sometimes physically, sometimes just emotionally) to distance herself from her husband, who simply wants to make love, as if he were her assailant. Then once the PTSD episode has passed, when she realizes she's hurt his feelings, she may feel terrible remorse and guilt. And, of course, her husband is feeling none too loved, satisfied, or happy either. He feels he's paying for another person's crime and that it is unfair. Many marriages don't survive this painful cycle, which is why it is so important to take custody of your past pain, proactively seek healing, and bring your best selves to the marriage bed.

IT TAKES TWO TO HEAL

In summary, healing from childhood sexual trauma is usually essential if true emotional and sexual energy is to be enjoyed. (The exception might be if a child confided in a trusted caregiver and there was a positive, healing, and proactive response at that time or soon after. If this happened, healing may already have been accomplished.) Both spouses will need understanding, supportive help through the process. In the meantime, however, we therapists can bring some great physical and mental relief to a wounded fear center through the judicial use of supplements or medication, along with whatever healing process is chosen.

EMDR THERAPY

One of the most researched and successful methods for healing trauma memory might sound like an idea that some mad scientist thought up. But to the mental health community's surprise, it works! Eye movement desensitization and reprocessing (see why we shorten it to EMDR?) works very well with a qualified therapist who is well trained and experienced in using it.

EMDR is a form of psychotherapy, pioneered by Francine Shapiro, PhD, that has proven to help people who struggle with PTSD symptoms. EMDR uses bilateral stimulation of the brain through the movement of the eyes, sound, or touch to help process trauma. By alternately stimulating both sides of the body, this therapy works to help process trauma that is stored in the neural networks of the brain and the body. It literally helps to release the "charge" that keeps a memory of past wounds impacting the present.[1] But what does that mean to you? Here's a simplified model that works for most.

We all have regular, weekly (if not daily) fears or upsets—a driver who cuts you off, a rude coworker, a stubbed toe—that are like little chunks of ice that flow through our emotional brain and eventually get processed and dealt with in a healthy way. The ice chips we can usually handle (especially if our brain is fairly balanced). These ice-chip-sized memories work their way through our brain's system—where they get melted, chewed, dissolved, or redistributed—and life returns to normal fairly quickly. This is our brain's way of helping our mind, in Mafia-speak, to "fuggedaboutit" and move on.

When we are hit with a tragedy or trauma, it's like being hit with a heavy block of ice rather than the little ice chips. We can handle and process the chips because, after all, since we were about two years old, we've learned that life isn't exactly fair or perfect. So a healthy brain deals with it or shrugs it off. Not so with big ice chunks of pain. Not only does the big chunk of ice stay put, but sometimes it sticks to other ice chunks and turns into an iceberg, especially if there are multiple traumas, a prolonged trauma, or a very severe trauma (soldiers in a war; losing multiple friends or family members; a long, frightening bout with cancer; a shocking or painful divorce; 9/11 survivors). This is an oversimplification, but it is a picture of post-traumatic stress disorder. I should mention here that one person's ice chip could be someone else's chunk of ice and, depending on a number of factors, can be just as stubborn to melt.

This much pain and shock literally changes your brain, and most people who've been there would wholeheartedly agree with that assessment. Then you have an iceberg of collective memories that gets stuck in the Basement of Giant Fears and refuses to budge, melt, or go anywhere—even though you'd love nothing more than to have it disappear or, at least, be able to minimize the painful memory to a normal size so your brain can deal with it.

Not all people who suffer get PTSD (though most do experience some form of PTSD for a little while after a trauma, even a relatively minor car accident; however, the trauma might just linger a day, a week, or a month). Some soldiers return from war and, after a reasonable period of time, are able to move

forward. Others are not so lucky, as we are hearing about in the soldiers returning from Iraq (particularly the ones who were in the National Guard, who
weren't prepared for the horrors of war). Some of the ability to rebound faster
has to do with genetic predisposition, and some of it involves the amount of
trauma and the amount of attachment to the person who was killed or who
died. Also, the amount of emotional and relational support that was given during and just after the crisis can play a role in our ability to recover.

Those who probably suffer the most are adults who were abused as children, when their brains really didn't have the resources to deal with such pain,
especially if their parents or clergy or teachers, when told, didn't respond in
soothing and proactive ways. This is often called a *sanctuary trauma*—when a
child looked for safety after a traumatizing experience and was turned away.
This has a way of driving the original hurt deeper into the soul.

When the iceberg gets lodged, we are hit with unwanted thoughts and
memories that may interrupt us at any moment. We're triggered easily by
anything that reminds us of the day that chunk of ice landed in our lives. We
have nightmares about every aspect of that iceberg, almost as if our Basement
of Giant Fears doesn't even take a break to sleep. Oh, our brain continues to
work around it as best it can, but it's not the same . . . our brain stays on
hyperalert even when we don't want to or mean to be.

Ultimately, EMDR works a bit like a high-powered blender. It breaks up
traumatic memories into manageable pieces using a variety of blender blades:
recalling painful memories and replacing them with new, improved thoughts
(with a trained counselor); slowing down or interrupting the story you've
been telling yourself (which helps remove some of its power over your brain);
and using alternating eye movement, tapping, or sounds (to break up and
disrupt thought patterns). Using these methods and more, we sort of whirl,
if you will, that big immovable hunk o' ice into smaller pieces that can then
be distributed through your brain and processed like other normal-sized
memories until they melt into the place where typical memories (without
major stress reactions attached) are stored. To simplify even more: we help
monster memories turn into medium-sized memories, so they can go through
the normal brain-drain system.

To find out more about what such a session looks like, check out www.
emdr.com.

BE HERE NOW

Another aspect to dealing with trauma in a clinical setting is to use *grounding* techniques. This simply means that we help a person process old pain while being firmly grounded in the present: by touching a chair and reminding the client where she is, who she is *today*. Because when one of those ice-chunk memories gets replayed, it often comes with its own set of dramatic devices. Sights, smells, and sounds can feel so real that it is easy to forget that this is now, and that was then. In fact, in reliving a painful memory, many people feel as though they are in a movie. What we do is help them to move from playing a part in the movie to playing the part of an observer—an adult— who is no longer in the scene.

The good news is that EMDR works so well that oftentimes it only takes a few sessions to dislodge the iceberg. Interestingly, we have scans from before and after PTSD. Time and again we can show in living color that EMDR is effective.

ADDITIONAL RESOURCES

• *Healing from Trauma* by Jasmin Lee Cori, MS, LPC.

What I most appreciate about this comprehensive guide to healing from trauma is that it isn't filled with lots of trauma stories (most people who've been through their own have had their fill). It focuses on what PTSD feels like and how it happens and then gives a comprehensive list of *all* the available treatments for recovery from trauma. Some solutions will probably seem to be "out there," but many more will be very helpful.

Jasmin Lee Cori does an admirable job of presenting the information objectively and concisely. She points out that the main task of most trauma interventions is to "break up" those patterns of thinking that continue to torment us.

EMDR is one treatment I've mentioned and that I use successfully, but she also discusses others. She also mentions Dr. Amen's book *Healing from Depression and Anxiety* and says she found his recommendation for supplementation to be especially helpful to her personally.

- *Door of Hope* and *Unclaimed Baggage*, both by Jan Franks.

She and her husband, Don, have a heart for helping couples, especially those who have had their marriages interrupted by unclaimed baggage or past trauma. They offer several helps at www.janfrank.com, and all materials come from a Christian-based point of view.

- *Redeeming Love* by Francine Rivers.

I would venture to say that this is probably the most beloved, absorbing, and helpful novel written from a Christian perspective for any woman who has suffered from abuse, neglect, or abandonment. You close the book feeling refreshed and loved at a deeper level than you ever dreamed.

INDEX

NOTES

Chapter One: My First Hug and Other Joyful Brain Matters
1. Garrison Keillor, *Lake Wobegon Days* (New York: Penguin, 1990), 7.
2. Daniel Amen, *Healing the Hardware of the Soul* (New York: Free Press, a division of Simon & Schuster, 2002), 16.

Chapter Three: A Head Trip to a Happier Life
1. Andrew Newberg, Eugene D'Aquili, Vince Rause, *Why God Won't Go Away: Brain Science and the Biology of Belief* (New York: Ballentine, 2002), 7.
2. Virginia Woolf, *A Writer's Diary*, Leonard Woolf, ed. (New York: Harcourt, 1953, 2003), 64.

Chapter Four: Testing, Testing . . . All Brains Need a Little Help Sometimes
1. Diane Ackerman, *An Alchemy of Mind: The Marvel and Mystery of the Brain* (New York: Scribner, 2004), 4.
2. Sharon Begley, *Train Your Mind, Change Your Brain: How a New Science Reveals Our Extraordinary Potential to Transform Ourselves* (New York: Ballantine Books, 2007).

Chapter Five: Joy Boosters: The Science Behind Pleasure Prescriptions
1. Summarized from *The Myth of the Drug-Induced Addiction* by Bruce K. Alexander, Department of Psychology, Simon Fraser University, Burnaby, BC, www.parl.gc.ca/37/1/parlbus/commbus/senate/Com-e/ille-e/presentation-e/alexender-e.htm (accessed 9 August 2008).
2. B. Egolf, J. Lasker, S. Wolf, and L. Potvin, "Featuring health risks and mortality: The Roseto effect: A 50-year comparison of mortality rates," *American Journal of Public Health*, 82(8), 1992, 1089–92.
3. T. D. Jakes, *The Lady, Her Lover, and Her Lord* (New York: G. P. Putnam's Sons, 1998), 32.
4. "Volunteering Boosts Community Happiness," *Society Guardian*, 20 September 2004, www.guardian.co.uk/society/2004/sep/20/research.highereducation (accessed 9 August 2008).
5. Randolph E. Schmid, "Giving Big Not Just for Oprah," *Denver Post*, 21 March 2008, http://www.denverpost.com/search/ci_8644814 (accessed 9 August 2008).
6. P. J. Pierson and Mary Shipley, *Aromatherapy for Everyone: Discover the Scents of Health and Happiness with Essential Oils* (Ridgefield, CT: Vital Health Publishing, 2004), 14.
7. *Web MD* Magazine, Jan/Feb 2008, 41.
8. Rachel St. John Gilbert, telephone interview conducted by Becky Johnson, August 12 2008. Used with permission.
9. Marci Shimoff, *Happy for No Reason* (New York: Free Press, a division of Simon & Schuster, 2008), 151.
10. Birgit Wolz, "Why cinema therapy works," www.cinematherapy.com/whyitworks.html (accessed 29 October 2008).
11. *Homecoming Magazine*, Jan/Feb 2008, 29.
12. Sara C. Mednick, *Take a Nap! Change Your Life* (New York: Workman, 2006), backcover.
13. Alan C. Logan, *The Brain Diet* (Nashville, TN: Cumberland House, 2007), 116.

Chapter Six: The Prefrontal Cortex: The Presidential Control Center
1. Mitford M. Mathews, ed. *A Dictionary of Americanisms on Historical Principles* (Chicago: University of Chicago Press, 1951), 198–199; www.trumanlibrary.org/buckstop.htm.
2. Stefan Klein, PhD, *The Science of Happiness* (New York: Marlow & Co., an imprint of Avalon Publishing, 2006), 35–37.
3. Used by permission from Dr. Daniel Amen, www.amenclinic.com.
4. Henry Emmons, MD, *The Chemistry of Joy* (Fireside, New York: Simon and Schuster, 2006), 63.
5. Daniel Amen, *Healing ADD* (New York: Berkley, a division of Penguin, 2002), 260.
6. The ADD Coaching Group, ADD Quotes, www.addcoachinggroup.com/content/quotes.html.
7. Sari Solden, *Women with Attention Deficit Disorder: Embrace Your Differences and Transform Your Life* (Nevada City, CA: Underwood Books, 2005).

Chapter Seven: The Cingulate Gyrus: The Circular Gerbil Wheel
1. Summarized from Dr. Jeffrey Schwartz, "Do I have Obsessive-Compulsive Disorder? A Checklist of Common OCD Symptoms," www.brainphysics.com/checklist.php.

2. "Count Your Blessings," words by Johnson Oatman Jr, 1856–1922, music by Edwin O. Excell, 1851–1921. First appeared in *Songs for Young People*, compiled and published by Edwin O. Excell in 1897.
3. Frederic Luskin, PhD, "9 Steps," *Forgive for Good*. Used with permission.

Chapter Eight: The Basal Ganglia: The Basement of Giant Fears
1. *The Wizard of Oz*, script by Noel Langley, Florence Ryerson, and Edgar Allen Woolf, © 1939.
2. "The Biscuit Hostage," TruthOrFiction.com, www.truthorfiction.com/rumors/b/biscuithostage.htm.
3. Paula Deen with Sherry Suib Cohen, *It Ain't All About the Cookin'*, (New York: Simon & Schuster, 2007), 43–45.
4. Ibid., 65.
5. Ibid., 67.
6. Sue Gilbert, "Eat for Wellness: Anti-Anxiety Diet," Your Total Health: Anti-Anxiety Diet Tips at iVillage.com, 14 July 2006, www.yourtotalhealth.ivillage.com/eat-wellness-anti-anxiety-diet.html?pageNum=1.
7. Ibid., www.yourtotalhealth.ivillage.com/eat-wellness-anti-anxiety-diet.html?pageNum=3.
8. Martha Beck, "Martha Beck's Five (New) Pieces of Advice," *Oprah*, March 2008, 74.
9. Ibid.
10. "Famous People Affected by an Anxiety Disorder," anxietycentre.com, www.anxietycentre.com/anxiety-famous-people.shtml.
11. See *The Pippi Longstocking Collection (Pippi Longstocking / Pippi Goes on Board / Pippi in the South Seas / Pippi on the Run)* (1975) Henstooth Video, Released October 2005.

Chapter Nine: The Deep Limbic System: The Depressed Low-Mood Space
1. Adapted from S. D. Block and L. Snyder, "Assessing and managing depression in the terminally ill patient," *Annals of Internal Medicine* 132(3) (2000): 209–218.
2. Tony Headley, "Luther on Depression," www.freemethodistchurch.org/Magazine/Articles/Nov-Dec%20Articles/N-D%20Headley%20Article.htm.
3. Roland Bainton, *Here I Stand—A Life of Martin Luther* (Nashville, TN: Abingdon-Cokesbury, 2007), 39.
4. Dwight Carlson, *Why Do Christians Shoot Their Wounded?* (Downers Grove, IL: InterVarsity Press, 1994), 47.
5. Julia Ross, *The Mood Cure* (New York: Penguin, 2003).
6. Jean Lush and Pam Vredevelt, *Women and Stress: Practical Ways to Manage Tension* (Grand Rapids: Fleming Revell, a division of Baker Book Group, 2008), 106–111.
7. "Bound to Come Some Trouble," written by Rich Mullins, Universal Music/BMG Songs Inc. © 1990.
8. depression-guide.com, Aromatherapy for Depression, www.depression-guide.com/aromatherapy-depression.htm.
9. C. S. Lewis, *The Four Loves* (New York: Harcourt, 1991), 121.

Chapter Ten: The Temporal Lobes: The Temper Lofts
1. Stephen Ambrose, *The Supreme Commander* (New York: Random House, 1999), 229–230.
2. Carlo Deste, *Patton: A Genius for War* (New York: HarperCollins, 1996), 465.
3. "Quotations About Anger," quotegarden.com, www.quotegarden.com/anger.html.
4. Daniel G. Amen, *Change Your Brain, Change Your Life* (New York: Three Rivers Press, 1998), 204.
5. "Quotations About Anger," ibid.

Chapter Eleven: An Apostle on Joy: The *Real* Secret
1. Viktor Frankl, *Man's Search for Meaning* (Boston: Beacon Press, 2006), 86.
2. Thornton Wilder, *The Collected Short Plays of Thornton Wilder, Volume T* (New York: Theatre Communications Group, 1998), 74.
3. Summarized from lecture by Martha Beck, *Finding Your Own North Star*, Audio CD, Sound True, 2005.
4. Arthur H. Stainback, *Illustrating the Lesson* (Grand Rapids: Fleming Revell, a division of Baker Book Group, 1968).
5. Henri Nouwen, "Journey to L'Arche," Program #3301, 1 October 1989, www.csec.org/csec/sermon/nouwen_33031.htm.
6. *Nouwen Then*, Christopher De Vinck, ed. (Grand Rapids, MI: Zondervan Publishing Company, 1999), 29.

***Appendix C*: A Different Kind of Diamond Head: Post-Traumatic Stress Disorder**
1. EMDR International Association, www.emdria.org/displaycommon.cfm?an=1&subarticlenbr=3.

Dr. Earl Henslin is a licensed counselor, former faculty member at Asuza Pacific University and at the Rosemead Graduate School of Psychology at Biola University, and author of five books and numerous professional articles. He is a member of several professional organizations and helped found Overcomers Outreach to aid churches in establishing support groups. For the past eight years—working closely with brain imaging research pioneer Daniel G. Amen, MD—Dr. Henslin has been integrating brain imaging into the treatment of psychological, physical, and spiritual problems at his counseling practice, Henslin and Associates, a Christian counseling group in Brea, California.

How to Contact Dr. Earl Henslin

- For speaking availability or speaking schedule
- To order other books and e-books by Dr. Henslin
- To sign up to receive the *Brain-Heart Matters Newsletter*

Please visit us at
www.drhenslin.com
or call us at
714-256-2807

- To schedule a personal counseling appointment, whether in person
  or by phone

Please go to
www.henslinandassoc.com
or contact us at
714-256-HOPE (714-256-4673)
Our offices are located in Brea, California.

For information about Amen Clinics or to see more SPECT images, please visit www.amenclinic.com. There are several Amen Clinics, but the one closest to our office is located in Newport Beach, California.

Printed in the USA
CPSIA information can be obtained
at www.ICGtesting.com
JSHW032021240624
65293JS00015B/198